O9-AIG-178

HE CHOSE THE NAILS

An In-Depth Study of the Cross

Participant's Workbook

by Max Luc

with Len Woods and Day

He Chose the Nails
An In-Depth Study of the Cross

Copyright © 2000 by Max Lucado. Published by Word Publishing, a Thomas Nelson Company, P.O. Box 141000, Nashville, TN 37214. All rights reserved. No portion of this book may be reproduced, stored in a retrieval system, or transmitted in any form or by any means—electronic, mechanical, photocopy, recording, or any other—except for brief quotations in printed reviews, without the prior permission of the publisher.

Scripture passages taken from:

The Holy Bible, New International Version® (NIV)
Copyright © 1973, 1978, 1984 by International Bible Society.

The Holy Bible, New King James Version (NKJV)
Copyright © 1979, 1980, 1982 by Thomas Nelson, Inc. Used by permission. All rights reserved.

Holy Bible, New Living Translation (NLT)
Copyright © 1996 by Tyndale Charitable Trust. All rights reserved.

The Holy Bible, New Century Version (NCV)
Copyright © 1987, 1988, 1991, 1996 by Word Publishing. All rights reserved.

The Good News Bible: The Bible in Today's English Version (TEV)
Copyright © 1976 by American Bible Society. All rights reserved.

The New American Standard Bible (NASB)
Copyright © 1960, 1962, 1963, 1968, 1971, 1972, 1973, 1975, 1977, 1995, 1997 by The Lockman Foundation. Used by permission.

w Revised Standard Version Bible (NRSV)
© 1989 Division of Christian Education of the National Council of the Churches
United States of America. All rights reserved.

stament with Psalms and Proverbs by Eugene H. Peterson (MSG).
995. Used by permission of NavPress Publishing Group.

ociety. Used by permission.

oration. Contributors: Len Woods, Dave

Comfort, Ph.D., D. Litt. of Phil.

TABLE OF CONTENTS

A Note from Max

Dear Friend,

The cross is the main event of history.

The timeline of mankind is dotted with many important moments. The first spark from the first flint. The rolling of the first wheel. The treating of the first wound. The slaying of the first soldier. Who dares minimize these events?

Yet who dares compare them with the cross? For if Jesus is who he claims to be and did what he claimed to do, then the cross towers over history like a Yosemite pine over its fallen cones.

History has only one main event.

Scripture has only one main event. Others matter, but only one is essential. The story of Jericho might stir you, but falling walls can't redeem you. Moses will give you direction for the wilderness but no solution for your sin. David's defeat of Goliath might reduce your timidity, but only the cross prepares you for eternity.

Scripture has only one main event.

Even in the life of Jesus, there is only one main event. What would it be? Not the manger of Jesus. For if there is no cross, then the manger is occupied by Mary's baby, not God's child. Not the miracles of Jesus, for if there is no cross, then the miracles are performed by history's greatest huckster, not heaven's highest hope. Not the teachings of Jesus, for if there is no cross, then his precepts are nice ideas, not the gospel truth. Not even the claims of Jesus. If there is no cross of Christ, then there is no truth to Christ, for he claimed to be the Savior of the world. With no cross, he is the hustler of the world.

In the drama we call Christ, the cross is the main act.

The same can be said for events that follow the cross. If there is no death and resurrection, then Paul was duped and his epistles are shams. John was a fool and his Revelation is an hallucination. If there is no cross, then the apostles founded a movement of lies rather than a movement of life.

When it comes to history, to Scripture, to Jesus, to the New Testament, there is only one main event. And when it comes to your life, the same is true.

To remove the cross is to remove the hinge-pin from the door of hope. The door of *your* hope. For if there is no cross, then there is no sacrifice for sin. If there is no sacrifice for sin, how will you face a sinless God? Will you cleanse your own sin?

If there is no cross, there is no resurrection of Jesus. And if there is no resurrection of Jesus, how will you live again? Will you open your own grave?

Forgiveness of sin. Deliverance from death. Those are the claims of the cross. Let there be no mistake. The cross is not an event in history. It is *the* event of history.

That's what makes this study so important. We are studying the grandest topic known to man.

Before we begin let me give a well-deserved pat on the back to Dave Veerman and the Livingstone team. They did the lion's share of this workbook. The questions, the quotes, the organization—all were born out of this creative group. Thanks, guys.

And thanks to you for choosing to dwell on the hill of Calvary. May God use these pages to show you Jesus: the One who chose the nails for you.

HE CHOSE THE NAILS

Introduction to the Workbook

Welcome to the workbook for *He Chose the Nails*. We hope that this will be a valuable experience for you as you make your way through the pages of this book. These twelve lessons have been written to encourage, inspire, and challenge as you journey by the *Via Dolorosa*, the "Way of Sorrows" that Christ took to Calvary. As you consider what Christ's sacrifice means, you will be able to look into his eyes, touch his wounds, hear his voice, recognize his pain, and realize that he did it all just for you.

This interactive study incorporates material from the book *He Chose the Nails*, but it can be used without ever reading the book. You can either use this workbook as part of a group study or on your own—both methods will help you grow significantly. To accompany this workbook, a leader's guide has been provided for leaders of small group studies. If you're studying this as an individual, use this workbook with the video and the CD. These may be purchased at a Christian bookstore.

You will notice that each lesson is divided into separate sections: Getting Started, Digging In, Going Deeper, Making It Real, Thinking It Through, and Taking It Home.

— "Getting Started" helps you to begin thinking about the topic of the lesson from your own experience.

— "Digging In" focuses on the topic and has several questions to probe your thoughts.

— "Going Deeper" includes a passage of Scripture and thought-provoking questions to plunge you into the meaning of the text. Special theological notes will elaborate on biblical concepts and help you comprehend the heart of the message.

— "Making It Real" unites the threads of your study and helps you apply what you have learned.

— "Thinking It Through" leads you in quiet reflection on Christ's sacrifice and encourages your prayerful response to God. You will find the printed lyrics from the powerful songs of worship on the *He Chose the Nails* music CD, which adds an exciting new dimension to your worship. Inspired by the message of *He Chose the Nails*, top Christian recording artists have written inspiring songs filled with intense emotion. Artists such as Twila Paris, Kim Hill, Wes King, Natalie Grant, Sonicflood, Jennifer Langford and the Oak Hills Church of Christ Choir will thrill your spirit with their music, ranging from acoustic contemporary, to edgy power ballads, to praise-style gospel.

— "Taking It Home" includes five homework segments for the following week to reinforce the ideas you have learned and help you make more connections with Scripture and your own life. Each day will introduce you to new passages in both the Old and New Testaments. Special boxes feature notes on biblical doctrine and key theological themes and words, and insightful quotes from leading Christians through the ages are sprinkled in the lessons. The questions will help you analyze the reading and respond to it, applying your thoughts to your actions.

In the video package, fourteen video segments feature Max sharing his experiences and reenacting scenes drawn from the book. Each lesson features one video segment, except for lesson 12, which has two. Segment 14 is a concluding message from Max. The scripts of the video have also been included in the back of the book, in case you do not have access to the video or you would simply like to follow along.

Max's original book, *He Chose the Nails,* takes a closer look at the meaning of Christ's sacrifice for you. He invites you to ponder the Cross by examining its many inanimate objects. The nails, the spear, the bitter sponge, and the thorny crowns each carry rich meaning and messages.

He Chose the Nails is a study and worship experience that will have a profound impact on your spiritual growth. With startling clarity, *He Chose the Nails* shows us that to truly understand who Jesus is, we must stand at the foot of the Cross. May God bless you as you take a closer look at the Cross and marvel that he did it all for you.

L E S S O N

1

"You Did This for Me?"

GETTING STARTED

VIDEO—In video segment number 1, Max tells the story of trying to find a gift for his wife. (The script is in reprinted on page 221.)

1. Think back over Christmases, birthdays, and anniversaries. What are some of the more memorable gifts you've been given? the more odd gifts? the more lavish gifts? the most treasured gifts?

_____

_____

_____

2. *Max says:* "Oh, the things we do to give gifts to those we love." What was one of your more extravagant gift-giving experiences?

_____

_____

_____

3. Which of the following types of gifts do you like to give most? Receive most? Why?
   gifts of time (attention) _____
   gifts of affection (expressions of endearment) _____
   gifts of praise (affirmation) _____
   gifts of touch (hugs, kisses, etc.)_____
   gifts of things (material) _____

4. *Max writes:*
"He splashed orange in the sunrise
and cast the sky in blue.
And if you love to see geese as they gather,
Chances are you'll see that, too.

"Did he have to make the squirrel's tail furry?
Was he obliged to make the birds sing?
And the funny way that chickens scurry
or the majesty of thunder when it rings?

"Why give a flower fragrance? Why give food its taste?
Could it be
he loves to see
that look upon your face?"

"If we give gifts to show our love, how much more would he? If we—speckled with foibles and greed—love to give gifts, how much more does God, pure and perfect God, enjoy giving gifts to us?"

What God-given gifts do you most appreciate and why?

_____

_____

_____

5. *Max writes*: "Have you ever wondered why God gives so much? We could exist on far less. He could have left the world flat and gray; we wouldn't have known the difference. But he didn't." Why do you think God gives so much?

_____

_____

_____

6. What aspects of God's creation most delight your own heart? What aspect of God's salvation thrills you most? Why?

_____

_____

> *Salvation is God-given, God-driven, God-empowered, and God-originated. The gift is not from man to God. It is from God to man.*
> *Max Lucado[1]*

7. *Max writes:* "Every gift reveals God's love . . . but no gift reveals his love more than the gifts of the cross. They came, not wrapped in paper, but in passion. Not placed around a tree, but a cross. And not covered with ribbons, but sprinkled in blood." To what "gifts of the cross" is Max referring?

_____

_____

_____

8. Have you ever considered the objects from the crucifixion scene (for example, the thorns, nails, garment, sponge, etc.) as "gifts" before? Why or why not?

_____

_____

_____

GOING DEEPER

Ephesians 1:4–11
⁴For he chose us in him before the creation of the world to be holy and blameless in his sight. In love
⁵he predestined us to be adopted as his sons through Jesus Christ, in accordance with his pleasure and will—
⁶to the praise of his glorious grace, which he has freely given us in the One he loves.
⁷In him we have redemption through his blood, the forgiveness of sins, in accordance with the riches of God's grace
⁸that he lavished on us with all wisdom and understanding.
⁹And he made known to us the mystery of his will according to his good pleasure, which he purposed in Christ,
¹⁰to be put into effect when the times will have reached their fulfillment—to bring all things in heaven and on earth together under one head, even Christ.
¹¹In him we were also chosen, having been predestined according to the plan of him who works out everything in conformity with the purpose of his will. (NIV)

9. How would you summarize this passage that speaks of the spiritual blessings that God has given to us?

_____

_____

10. What specific words or phrases does the apostle Paul use here that indicate God is eager to pour out blessings on his children and is generous in doing so?

_____

_____

Ephesians 1

Spiritual blessings begin with and are based on election (he chose us), of which God is the subject and believers are the object. Election is God's sovereign work of choosing some to believe (see Rom. 8:30; Eph. 1:11; 1 Thess. 1:4; 2 Thess. 2:13; Titus 1:1). Salvation is God's doing, not man's (Eph. 2:8–9). Though it is an act of grace (Rom. 11:5–6; 2 Tim. 1:9), based on his will (Eph. 1:5, 9, 11), a person is responsible to believe (v. 13). "God chose you to be saved . . . through belief in the truth" (2 Thess. 2:13, NIV).

(adapted from Harold Hoehner, *The Bible Knowledge Commentary–New Testament* [Wheaton. IL: Victor Books, 1983], 617)

11. Romans 6:23 states: "For the wages of sin is death, but the gift of God is eternal life in Christ Jesus our Lord" (NIV). What gift from God is described here?

_____

_____

_____

12. What does it mean to you that the word "gift" is used instead of "wages" in this verse?

_____

_____

_____

13. What is Jesus' connection to this gift?

_____

_____

_____

The Terms of Salvation

The Book of Romans, called by the poet Coleridge "the most profound book in existence" and by Martin Luther "the very purest gospel" clearly portrays God's plan of salvation through Christ. Here are the key terms used in the book.

Term	Number of References	Meaning
Gospel	13	"Good news"; used by Paul to refer to the wonderful message of forgiveness and eternal life in Christ.
Faith	39	"Belief, trust"; the means by which sinful people (all of us) can experience and enjoy all the blessings of salvation.
Righteousness	36	God's standard of purity which must be met if we are to have fellowship with God. It is through Jesus Christ alone (and our faith in him) that we find this righteousness and become acceptable to God. Through a process called "imputation," Christ not only takes away our sin, but he grants us his per-fect purity!
Sin	45	Paul used several different Greek words to describe the human tendency to rebel against God. Broadly we may define sin as "any attitude or action that opposes the character and will of God." Sin is what brings death (that is, separation from God).
Salvation	4	Deliverance; often used in the Bible to describe a rescue from physical harm; used chiefly by Paul to

Term	Number of References	Meaning
		denote deliverance from sin and its deadly consequences.
Justification	3	The act of being declared "righteous"; a legal term used by Paul to describe the spiritual transaction whereby God (the Judge) declares those who trust in Christ and what he has done for them on the cross to be acceptable before him. Such a verdict is possible only because Christ has settled all the claims of the Law against sinners.
Grace	24	The unmerited favor of God; this term refers to God's inexplicable giving of good things (especially salvation) to people who do not deserve and could never earn such. It is a free gift made possible by Christ's death on our behalf.
Redemption	2	The act of freeing something or someone by paying a purchase price; this economic term is used by Paul in a theological sense to describe how Christ paid the penalty required by God for our sins (that is, death) by giving his own life on the cross. He redeemed us from sin—its power and effects.
Propitiation	1	The satisfaction of God's holy wrath against sin; human rebellion against God (that is, sin) results in the wrath of God and must be met with judgment. By dying in our place and taking our sins upon himself, Christ satisfied God's righteous anger against all who believe.
Law	78	The body of commandments and rules for living given to Israel by God through Moses; Romans emphasizes the holy character of the Law as well as the inability of sinful people to live according to it. Thus the Law becomes a burden and a curse, until we allows it to point us to Christ, who perfectly fulfills all its requirements.

(adapted from *The Nelson Study Bible* [Nashville, TN: Thomas Nelson Publishers, 1997], 1904)

14. Second Corinthians 9:15 says: "Thanks be to God for his indescribable gift!" (NIV). What gift from God is described here?

_____

_____

Why is this gift called "indescribable"?

_____

_____

How are we to respond to this gift?

_____

_____

_____

15. *Max writes:* "We are at our best when we are giving. In fact, we are most like God when we are giving." What do you think Max means by this statement?

_____

_____

_____

16. How have you felt when you've been particularly generous? What happened as a result of your giving?

_____

_____

_____

_____

MAKING IT REAL

1 Peter 1:3—5

³Praise be to the God and Father of our Lord Jesus Christ! In his great mercy he has given us new birth into a living hope through the resurrection of Jesus Christ from the dead, ⁴and into an inheritance that can never perish, spoil or fade—kept in heaven for you, ⁵who through faith are shielded by God's power until the coming of the salvation that is ready to be revealed in the last time." (NIV)

Overcome by pride, the Starmaker turns to us, one by one, and says, "You are my child. I love you dearly. I'm aware that someday you'll turn from me and walk away. But I want you to know, I've already provided you a way back."
Max Lucado²

17. How does the apostle Peter describe the "inheritance" that is ours in Christ?

_____

_____

_____

_____

18. Find words in this short passage that reveal what God has done or will do for us, and record them below.

_____

_____

_____

_____

Max writes: "Perchance you will hear him whisper: 'I did it just for you.'"

Take a few minutes to list some of God's gifts to you. When you are finished with this exercise, pour out your heart in thanksgiving to God for the abundance of his rich gifts. Try hard not to bring up any prayer requests during this time; instead concentrate only on expressing gratitude.

THINKING IT THROUGH

Spend a few moments in quiet reflection as you listen to the song "Because of Love" by Natalie Grant and Bernie Herms on the CD. Then thank God for the inexplicable love he has for you, the love that prompted him to give you the most precious gift—his one and only Son.

TAKING IT HOME

Memory Verse
Romans 6:23
For the wages of sin is death, but the gift of God is eternal life in Christ Jesus our Lord. (NIV)
For the wages of sin is death, but the gift of God is eternal life in Christ Jesus our Lord. (NKJV)
For the wages of sin is death, but the free gift of God is eternal life through Christ Jesus our Lord. (NLT)

During the next week, study the following passages.

Day 1) *The Gifts of Creation and Material Blessings*

Read
Psalm 104

1 Praise the LORD, O my soul.
O LORD my God, you are very great;
you are clothed with splendor and majesty.
2 He wraps himself in light as with a garment;
he stretches out the heavens like a tent
3 and lays the beams of his upper chambers on their waters.
He makes the clouds his chariot
and rides on the wings of the wind.
4 He makes winds his messengers,
flames of fire his servants.
5 He set the earth on its foundations;
it can never be moved.
6 You covered it with the deep as with a garment;
the waters stood above the mountains.
7 But at your rebuke the waters fled,
at the sound of your thunder they took to flight;
8 they flowed over the mountains,
they went down into the valleys,
to the place you assigned for them.
9 You set a boundary they cannot cross;
never again will they cover the earth.
10 He makes springs pour water into the ravines;
it flows between the mountains.
11 They give water to all the beasts of the field;
the wild donkeys quench their thirst.
12 The birds of the air nest by the waters;
they sing among the branches.
13 He waters the mountains from his upper chambers;
the earth is satisfied by the fruit of his work.
14 He makes grass grow for the cattle,
and plants for man to cultivate—
bringing forth food from the earth:
15 wine that gladdens the heart of man,
oil to make his face shine,
and bread that sustains his heart.
16 The trees of the LORD are well watered,
the cedars of Lebanon that he planted.
17 There the birds make their nests;
the stork has its home in the pine trees.
18 The high mountains belong to the wild goats;
the crags are a refuge for the coneys.

^{19} *The moon marks off the seasons,*
and the sun knows when to go down.
^{20} *You bring darkness, it becomes night,*
and all the beasts of the forest prowl.
^{21} *The lions roar for their prey*
and seek their food from God.
^{22} *The sun rises, and they steal away;*
they return and lie down in their dens.
^{23} *Then man goes out to his work,*
to his labor until evening.
^{24} *How many are your works, O LORD!*
In wisdom you made them all;
the earth is full of your creatures.
^{25} *There is the sea, vast and spacious,*
teeming with creatures beyond number—
living things both large and small.
^{26} *There the ships go to and fro,*
and the leviathan, which you formed to frolic there.
^{27} *These all look to you*
to give them their food at the proper time.
^{28} *When you give it to them,*
they gather it up;
when you open your hand,
they are satisfied with good things.
^{29} *When you hide your face,*
they are terrified;
when you take away their breath,
they die and return to the dust.
^{30} *When you send your Spirit,*
they are created,
and you renew the face of the earth.
^{31} *May the glory of the LORD endure forever;*
may the LORD rejoice in his works—
^{32} *he who looks at the earth, and it trembles,*
who touches the mountains, and they smoke.
^{33} *I will sing to the LORD all my life;*
I will sing praise to my God as long as I live.
^{34} *May my meditation be pleasing to him,*
as I rejoice in the LORD.
^{35} *But may sinners vanish from the earth*
and the wicked be no more.
Praise the LORD, O my soul.
Praise the LORD (NIV).

Ever feel like you have nothing? Just look at the gifts God has given you: He sent his angels to care for you, his Holy Spirit to dwell in you, his church to encourage you, and his Word to guide you. . . . Anytime you speak, he listens; make a request and he responds. He will never let you be tempted too much or stumble too far. Let a tear appear on your cheek, and he is there to wipe it. Let a love sonnet appear on your lips, and he is there to hear it. As much as you want to see him, he wants to see you more. . . . You have been chosen by Christ. . . . He has claimed you as his beloved.
Max Lucado[3]

Realize

1. For what amazing aspects of creation does the psalmist praise God?

_____

_____

_____

2. What verses or phrases depict God's great power?

_____

_____

3. What verses or phrases demonstrate God's sovereignty (his "being in control of all things")?

_____

_____

4. How does this psalm indicate God's specific care for animals and people?

_____

_____

_____

Respond

5. How can focusing on God's revelation through creation change the way we think and live?

_____

_____

_____

6. How often do you stop and acknowledge God's creative gifts all around you? How could you develop this habit?

_____

_____

_____

7. What specific items or creatures from nature fill you with awe and prompt you to remember God? Why?

_____

_____

_____

Day 2) *The Gift of Salvation*

Read
Psalm 103

¹ *Praise the LORD, O my soul;*
   all my inmost being, praise his holy name.
² *Praise the LORD, O my soul,*
   and forget not all his benefits—
³ *who forgives all your sins*
   and heals all your diseases,
⁴ *who redeems your life from the pit*
   and crowns you with love and compassion,
⁵ *who satisfies your desires with good things*
   so that your youth is renewed like the eagle's.
⁶ *The LORD works righteousness*
   and justice for all the oppressed.
⁷ *He made known his ways to Moses,*
   his deeds to the people of Israel:
⁸ *The LORD is compassionate and gracious,*
   slow to anger, abounding in love.
⁹ *He will not always accuse,*
   nor will he harbor his anger forever;
¹⁰ *he does not treat us as our sins deserve*
   or repay us according to our iniquities.
¹¹ *For as high as the heavens are above the earth,*
   so great is his love for those who fear him;
¹² *as far as the east is from the west,*
   so far has he removed our transgressions from us.
¹³ *As a father has compassion on his children,*
   so the LORD has compassion on those who fear him;

¹⁴ for he knows how we are formed,
he remembers that we are dust.
¹⁵ As for man, his days are like grass,
he flourishes like a flower of the field;
¹⁶ the wind blows over it and it is gone,
and its place remembers it no more.
¹⁷ But from everlasting to everlasting
the LORD's love is with those who fear him,
and his righteousness with their children's children—
¹⁸ with those who keep his covenant
and remember to obey his precepts.
¹⁹ The LORD has established his throne in heaven,
and his kingdom rules over all.
²⁰ Praise the LORD, you his angels,
you mighty ones who do his bidding,
who obey his word.
²¹ Praise the LORD, all his heavenly hosts,
you his servants who do his will.
²² Praise the LORD, all his works
everywhere in his dominion.
Praise the LORD, O my soul. (NIV)

Realize

1. What does it mean to "praise the Lord"?

_____

_____

_____

2. Below, write the three "benefits" from God that touch your heart most today.

_____

_____

_____

3. What words and phrases does David use to describe humans?

_____

_____

_____

Next time a sunset steals your breath or a meadow of flowers leaves you speechless, remain that way. Say nothing and listen as heaven whispers, "Do you like it? I did it just for you."
Max Lucado[4]

4. What words and phrases does David use to describe God himself?

_____

_____

_____

5. What does this psalm say that God does with our sin? (Hint: See verses 3, 10–12.)

_____

_____

_____

Respond

6. If you were going to make a list of God's most meaningful gifts to you, what items would top the list and why?

Take some time to write out a short prayer (or psalm) to God expressing your gratitude for his salvation.

_____

_____

_____

Day 3) *The Gift of the Holy Spirit*

Read

Ezekiel 11:19
I will give them an undivided heart and put a new spirit in them; I will remove from them their heart of stone and give them a heart of flesh. (NIV)

Acts 2:38
Peter replied, "Repent and be baptized, every one of you, in the name of Jesus Christ for the forgiveness of your sins. And you will receive the gift of the Holy Spirit." (NIV)

Luke 11:13
If you then, though you are evil, know how to give good gifts to your children, how much more will your Father in heaven give the Holy Spirit to those who ask him! (NIV)

Romans 5:5
And hope does not disappoint us, because God has poured out his love into our hearts by the Holy Spirit, whom he has given us. (NIV)

Ephesians 1:13
And you also were included in Christ when you heard the word of truth, the gospel of your salvation. Having believed, you were marked in him with a seal, the promised Holy Spirit. (NIV).

Jesus Christ broke the power of sin and death, but the converse is not true. Sin and death cannot break the power of Jesus Christ. The condemnation of Adam's sin is reversible, the redemption of Jesus Christ is not. The effect of Adam's act is permanent only if not nullified by Christ. The effect of Christ's act, however, is permanent for believing individuals and not subject to reversal or nullification. We have the great assurance that once we are in Jesus Christ, we are in him forever.
John MacArthur[5]

Realize

1. In the prophecy revealed by Ezekiel, what hopeful promise did God give his people?

_____

_____

_____

2. When Peter preached at Pentecost, what did he promise as the result of repentance and baptism?

_____

_____

_____

3. How would this new relationship with the Spirit of God be different from the old life before Pentecost?

_____

_____

_____

4. What is significant about Luke's quote of Jesus (11:13)? To what does he compare the Holy Spirit?

_____

_____

_____

5. According to Paul (Romans 5:5), how is it that we come to know and appreciate God's love?

_____

_____

6. What does Ephesians 1:13 say about the Holy Spirit and salvation?

_____

_____

Ephesians 1:13–14

The Holy Spirit is God's seal that we belong to him and his deposit guaranteeing that he will do what he has promised. The Holy Spirit is like a down payment, a deposit, a validating signature on the contract. The presence of the Holy Spirit in us demonstrates the genuineness of our faith, proves that we are God's children, and secures eternal life for us. His power works in us to transform us now, and what we experience now is a taste of the total change we will experience in eternity.

(adapted from the *Life Application Bible/NLT*, [Wheaton, IL: Tyndale House Publishers, Inc., 1996], 1872)

Respond

7. What evidence do you have of the presence and power of the Holy Spirit in your life?

_____

_____

_____

_____

8. In what ways does the indwelling Spirit assure us of our salvation?

_____

_____

_____

_____

God gives us many benefits even against our will and maybe even without our knowing it. When we pray for one thing and He does the reverse, it is plain that He is doing good even when we don't know it.
Chrysostom

Day 4) *The Gift of the Word*

Read
Psalm 119:1–18
1Blessed are they whose ways are blameless, who walk according to the law of the LORD.
2Blessed are they who keep his statutes and seek him with all their heart.
3They do nothing wrong; they walk in his ways.
4You have laid down precepts that are to be fully obeyed.
5Oh, that my ways were steadfast in obeying your decrees!
6Then I would not be put to shame when I consider all your commands.
7I will praise you with an upright heart as I learn your righteous laws.
8I will obey your decrees; do not utterly forsake me.
9How can a young man keep his way pure? By living according to your word.
10I seek you with all my heart; do not let me stray from your commands.
11I have hidden your word in my heart that I might not sin against you.
12Praise be to you, O LORD; teach me your decrees.
13With my lips I recount all the laws that come from your mouth.
14I rejoice in following your statutes as one rejoices in great riches.
15I meditate on your precepts and consider your ways.
16I delight in your decrees; I will not neglect your word.
17Do good to your servant, and I will live; I will obey your word.
18Open my eyes that I may see wonderful things in your law. (NIV)

Realize

1. What different words does the psalmist use to describe God's revelation?

_____

_____

_____

_____

2. Underline each occurrence of the word "your" in verses 1–18. What does this say about the source of truth?

_____

_____

_____

3. According to this passage, what are some of the benefits of knowing and obeying God's word?

_____

_____

_____

EIGHT WORDS FOR LAW

Hebrew law served as the personal and national guide for living under God's authority. It directed the moral, spiritual, and social life. Its purpose was to produce better understanding of God and greater commitment to him.

Word	Meaning	Examples	Significance
Torah	Directions, Guidance, Instruction	Exod. 24:12; Isa. 30:20	Need for law in general; a command from a higher person to a lower
Mitswah	Commandment, Command	Gen 25:5; Exod. 15:26; 20:2–17; Deut. 5:6–21	God's specific instruction to be obeyed rather than a general law; used of the Ten Commandments
Mishpat	Judgment, Ordinance	Gen. 13:19; Deut. 34:2; Deut. 16:18; 17:9	Refers to civil, social, and sanitation laws
Eduth	Admonition, Testimony	Exod. 25:22	Refers to God's law as he deals with his people
Huqqim	Statutes, Oracles	Lev. 18:4;' Deut. 4:1	Dealt with the royal pronouncements; mainly connected to worship and feasts
Piqqudim	Orders, Precepts	Psa. 19:8; 103:8	Used often in the psalms to describe God's orders and assignments
Dabar	Word	Exod. 34:28; Deut. 4:13	Used to indicate divine oracles or revelations of God
Dath	Royal Edict, Public Law	Ezek. 7:26; Dan. 2:3, 15; Dan. 6:8, 12	Refers to the divine law or Jewish religious traditions in general

(adapted from the *Life Application Bible/NLT* [Wheaton, IL: Tyndale House Publishers, 1996], 257)

4. How can we live pure lives and keep from sin?

_____

_____

_____

_____

5. What is the psalmist's attitude toward all that God has said? How would you describe his attitude toward the things of God?

_____

_____

_____

_____

6. How much do you hunger and thirst for God's truth?

_____
_____
_____

7. The psalmist mentioned hiding God's Word in his heart. What is another way of saying this? How much do you do this?

_____
_____
_____

8. What does it mean to meditate on God's precepts? Is this a regular practice of yours?

_____
_____
_____

9. Write five adjectives that you think would describe your life if you did not possess the gift of God's Word.

_____
_____
_____

Day 5) Appreciating God's Great Gifts

Read
Luke 11:13
(Jesus is speaking) "Even though you are bad, you know how to give good things to your children. How much more will your heavenly Father will give the Holy Spirit to those who ask him!" (NCV)

James 1:17
Every good and perfect gift is from above, coming down from the Father of the heavenly lights, who does not change like shifting shadows. (NIV)

Ecclesiastes 5:19–20
¹⁹Moreover, when God gives any man wealth and possessions, and enables him to enjoy them, to accept his lot and be happy in his work—this is a gift of God.
²⁰He seldom reflects on the days of his life, because God keeps him occupied with gladness of heart. (NIV)

Realize
1. What does Luke 11:13 suggest about gift-giving tendencies of earthly parents? about the Father heart of God?

_____
_____
_____

2. According to James 1:17, what is the source of all the good gifts in life? How can this be so?

_____
_____

3. How does this verse describe the character or nature of God?

_____

_____

_____

4. What gifts or blessings are cited in Ecclesiastes 5?

_____

_____

5. Would you agree that health and wealth are relative terms? Though you can, no doubt, list many who have these to a greater degree, what specific gifts have you been granted in these areas?

_____

_____

_____

Respond

6. How is God's grace a gift to you?

_____

_____

_____

GRACE—favor or kindness shown without regard to the worth or merit of the one who receives it and in spite of what that person deserves

Grace is one of the key attributes of God. The Lord God is "merciful and gracious, long-suffering, and abounding in goodness and truth" (Exod. 34:6, NKJV). Therefore, grace is almost always associated with mercy, love, compassion, and patience.

In the Old Testament, the supreme example of grace was the redemption of the Hebrew people from Egypt and their establishment in the Promised Land. This did not happen because of any merit on Israel's part, but in spite of their unrighteousness (Deut. 7:7–8; 9:5–6). Although the grace of God is always free and undeserved, it must not be taken for granted. Grace is enjoyed only within the Covenant—the gift is given by God, and the gift is received by people through repentance and faith (Amos 5:15). Grace is to be humbly sought through the prayer of faith (Mal. 1:9).

The grace of God was supremely revealed and given in the person and work of Jesus Christ. Jesus was not only the beneficiary of God's grace (Luke 2:40) but was also its very embodiment (John 1:14), bringing it to humankind for salvation (Titus 2:11). By his death and resurrection, Jesus restored the broken fellowship between God and his people, both Jew and Gentile. The only way of salvation for any person is "through the grace of the Lord Jesus Christ" (Acts 15:11, NKJV).

The grace of God revealed in Jesus Christ is applied to human beings for their salvation by the Holy Spirit, who is called "the Spirit of grace" (Heb. 10:29, NKJV). The Spirit is the One who binds Christ to his people so that they receive forgiveness, adoption to sonship, and newness of life, as well as every spiritual gift or grace (Eph. 4:7).

The theme of grace is especially prominent in the letters of Paul. He sets grace radically over against the Law and the works of the Law (Rom. 3:24, 28). Paul makes it abundantly clear that salvation is not something that can be earned; it can be received only as a gift of grace (Rom. 4:4). Grace, however, must be accompanied by faith; a person must trust in the mercy and favor of God, even while it is undeserved (Rom. 4:16; Gal. 2:16).

The Law of Moses revealed the righteous will of God in the midst of pagan darkness; it was God's gracious gift to Israel (Deut. 4:8). But his will was made complete when Jesus brought the gospel of grace into the world (John 1:17).

(adapted from Ronald F. Youngblood, Ed., *Nelson's New Illustrated Bible Dictionary* [Nashville, TN: Thomas Nelson Publishers) 1997, c1995], CD-ROM)

7. How (specifically and practically) can you develop a more thankful heart this week?

_____

_____

_____

8. *If, as Max writes,* "we are most like God when we are giving," how can you be "like God" this week?

_____

_____

_____

9. Who can you bless with an unexpected gift? What kind of gift should this be? When can you give it? How can you present it to make the moment extra special?

_____

_____

Plan out the details of your gift giving and then carry it out before the end of the week.

L E S S O N

2

"I Will Become One of You and Bear Your Dark Side"

God's Promise in the Crown of Thorns and the Soldier's Spit

LOOKING BACK

Lesson 1 looked at God's amazing generosity—his willingness (eagerness, even) to shower us with good and perfect gifts. See if you can say Romans 6:23 by memory, our memory verse for that first lesson.

1. *Max writes:* "God's gifts shed light on God's heart, God's good and generous heart. . . . Every gift reveals God's love . . . but no gift reveals his love more than the gifts of the cross." For what gifts of God do you have the greatest appreciation? What divine gifts do you feel the need to understand more deeply?

   _____

   _____

   _____

2. What new insights into God's generosity did you get from your daily study?

   _____

   _____

   _____

GETTING STARTED

VIDEO—In video segment number 2, Max tells about his feelings of anger during his traffic duel with another driver. (The script is reprinted on page 222.)

3. When did you have a similar experience in traffic?

   _____

   _____

   _____

4. What other experiences have dramatically reminded you of your sinful nature?

   _____

   _____

   _____

5. *Max says:* "Want to know the coolest thing about the one who gave up the crown of heaven for a crown of thorns? He did it for you. Just for you." What makes this so "cool"?

   _____

   _____

   _____

DIGGING IN

6. *Max writes:* "Ever since the curse, we've been different. Beastly. Ugly. Defiant. Angry. We do things we know we shouldn't do and wonder why we did them." To what event does

Max refer when he speaks of "the curse"? How did this event change everything about the world and about humanity?

_____

_____

_____

7. In what kinds of situations is your own sin nature most likely to surface? (If you feel comfortable doing so, describe a recent occasion in which you did something you knew you shouldn't do, only to wonder later why you did it.)

8. Max issues the following challenge: "For the next twenty-four hours, lead a sinless life." What do you think would happen if you attempted this experiment?

_____

_____

_____

9. What are some of the explanations irreligious people typically give for the evil actions of humankind?

_____

_____

_____

The moment the forbidden fruit touched the lips of Eve, the shadow of a cross appeared on the horizon. And between that moment and the moment the man with a mallet placed the spike against the wrist of God, a master plan was fulfilled.
Max Lucado[1]

10. What are some human solutions to which irreligious people look in their attempts to overcome humanity's propensity for evil?

_____

_____

_____

The scriptural evidence provides the basis for what has been commonly called total depravity. The English word "depravity" means perverted or crooked. It is not used in the translation of the King James Version, but some modern translations do use it to translate *adokimos* in Romans 1:28. This word means "not standing the test," and gives us a clue as to how to define the concept of depravity. Depravity means that man fails the test of pleasing God. He denotes his unmeritoriousness in God's sight. This failure is total in that (a) it affects all aspects of a person's being, and (b) it affects all people.

Negatively, the concept of total depravity does not mean (a) that every person has exhibited his or her depravity as thoroughly as he or she could; (b) that sinners do not have a conscience or a "native induction" concerning God; (c) that sinners will indulge in every form of sin; (d) that depraved people do not perform actions that are good in the sight of others and even in the sight of God.

Positively, total depravity means (a) that corruption extends to every facet of human nature and faculties; (b) that there is nothing in anyone that can commend a person to a righteous God.

Total depravity must always be measured against God's holiness. Relative goodness exists in people. They can do good works which are appreciated by others. But nothing that anyone can do will gain salvational merit or favor in the sight of a holy God.

(© 1986 Cook Communications Ministries. *Bible Knowledge Commentary* by Walvoord and Zuck. Reprinted with permission. May not be further reproduced. All rights reserved.)

11. *Max writes:* "When God entered time and became a man, he who was boundless became bound. Imprisoned in flesh. Restricted by weary-prone muscles and eyelids. For more than three decades, his once limitless reach would be limited to the stretch of an arm; his speed checked to the pace of human feet." What do you think would be the hardest part about exchanging boundlessness for being confined to a finite human body? Why?

12. Is it easy for you to think of Jesus as completely human (although without sin)? Explain.

_____

_____

_____

He sat in silence while the sins of the world were placed upon his Son. And he did nothing while a cry a million times bloodier than John's echoed in the black sky: "My God, my God, why have you forsaken me?"
Was it right? No.
Was it fair? No.
Was it love? Yes.
Max Lucado[1]

13. Why would Jesus exchange the limitless conditions he knew in heaven for the severe limits of earth?

_____

_____

GOING DEEPER

Mark 15:17–19
They put a purple robe on him, then twisted together a crown of thorns and set it on him. 18And they began to call out to him, "Hail, king of the Jews!" 19Again and again they struck him on the head with a staff and spit on him. Falling on their knees, they paid homage to him (NIV).

14. Why do you suppose the soldiers did these things?

_____

15. *Max writes:* "Throughout Scripture thorns symbolize, not sin, but the consequences of sin. Remember Eden? After Adam and Eve sinned, God cursed the land. Brambles on the earth are the product of sin in the heart." How are thorns an appropriate symbol for the consequences of sin? Why do you think the thorns placed on Jesus' head were called a "crown" instead of a wreath or a circle?

_____

_____

_____

Psalm 36:1
Sin whispers to the wicked, deep within their hearts. They have no fear of God to restrain them. (NLT)

16. How is sin described in this passage? Is it a superficial issue? Why or why not?

_____

_____

_____

Jeremiah 17:9
The heart is deceitful above all things and beyond cure. Who can understand it? (NIV)

17. How has sin affected the heart of each individual? Is it fair to describe sin as a "spiritual disease"? Why or why not?

_____

_____

_____

Romans 3:23
For all have sinned and fall short of the glory of God. (NKJV)

18. What does this verse say about the extent of sin?

_____

_____

19. What is the result of human sinfulness?

_____

_____

_____

John 1:1–2, 14
1In the beginning the Word already existed. He was with God, and he was God.
2He was in the beginning with God.
14So the Word became human and lived here on earth among us. He was full of unfailing love and faithfulness. And we have seen his glory, the glory of the only Son of the Father. (NLT)

20. What does John 1 say about the essential nature of Christ? Is he God, man, or both?

_____

_____

_____

21. Why is it significant that Christ took on human flesh?

_____

_____

_____

SIN—lawlessness (1 John 3:4) or transgression of God's will, either by omitting to do what God's law requires or by doing what it forbids. The transgression can occur in thought (1 John 3:15), word (Matt. 5:22), or deed (Rom. 1:32).

Humankind was created without sin, morally upright and inclined to do good (Eccles. 7:29). But sin entered into human experience when Adam and Eve violated the direct command of God by eating the forbidden fruit in the Garden of Eden (Gen. 3:6). Because Adam was the head and representative of the whole human race, his sin affected all future generations (Rom. 5:12–21). Associated with this guilt is a corrupted nature passed from Adam to all his descendants. Out of this perverted nature arise all the sins that people commit (Matt. 15:19); no person is free from involvement in sin (Rom. 3:23).

God is holy and cannot sin (James 1:13). Jesus Christ, the Son of God who came to earth in human form, is also sinless. His perfection arises from his divine nature, as well as his human nature (1 Pet. 2:22). Although the story of the Bible focuses on the sin of humankind and God's provision for our redemption, the angels are also described as capable of sinning. Some have fallen away from God's service (Jude 6). But animals are not morally responsible creatures; so they cannot sin.

Humankind originally fell into sin at the temptation of Satan. As the tempter, he continues to lure people into sin (1 Pet. 5:8); nevertheless, people remain fully responsible for what they do. God is not the author of sin, but his plan for world redemption does include his dealing with the reality of sin (2 Sam. 24:1; 1 Chron. 21:1). This truth is dramatically witnessed in the death of Jesus Christ. The crucifixion happened according to God's will; but at the same time, it was the worst crime of human history (Acts 2:23).

Sin is not represented in the Bible as the absence of good or as an illusion that stems from our human limitations. Sin is portrayed as a real and positive evil. Sin is more than unwise, inexpedient, calamitous behavior that produces sorrow and distress. It is rebellion against God's law—the standard of righteousness (Ps. 119:160).

Since God demands righteousness, sin must be defined in terms of humankind's relation to God. Sin is thus the faithless rebellion of creatures against the just authority of their Creator. For this reason, breaking God's law at any point involves transgression at every point (James 2:10).

Violation of the law of God in thought, word, and deed shows the sinfulness of the human heart. Sin is actually a contradiction to the holiness of God, whose image human beings bear. This depraved condition is called "original sin" because it comes from Adam and characterizes all persons from the moment of their birth.

Human moral depravity is total in that "the carnal mind is enmity against God; for it is not subject to the law of God, nor indeed can be" (Rom. 8:7, NKJV). Apart from Christ, all are "dead in trespasses and sins" (Eph. 2:1, NKJV). But this does not mean that people behave as wickedly as they might, for God restrains the outworkings of the sinful heart. At times he even helps sinners to do things that conform to the law (Gen. 20:6). The corruption of sin is not developed or expressed to the same degree in every person. Neither is it expressed in the same way in any person at all times.

Sin involves the denial of the living God from whom human beings draw their life and existence (Acts 17:28); the consequence of this revolt is death and the torment of hell. Death is the ultimate penalty imposed by God for sin (Rom. 6:23).

Against this dark background of sin and its reality, the gospel comes as the good news of the deliverance that God has provided through his Son. Jesus bears the penalty of sin in place of his people (Mark 10:45). He also redeems us from lawlessness and makes us long for good works in service to God and others (Titus 2:14).

(adapted from Ronald F Youngblood, Ed., *Nelson's New Illustrated Bible Dictionary* [Nashville, TN: Thomas Nelson Publishers, 1997, c1995], CD-ROM)

22. *Max writes:* "It's not that we *can't* do good. We do. It's just that we can't keep from doing bad. In theological terms, we are 'totally depraved.' Though made in God's image, we have fallen. We're corrupt at the core. The very center of our being is selfish and perverse." In your own terms, how would you describe humankind's fallen condition?

_____

_____

_____

23. Do you agree that it's impossible for us to keep from doing bad? Explain.

_____

_____

_____

MAKING IT REAL

24. *Max writes:* "What is the fruit of sin? Step into the briar patch of humanity and feel a few thistles. Shame. Fear. Disgrace. Discouragement. Anxiety. Haven't our hearts been caught in these brambles?

"The heart of Jesus, however, had not. He had never been cut by the thorns of sin. What you and I face daily, he never knew. Anxiety? He never worried! Guilt? He was never guilty! Fear? He never left the presence of God! Jesus never knew the fruits of sin . . . until he became sin for us.

"And when he did, all the emotions of sin tumbled in on him like shadows in the forest. He felt anxious, guilty, and alone. Can't you hear the emotions in his prayer? 'My God, my God why have you rejected me?' (Mt. 27:46). These are not the words of a saint. This is the cry of a sinner."

What does it mean to you that Jesus, knowing our utter sinfulness, still chose to enter our fallen world and take our sin upon himself?

_____

_____

_____

THINKING IT THROUGH

Quietly ponder the truths you've just studied. Consider the awfulness of sin and the wonder of a God who would come to deliver you from sin's effects as you contemplate the words of "The Thread of Scarlet" by Wes King on the CD.

TAKING IT HOME

Memory Verse:
Romans 3:23
For all have sinned and fall short of the glory of God. (NIV)

For all have sinned and fall short of the glory of God. (NKJV)

For all have sinned; all fall short of God's glorious standard. (NLT)

During the next week, study the following passages.

Day 1) *The Fall*

Read
Genesis 3
¹*Now the serpent was more cunning than any beast of the field which the LORD God had made. And he said to the woman, "Has God indeed said, 'You shall not eat of every tree of the garden'?"*
²*And the woman said to the serpent, "We may eat the fruit of the trees of the garden;*
³*but of the fruit of the tree which is in the midst of the garden, God has said, 'You shall not eat it, nor shall you touch it, lest you die.'"*
⁴*Then the serpent said to the woman, "You will not surely die.*
⁵*For God knows that in the day you eat of it your eyes will be opened, and you will be like God, knowing good and evil."*
⁶*So when the woman saw that the tree was good for food, that it was pleasant to the eyes, and a tree desirable to make one wise, she took of its fruit and ate. She also gave to her husband with her, and he ate.*
⁷*Then the eyes of both of them were opened, and they knew that they were naked; and they sewed fig leaves together and made themselves coverings.*
⁸*And they heard the sound of the LORD God walking in the garden in the cool of the day, and Adam and his wife hid themselves from the presence of the LORD God among the trees of the garden.*
⁹*Then the LORD God called to Adam and said to him, "Where are you?"*
¹⁰*So he said, "I heard Your voice in the garden, and I was afraid because I was naked; and I hid myself."*
¹¹*And He said, "Who told you that you were naked? Have you eaten from the tree of which I commanded you that you should not eat?"*
¹²*Then the man said, "The woman whom You gave to be with me, she gave me of the tree, and I ate."*
¹³*And the LORD God said to the woman, "What is this you have done?" The woman said, "The serpent deceived me, and I ate."*
¹⁴*So the LORD God said to the serpent: "Because you have done this, you are cursed more than all cattle, and more than every beast of the field; On your belly you shall go, And you shall eat dust all the days of your life.*
¹⁵*And I will put enmity Between you and the woman, and between your seed and her Seed; He shall bruise your head, and you shall bruise His heel."*
¹⁶*To the woman He said: "I will greatly multiply your sorrow and your conception; in pain you shall bring forth children; your desire shall be for your husband, and he shall rule over you."*
¹⁷*Then to Adam He said, "Because you have heeded the voice of your wife, and have eaten from the tree of which I commanded you, saying, 'You shall not eat of it': Cursed is the ground for your sake; in toil you shall eat of it all the days of your life.*
¹⁸*Both thorns and thistles it shall bring forth for you, and you shall eat the herb of the field.*
¹⁹*In the sweat of your face you shall eat bread till you return to the ground, for out of it you were taken; for dust you are, and to dust you shall return."*
²⁰*And Adam called his wife's name Eve, because she was the mother of all living.*

²¹*Also for Adam and his wife the* LORD *God made tunics of skin, and clothed them.*
²²*Then the* LORD *God said, "Behold, the man has become like one of Us, to know good and evil. And now, lest he put out his hand and take also of the tree of life, and eat, and live forever"—*
²³*therefore the* LORD *God sent him out of the garden of Eden to till the ground from which he was taken.*
²⁴*So He drove out the man; and He placed cherubim at the east of the garden of Eden, and a flaming sword which turned every way, to guard the way to the tree of life. (NKJV)*

Realize

1. How did the serpent entice the man and woman to disobey God?

_____

_____

_____

2. Given the perfection of the setting, what does this say about the seductiveness and deceptiveness of the enemy?

_____

_____

_____

Genesis 3

Eve either did not know God's command very well or did not want to remember it. By contrast, Christ gained victory over Satan by his precise knowledge of God's Word (Matt. 4:4, 7, 10). Eve disparaged the privileges, added to the prohibition, and weakened the penalty—all seen by contrasting her words (Gen. 3:3) with God's original commands (2:16–17). After Satan heard this, he blatantly negated the penalty of death that God had given (3:4). Satan is a liar from the beginning (John 8:44), and this is his lie: one can sin and get away with it. But death is the penalty for sin (Gen. 2:17).

The tempter also cast doubt over God's character, suggesting that God was jealous, holding them back from their destiny (3:5). They would become like God when they ate—and God knew that, according to Satan. So Satan held out to them the promise of divinity—knowing good and evil.

The results, of course, were anticlimactic. The promise of divine enlightenment did not come about. They both ate and saw, but they were spoiled by so doing. They were ill at ease with one another (mistrust and alienation) and they were ill at ease with God (fearful and hiding from him).

Satan's promises never come true. Wisdom is never attained by disobeying God's Word. Instead the fear of the Lord is the beginning of wisdom (Prov. 1:7).

(© 1986 Cook Communications Ministries. *Bible Knowledge Commentary Old Testament* by Walvoord and Zuck. Reprinted with permission. May not be further reproduced. All rights reserved.)

3. Immediately following their eating of the forbidden fruit, what did Adam and Eve do when they heard the "sound of the LORD God walking in the garden"? Why do you think?

_____

_____

_____

4. What were the emotional consequences of sin? (see verse 10)

_____

_____

_____

5. What were the relational consequences of sin? (see verses 11, 12, 16)

_____

_____

_____

6. In what specific ways did the curse affect Eve?

_____

_____

7. In what specific ways did the curse affect Adam?

_____

_____

What sort of garland did Christ Jesus . . . submit to on behalf of humanity? One made of thorns and thistles—a symbol of our sins, produced by the soil of the flesh. However, the power of the cross removed these thorns, blunting death's every sting in the Lord's enduring head. Yes, even beyond this symbol, contempt, shame, disgust, and fierce cruelty disfigured and lacerated the Lord's temples. . . . If you can't be crowned with thorns, you may never be crowned with flowers.

Tertillian

8. What glimpses of hope and mercy do you see in Genesis 3?

_____

_____

_____

Respond

9. Why could you say that Genesis 3:10 is one of the saddest verses in the entire Bible?

_____

_____

_____

10. Do you agree, as some commentators on this passage have argued, that people sin and go against the will of God because they have deep doubts about the goodness of God? Give an example of this from your own life.

_____

_____

_____

Day 2) The Results of the Fall

Read

Romans 1:18–25

18The wrath of God is being revealed from heaven against all the godlessness and wickedness of men who suppress the truth by their wickedness,

19since what may be known about God is plain to them, because God has made it plain to them.

20For since the creation of the world God's invisible qualities—his eternal power and divine nature—have been clearly seen, being understood from what has been made, so that men are without excuse.

21For although they knew God, they neither glorified him as God nor gave thanks to him, but their thinking became futile and their foolish hearts were darkened.

22Although they claimed to be wise, they became fools

23and exchanged the glory of the immortal God for images made to look like mortal man and birds and animals and reptiles.

24Therefore God gave them over in the sinful desires of their hearts to sexual impurity for the degrading of their bodies with one another.

25They exchanged the truth of God for a lie, and worshiped and served created things rather than the Creator—who is forever praised. Amen. (NIV)

Romans 3:10–20

10As it is written: "There is no one righteous, not even one;

11there is no one who understands, no one who seeks God.

12All have turned away, they have together become worthless; there is no one who does good, not even one."

¹³"Their throats are open graves; their tongues practice deceit." "The poison of vipers is on their lips."
¹⁴"Their mouths are full of cursing and bitterness."
¹⁵"Their feet are swift to shed blood;
¹⁶ruin and misery mark their ways,
¹⁷and the way of peace they do not know."
¹⁸"There is no fear of God before their eyes."
¹⁹Now we know that whatever the law says, it says to those who are under the law, so that every mouth may be silenced and the whole world held accountable to God.
²⁰Therefore no one will be declared righteous in his sight by observing the law; rather, through the law we become conscious of sin. (NIV)

Realize

1. What claims do these passages make about the human race?

_____

_____

_____

2. Is the thrust of these verses that people "mess up" and "make mistakes" or that people "willfully choose what is evil"? Why do you say that?

_____

_____

_____

3. In what ways do these passages paint us, in Max's term, as "beastly"?

_____

_____

_____

_____

4. Does Romans teach that all people are equally evil? If not, what does it teach?

_____

_____

_____

_____

Jesus Christ was crucified between two thieves on a rugged cross on Calvary. Jesus gave His head to the crown of thorns for us. He gave His face to the spittle for us. He gave His cheeks and His beard to be plucked off for us. He gave His back for the lash for us. He gave His side to the spear for us. He gave His hands and feet to the spikes for us. He gave His blood for us. Jesus Christ, dying in our place, taking our sins on that cross, is love.
Billy Graham[3]

5. What does it mean to fear God (Romans 3:18)?

_____

_____

_____

Respond

6. How are these passages from Romans at odds with most cultural ideas about the nature of humanity?

_____

_____

_____

7. Many (in our day of pluralism and tolerance) call these statements from the pen of the apostle Paul "offensive." How do you respond?

_____

_____

_____

Day 3) *We Cannot Save Ourselves*

Read

Jeremiah 13:23
Can an Ethiopian change the color of his skin? Can a leopard take away its spots? Neither can you start doing good, for you always do evil. (NLT)

Romans 8:7
Because the carnal mind is enmity against God; for it is not subject to the law of God, nor indeed can be. (NKJV)

Galatians 3:10–14
¹⁰All who rely on observing the law are under a curse, for it is written: "Cursed is everyone who does not continue to do everything written in the Book of the Law."
¹¹Clearly no one is justified before God by the law, because, "The righteous will live by faith."
¹²The law is not based on faith; on the contrary, "The man who does these things will live by them."
¹³Christ redeemed us from the curse of the law by becoming a curse for us, for it is written: "Cursed is everyone who is hung on a tree."
¹⁴He redeemed us in order that the blessing given to Abraham might come to the Gentiles through Christ Jesus, so that by faith we might receive the promise of the Spirit. (NIV)

Romans 6:23
For the wages of sin is death, but the free gift of God is eternal life through Christ Jesus our Lord. (NLT)

Ephesians 2:8–9
⁸For it is by grace you have been saved, through faith—and this not from yourselves, it is the gift of God—
⁹not by works, so that no one can boast. (NIV)

Realize

1. What does Jeremiah 13:23 say about fundamental (not superficial) change?

_____

_____

2. What does it mean to have a "carnal" mind?

_____

_____

3. How does Romans 8 describe the mind of one who does not know Christ?

_____

_____

_____

4. What does Galatians 3 say to the person who thinks he or she can earn God's approval by living a moral life?

_____

_____

_____

5. What are "the wages of sin"? What does that phrase mean?

_____

_____

_____

6. If we could save ourselves, what would we be able to do, according to Ephesians 2:9?

_____

_____

_____

Respond

7. When have you tried to change by relying on mere human effort? What happened?

_____

_____

_____

8. Since the Bible is clear that we cannot save ourselves, what would our situation be if Christ had not died for us?

_____

_____

_____

> *Not only have we sinned, but we also continue to sin. Because of the weakness of our sinful, corrupt nature, which we will have as long as we have these bodies, there is an ongoing battle between the corrupt nature and the Spirit.*
> Martin Luther

Day 4) *The Incomparable Christ*

Read

Colossians 1:13–23

¹³*He has delivered us from the power of darkness and conveyed us into the kingdom of the Son of His love,*

¹⁴*in whom we have redemption through His blood, the forgiveness of sins.*

¹⁵*He is the image of the invisible God, the firstborn over all creation.*

¹⁶*For by Him all things were created that are in heaven and that are on earth, visible and invisible, whether thrones or dominions or principalities or powers. All things were created through Him and for Him.*

¹⁷*And He is before all things, and in Him all things consist.*

¹⁸*And He is the head of the body, the church, who is the beginning, the firstborn from the dead, that in all things He may have the preeminence.*

¹⁹*For it pleased the Father that in Him all the fullness should dwell,*

²⁰*and by Him to reconcile all things to Himself, by Him, whether things on earth or things in heaven, having made peace through the blood of His cross.*

²¹*And you, who once were alienated and enemies in your mind by wicked works, yet now He has reconciled*

²²*in the body of His flesh through death, to present you holy, and blameless, and above reproach in His sight—*

²³*if indeed you continue in the faith, grounded and steadfast, and are not moved away from the hope of the gospel which you heard, which was preached to every creature under heaven, of which I, Paul, became a minister. (NKJV)*

Realize

1. Where does this passage suggest redemption and forgiveness are found?

_____

_____

_____

2. How is Christ described in this passage?

_____

_____

_____

3. What does it mean that Christ is "the image of the invisible God" or that "in Him all the fullness dwells"?

_____

_____

_____

_____

4. What does this passage say made reconciliation possible between a holy God and sinful humanity?

_____

_____

_____

_____

> There are two causes leading to sin: either we don't know our duty, or we don't perform the duty we know. The former is the sin of ignorance, the latter of weakness.
> *Augustine*

5. What is the significance of the fact that unredeemed people are called "alienated and enemies"?

_____

_____

Respond

6. Given the exalted description of Christ in this passage, how should your attitudes and actions change this week?

_____

_____

7. What is the proper response for someone who has been rescued from death? from *eternal* death?

_____

_____

_____

Day 5) *What Jesus Endured and Did for Us*

Read
Matthew 27:45–46
⁴⁵*From the sixth hour until the ninth hour darkness came over all the land.*
⁴⁶*About the ninth hour Jesus cried out in a loud voice, "Eloi, Eloi, lama sabachthani?"—which means, "My God, my God, why have you forsaken me?" (NIV)*

Psalm 22
¹*My God, My God, why have You forsaken Me? Why are You so far from helping Me, and from the words of My groaning?*
²*O My God, I cry in the daytime, but You do not hear; and in the night season, and am not silent.*
³*But You are holy, who inhabit the praises of Israel.*
⁴*Our fathers trusted in You; they trusted, and You delivered them.*
⁵*They cried to You, and were delivered; they trusted in You, and were not ashamed.*
⁶*But I am a worm, and no man; a reproach of men, and despised of the people.*
⁷*All those who see Me laugh Me to scorn; they shoot out the lip, they shake the head, saying,*
⁸*"He trusted in the LORD, let Him rescue Him; Let Him deliver Him, since He delights in Him!"*
⁹*But You are He who took Me out of the womb; You made Me trust when I was on My mother's breasts.*
¹⁰*I was cast upon You from birth. From My mother's womb You have been My God.*
¹¹*Be not far from Me, for trouble is near; for there is none to help.*
¹²*Many bulls have surrounded Me; strong bulls of Bashan have encircled Me.*
¹³*They gape at Me with their mouths, as a raging and roaring lion.*

14I am poured out like water, and all My bones are out of joint; My heart is like wax; it has melted within Me.

15My strength is dried up like a potsherd, and My tongue clings to My jaws; You have brought Me to the dust of death.

16For dogs have surrounded Me; the assembly of the wicked has enclosed Me. They pierced My hands and My feet;

17I can count all My bones. They look and stare at Me.

18They divide My garments among them, and for My clothing they cast lots.

19But You, O Lord, do not be far from Me; O My Strength, hasten to help Me!

20Deliver Me from the sword, My precious life from the power of the dog.

21Save Me from the lion's mouth and from the horns of the wild oxen! You have answered Me.

22I will declare Your name to My brethren; in the midst of the congregation I will praise You.

23You who fear the Lord, praise Him! All you descendants of Jacob, glorify Him, and fear Him, all you offspring of Israel!

24For He has not despised nor abhorred the affliction of the afflicted; nor has He hidden His face from Him; but when He cried to Him, He heard.

25My praise shall be of You in the great assembly; I will pay My vows before those who fear Him.

26The poor shall eat and be satisfied; those who seek Him will praise the Lord. Let your heart live forever!

27All the ends of the world shall remember and turn to the Lord, and all the families of the nations shall worship before You.

28For the kingdom is the Lord's, and He rules over the nations.

29All the prosperous of the earth shall eat and worship; all those who go down to the dust shall bow before Him, even he who cannot keep himself alive.

30A posterity shall serve Him. It will be recounted of the Lord to the next generation,

31They will come and declare His righteousness to a people who will be born, that He has done this. (NKJV)

Galatians 3:13a
But Christ has rescued us from the curse pronounced by the law. When he was hung on the cross, he took upon himself the curse for our wrongdoing. (NLT)

Realize
1. What is the significance of the "darkness" described in the Matthew passage?

2. How does Jesus' cry correspond to the heart cries of repentant sinners?

3. Why had God forsaken Jesus at that point?

4. How does the background of David's experience in Psalm 22 give you a fuller understanding of Jesus' awful cry?

5. List some of the more obvious parallels between Psalm 22 and the crucifixion of Christ.

30

6. What does Galatians 3 say that Jesus did for us?

_____

_____

_____

The finished work of sin is to kill the soul.
Max Lucado[4]

Respond

7. While on the cross, Jesus willingly endured a terrible separation from the Father—something he had never experienced in all eternity. How does it make you feel to realize that your sin required a rupture in the Trinity?

_____

_____

_____

Get by yourself in a quiet part of your house, sit down, close your eyes, and try to put yourself in Jesus' place during the awful moments when the soldiers abused him. Imagine the beard being plucked from your face; the hard slaps across your mouth; the cruel mocking and jeering; the spit dripping down your cheeks. What do you feel? What are you thinking? Remember: Jesus did all this not only for the soldiers who beat him, but for you. Be sure to give him thanks for choosing to suffer such dreadful abuse for you.

L E S S O N
3

"I Forgive You"

God's Promise in the Nails

LOOKING BACK

The previous lesson concerned the ugliness of sin and the awfulness of its effects. You memorized Romans 3:23. Say this verse to yourself several times, focusing on each word.

1. Have you ever been spat upon? What were the circumstances? How did you feel? Or, have you witnessed someone else being treated this way? Describe the situation and your reaction.

   _____

   _____

2. Why is the crucifixion scene of burly soldiers spitting in the face of Christ an accurate picture of sin?

   _____

   _____

3. *Max writes:* "If the fruit of sin is thorns, isn't the thorny crown on Christ's brow a picture of the fruit of our sin that pierced his heart?" What five adjectives best describe how you feel as you ponder the truth that it was, in part, your sin that Christ took upon himself?

   _____

   _____

   _____

4. As you worked through the Taking It Home lessons from the last lesson, what insights into sin (and the effects of sin) had the biggest impact on you personally? Why?

   _____

   _____

   _____

GETTING STARTED

VIDEO—In video segment number 3, Max tells about the list of flaws in his new home. (The script is reprinted on page 223.)

5. If you, like Max, were to make a list of all the flaws in your home, what would be the top items on that list? How fixable are these items? Could you address these imperfections personally, or would you have to call in experts? Why?

   _____

   _____

6. If you were asked to list your top personal weaknesses, what items would come to mind first? Why? Are these new developments or long-term flaws?

   _____

   _____

7. Why is it that most people first notice imperfections (in a house, church, community, person, etc.), rather than good features?

_____

_____

_____

8. Imagine that in your community lived an individual who could meet someone and immediately read his or her mind and know all shortcomings and secrets. Would you try to avoid this person? Why or why not?

_____

_____

_____

For all at once all sin is atoned for on the Cross, the entire Fall erased, and the whole obligation to Satan and the entire sentence passed upon the fall of Adam is torn up, canceled, and annulled by the nails of Jesus.
Count Nicholas Ludwig von Zinzendorf[1]

9. What are some of the most common myths and misunderstandings about God's forgiveness?

_____

_____

_____

JUSTIFICATION—the process by which sinful human beings are made acceptable to a holy God

Justification by Grace
Christianity is unique because of its teaching of justification by grace (Rom. 3:24). Justification is God's declaration that the demands of his Law have been fulfilled in the righteousness of his Son. The basis for this justification is the death of Christ. Paul tells us that "God was in Christ reconciling the world to Himself, not imputing their trespasses to them" (2 Cor. 5:19, NKJV). This reconciliation covers all sin: "For by one offering He has perfected forever those who are being sanctified" (Heb. 10:14, NKJV). Justification, then, is based on the work of Christ, accomplished through his blood (Rom. 5:9), and brought to his people through his resurrection (Rom. 4:25).

When God justifies, he charges the sin of the person to Christ and credits the righteousness of Christ to the believer (2 Cor. 5:21). Thus, "through one Man's righteous act, the free gift came to all men, resulting in justification of life" (Rom. 5:18, NKJV). Because this righteousness is "the righteousness of God" which is "apart from the law" (Rom. 3:21, NKJV), it is thorough; a believer is "justified from all things" (Acts 13:39, NKJV). God is "just" because his holy standard of perfect righteousness has been fulfilled in Christ, and he is the "justifier," because this righteousness is freely given to the believer (Rom. 3:26; 5:16).

Justification by Faith
Although the Lord Jesus has paid the price for our justification, it is through our faith that he is received and his righteousness is experienced and enjoyed (Rom. 3:25–30). Faith is considered righteousness (Rom. 4:3, 9), not as the work of human beings (Rom. 4:5), but as the gift and work of God (John 6:28–29; Eph. 2:8; Phil. 1:29).

The New Testament sometimes seems to speak of justification by works. For example, Jesus spoke of justification (and condemnation) "by your words" (Matt. 12:37, NKJV). Paul said, "The doers of the law will be justified" (Rom. 2:13, NKJV). And James concluded that "a man is justified by works, and not by faith only" (James 2:24, NKJV).

These statements seem to conflict with Paul's many warnings that "by the deeds of the law no flesh will be justified in His sight" (Rom. 3:20, NKJV) and that the attempt to be justified through law is equivalent to being "estranged from Christ" and "fallen from grace" (Gal. 5:4, NKJV).

The solution to this problem lies in the distinction between the works of the flesh and the fruit of the Spirit (Gal. 5:16–25). Not only is Christ's righteousness legally accounted to the believer, but Christ also dwells in the believer through the Holy Spirit (Rom. 8:10), creating works of faith (Eph. 2:10). Certainly God's works may be declared righteous (Is. 26:12). If this is true, then the order of events in justification is grace, faith, and works; or, in other words, by grace, through faith, resulting in works (Eph. 2:8–10).

The Results of Justification
The negative result of justification is what we are saved from: "Having now been justified . . . we shall be saved from wrath" (Rom. 5:9, NKJV). The positive result is what we are saved to: "Whom He justified, these He also glorified" (Rom. 8:30, NKJV).

Paul also notes peace with God (Rom. 5:1) and access to God's grace (Rom. 5:2) as positive benefits. The believer in Christ may look forward to the redemption of his body (Rom. 8:23) and an eternal inheritance (Rom. 8:17; 1 Pet. 1:4).

(adapted from Ronald F. Youngblood, Ed., *Nelson's New Illustrated Bible Dictionary* [Nashville, TN: Thomas Nelson Publishers, 1997, c1995], CD-ROM)

DIGGING IN

10. *Max writes:* "The list of our weaknesses. Would you like anyone to see yours? Would you like them made public? How would you feel if they were posted high so that everyone, including Christ himself, could see?" How do you respond to each of these questions?

_____

_____

_____

11. How would it change society if every person were required to publicly wear a sandwich sign listing his or her worst failures from the previous week?

_____

_____

_____

> When human hands fastened the divine hands to the cross with spikes, it wasn't the soldiers who held the hands of Jesus steady. It was God who held them steady. Those same hands that formed the oceans and built the mountains. Those same hands that designed the dawn and crafted each cloud. Those same hands that blueprinted one incredible plan for you and me.
> *Max Lucado[2]*

12. *Max continues:* "May I take you to the moment when it was? Yes, there is a list of your failures. Christ has chronicled your shortcomings. And, yes, that list has been made public. But you've never seen it. Neither have I. Come with me to the hill of Calvary, and I'll tell you why." What would it be like to have before you a comprehensive list of all the sin and ugliness ever perpetrated by the entire human race? How would such a catalog of evil affect you?

_____

_____

_____

13. How do you imagine Christ felt as he pondered this listing?

_____

_____

_____

GOING DEEPER

Mark 15:24a
And they crucified him. (NIV)

14. What was involved in the specific act of crucifixion? How does John 20:25 shed light on the awfulness of this form of execution?

_____

_____

_____

Colossians 2:13–15
[13]When you were dead in your sins and in the uncircumcision of your sinful nature, God made you alive with Christ. He forgave us all our sins,

14having canceled the written code, with its regulations, that was against us and that stood opposed to us; he took it away, nailing it to the cross.
15And having disarmed the powers and authorities, he made a public spectacle of them, triumphing over them by the cross. (NIV)

15. What in this passage suggests that salvation is totally God's work?

_____

_____

_____

16. What is the picture here? What is it that the apostle Paul says was nailed to the cross?

_____

_____

_____

_____

17. What is the significance that this "code . . . that stood opposed to us" was nailed to the cross?

_____

_____

_____

> *Some people object to terms such as salvation and being saved, claiming that the ideas they convey are out of date and meaningless to contemporary men. But salvation is God's term, and there is no better one to describe what he offers fallen mankind through the sacrifice of his Son. Through Christ, and Christ alone, men can be saved from sin, from Satan, from judgment, from wrath, and from spiritual death.*
> John MacArthur[3]

Romans 3:21–25

21But now God has shown us a different way of being right in his sight—not by obeying the law but by the way promised in the Scriptures long ago.
22We are made right in God's sight when we trust in Jesus Christ to take away our sins. And we all can be saved in this same way, no matter who we are or what we have done.
23For all have sinned; all fall short of God's glorious standard.
24Yet now God in his gracious kindness declares us not guilty. He has done this through Christ Jesus, who has freed us by taking away our sins.
25For God sent Jesus to take the punishment for our sins and to satisfy God's anger against us. We are made right with God when we believe that Jesus shed his blood, sacrificing his life for us. God was being entirely fair and just when he did not punish those who sinned in former times. (NLT)

18. According to this passage, what is the only basis for sinful humanity to be forgiven and acquitted by a holy God?

_____

_____

_____

_____

19. This passage speaks of God's anger and wrath. What does this mean? What precipitates such a stern divine response?

_____

_____

_____

_____

20. How can people escape such devastating punishment?

_____

_____

_____

In the Book of Romans we have the apostle Paul's clearest and most detailed explanation of the gospel. After his customary salutation, Paul explains his unashamed passion for taking that good news to the ends of the earth: it is the power of God to salvation for everyone who believes (v. 1:16).

Salvation. When one ponders the full implications of this word, the results are mind-boggling. Unfortunately, too few believers ever stop to consider what all is conveyed in this rich term. The Greek word used by Paul, *soteria*, literally means deliverance or preservation. Used in a religious context, it is intended to suggest the idea of being rescued from the power and dominion of sin and all its consequences.

Both Paul and the other New Testament writers portray Jesus Christ, on the basis of his sacrificial death on the cross in the place of sinners, as the author/provider of salvation (Rom. 3:24–25; 5:21; Heb. 12:2; Acts 4:12). This spiritual deliverance is graciously and lovingly offered by God to all people, but only those who repent and trust in Christ experience its blessings (John 3:16; Heb. 2:3; Eph. 2:8–9).

What exactly are those blessings? Some Bible teachers summarize them as salvation from the penalty of sin, salvation from the power of sin, and salvation from the presence of sin. Theologians prefer to use the terms justification, sanctification, and glorification.

Justification is that divine act in which sinners are declared righteous because of their faith in the One who paid fully and finally for their sins on the cross (Rom. 3:21; 4:5; 5:1). Closely related to justification—and occurring almost simultaneously—is the truth of *regeneration*. This is the event in which the Spirit of God indwells a repentant sinner and imparts eternal life to his or her spiritually dead soul (Eph. 2:1–5).

Sanctification is that process in which God develops the new life of the believer and gradually brings it to perfection (Rom. 6:11; 12:1; Phil. 1:6).

Glorification is the ultimate redemption of the whole person. It occurs when we come face-to-face with our Savior and results in our total conformity to the image of Christ (Rom. 8:29–30; Phil. 3:21).

Salvation has other benefits. Let us not forget the marvelous truths of reconciliation and adoption. At the most basic level, when our sins are forgiven, we move from a position of being the alienated enemies of God to being the beloved sons of God (John 1:12; Gal. 4:4–5; Eph. 1:5)! And, of course, there is the additional promise of heaven (John 14:1–3; Rev. 21:1–22:7).

No wonder the apostle Paul was so excited about the gospel and its power to save. The more we consider the marvelous truth of salvation, the more enthused we will be—thankful to God and eager to share with others the hope that is in us (1 Pet. 3:15).

(adapted from *The Prophecy Study Bible* [Nashville, TN: Thomas Nelson Publishers, 1997], CD-ROM)

21. *Max writes:* "God has penned a list of our faults. The list God has made, however, cannot be read. The words can't be deciphered. The mistakes are covered. The sins are hidden. Those at the top are hidden by his hand; those down the list are covered by his blood. Your sins are 'blotted out' by Jesus." If such a list is hidden and covered, why have such a list at all?

_____

_____

_____

22. How does it make you feel to know that this list is hidden and covered? Why?

_____

_____

_____

MAKING IT REAL

23. *Max writes:* "Watch as the soldiers shove the Carpenter to the ground and stretch his arms against the beams. One presses a knee against a forearm and a spike against a

hand. Jesus turns his face toward the nail just as the soldier lifts the hammer to strike it.

"Couldn't Jesus have stopped him? With a flex of the biceps, with a clench of the fist, he could have resisted. Is this not the same hand that stilled the sea? Cleansed the Temple? Summoned the dead?

"But the fist doesn't clench . . . and the moment isn't aborted.

"The mallet rings and the skin rips and the blood begins to drip, then rush. Then the questions follow. Why? Why didn't Jesus resist?"

What about Jesus' actions suggest that they were deliberate?

_____

_____

_____

24. How does it make you feel to know that he voluntarily chose his suffering and death?

_____

_____

_____

THINKING IT THROUGH

Take some time for silent reflection. Thank the Lord for his willingness to endure the agony of crucifixion, the one and only act that could blot out your list of failures and rebellious acts. Then ponder the powerful lyrics of "He Chose the Nails" by Wes King as you listen to it on the CD.

Memory Verse:
Ephesians 1:7
In him we have redemption through his blood, the forgiveness of sins, in accordance with the riches of God's grace. (NIV)

In Him we have redemption through His blood, the forgiveness of sins, according to the riches of His grace. (NKJV)

He is so rich in kindness that he purchased our freedom through the blood of his Son, and our sins are forgiven. (NLT)

During the next week, study the following passages.

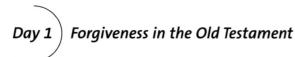

Day 1 ⟩ **Forgiveness in the Old Testament**

Read
Leviticus 16:1–34
¹Now the LORD spoke to Moses after the death of the two sons of Aaron, when they offered profane fire before the LORD, and died;
²and the LORD said to Moses: "Tell Aaron your brother not to come at just any time into the Holy Place inside the veil, before the mercy seat which is on the ark, lest he die; for I will appear in the cloud above the mercy seat.
³Thus Aaron shall come into the Holy Place: with the blood of a young bull as a sin offering, and of a ram as a burnt offering.
⁴He shall put the holy linen tunic and the linen trousers on his body; he shall be girded with a linen sash, and with the linen turban he shall be attired. These are holy garments. Therefore he shall wash his body in water, and put them on.
⁵And he shall take from the congregation of the children of Israel two kids of the goats as a sin offering, and one ram as a burnt offering.
⁶Aaron shall offer the bull as a sin offering, which is for himself, and make atonement for himself and for his house.
⁷He shall take the two goats and present them before the LORD at the door of the tabernacle of meeting.
⁸Then Aaron shall cast lots for the two goats: one lot for the LORD and the other lot for the scapegoat.
⁹And Aaron shall bring the goat on which the LORD's lot fell, and offer it as a sin offering.
¹⁰But the goat on which the lot fell to be the scapegoat shall be presented alive before the LORD, to make atonement upon it, and to let it go as the scapegoat into the wilderness.
¹¹"And Aaron shall bring the bull of the sin offering, which is for himself, and make atonement for himself and for his house, and shall kill the bull as the sin offering which is for himself.
¹²Then he shall take a censer full of burning coals of fire from the altar before the LORD, with his hands full of sweet incense beaten fine, and bring it inside the veil.
¹³"And he shall put the incense on the fire before the LORD, that the cloud of incense may cover the mercy seat that is on the Testimony, lest he die.
¹⁴He shall take some of the blood of the bull and sprinkle it with his finger on the mercy seat on the east side; and before the mercy seat he shall sprinkle some of the blood with his finger seven times.
¹⁵Then he shall kill the goat of the sin offering, which is for the people, bring its blood inside the veil, do with that blood as he did with the blood of the bull, and sprinkle it on the mercy seat and before the mercy seat.
¹⁶So he shall make atonement for the Holy Place, because of the uncleanness of the children of Israel, and because of their transgressions, for all their sins; and so he shall do for the tabernacle of meeting which remains among them in the midst of their uncleanness.
¹⁷"There shall be no man in the tabernacle of meeting when he goes in to make atonement

in the Holy Place, until he comes out, that he may make atonement for himself, for his household, and for all the assembly of Israel.

¹⁸And he shall go out to the altar that is before the LORD, and make atonement for it, and shall take some of the blood of the bull and some of the blood of the goat, and put it on the horns of the altar all around.

¹⁹Then he shall sprinkle some of the blood on it with his finger seven times, cleanse it, and consecrate it from the uncleanness of the children of Israel.

²⁰And when he has made an end of atoning for the Holy Place, the tabernacle of meeting, and the altar, he shall bring the live goat.

²¹Aaron shall lay both his hands on the head of the live goat, confess over it all the iniquities of the children of Israel, and all their transgressions, concerning all their sins, putting them on the head of the goat, and shall send it away into the wilderness by the hand of a suitable man.

²²The goat shall bear on itself all their iniquities to an uninhabited land; and he shall release the goat in the wilderness.

²³Then Aaron shall come into the tabernacle of meeting, shall take off the linen garments which he put on when he went into the Holy Place, and shall leave them there.

²⁴And he shall wash his body with water in a holy place, put on his garments, come out and offer his burnt offering and the burnt offering of the people, and make atonement for himself and for the people.

²⁵The fat of the sin offering he shall burn on the altar.

²⁶And he who released the goat as the scapegoat shall wash his clothes and bathe his body in water, and afterward he may come into the camp.

²⁷The bull for the sin offering and the goat for the sin offering, whose blood was brought in to make atonement in the Holy Place, shall be carried outside the camp. And they shall burn in the fire their skins, their flesh, and their offal.

²⁸Then he who burns them shall wash his clothes and bathe his body in water, and afterward he may come into the camp.

²⁹This shall be a statute forever for you: In the seventh month, on the tenth day of the month, you shall afflict your souls, and do no work at all, whether a native of your own country or a stranger who dwells among you.

³⁰For on that day the priest shall make atonement for you, to cleanse you, that you may be clean from all your sins before the LORD.

³¹It is a sabbath of solemn rest for you, and you shall afflict your souls. It is a statute forever.

³²And the priest, who is anointed and consecrated to minister as priest in his father's place, shall make atonement, and put on the linen clothes, the holy garments;

³³then he shall make atonement for the Holy Sanctuary, and he shall make atonement for the tabernacle of meeting and for the altar, and he shall make atonement for the priests and for all the people of the assembly.

³⁴This shall be an everlasting statute for you, to make atonement for the children of Israel, for all their sins, once a year." And he did as the LORD commanded Moses. (NKJV)

Realize

1. Why was the high priest warned (verse 2) not to come at just any time into the Holy Place inside the veil?

_____

_____

_____

On the eve of the cross, Jesus made his decision. He would rather go to hell for you than go to heaven without you.
Max Lucado

2. Before the high priest could offer a sacrifice for the people, what did he have to do first?

_____

_____

3. What is a scapegoat?

_____

_____

4. What specific acts did atonement include?

_____

_____

_____

5. How often did the high priest make atonement for the children of Israel?

_____

_____

_____

WordFocus

MAKE ATONEMENT (Heb. *kaphar*) (Lev. 1:4; 9:7; 14:18; 2 Sam. 21:3)

In its various uses, this word can mean to cover, to appease, or to ransom. It can refer to monetary transactions, but in the Scriptures it more commonly speaks of payment for sin. All of the various offerings in the Jewish sacrificial system are described as effecting atonement. The key idea is that these offerings gained the favor of God, and God removed the worshiper's guilt. The sacrifice was presented as a substitute for the life of the offender. The sacrifice of an animal atoned for the offender's sin and turned aside God's wrath. Like the lamb's offered to atone for the sins of the Israelites, Jesus' life was offered as a substitute for ours. His death turned away God's wrath and atoned for our sin (Rom. 3:25).

(adapted from *The Nelson Study Bible,* [Nashville: Thomas Nelson Publishers, 1997], 188)

Respond

6. How might your view of sin and judgment and forgiveness be altered if you were able to travel back in time and witness the events of the Jewish Day of Atonement?

_____

_____

_____

ATONEMENT—the act by which God restores a relationship of harmony and unity between himself and human beings. The word can be broken into three parts that express this great truth in simple but profound terms: "at-one-ment." Through God's atoning grace and forgiveness, we are reinstated to a relationship of at-one-ment with God, in spite of our sin.

Human Need

Because of Adam's sin (Rom. 5:18; 1 Cor. 15:22) and our own personal sins (Col. 1:21), no one is worthy of relationship with a holy God (Eccles. 7:20; Rom. 3:23). Since we are helpless to correct this situation (Prov. 20:9) and can do nothing to hide our sin from God (Heb. 4:13), we all stand condemned by sin (Rom. 3:19). It is human nature (our sinfulness) and God's nature (his holy wrath against sin) that makes us "enemies" (Rom. 5:10).

God's Gift

God's gracious response to the helplessness of his chosen people, the nation of Israel, was to give them a means of reconciliation through Old Testament covenant Law. This came in the sacrificial system where the death or "blood" of the animal was accepted by God as a substitute for the death (Ezek. 18:20) the sinner deserved: "For the life of the flesh is in the blood, and I have given it to you upon the altar to make atonement for your souls" (Lev. 17:11, NKJV).

The Law required that the sacrificial victims must be free from defect, and buying them always involved some cost to the sinner. But an animal's death did not automatically make people right with God in some simple, mechanical way. The hostility between God and people because of sin is a personal matter. God for his part personally gave the means of atonement in the sacrificial system; men and women for their part personally are expected to recognize the seriousness of their sin (Lev. 16:29–30; Mic. 6:6–8). They must also identify themselves personally with the victim that dies: "Then he shall put his hand on the head of the burnt offering, and it will be accepted on his behalf to make atonement for him" (Lev. 1:4, NKJV).

In the Old Testament, God himself brought about atonement by graciously providing the appointed sacrifices. The priests represented God in the atonement ritual, and the sinner received the benefits of being reconciled to God in forgiveness and harmony.

Although Old Testament believers were truly forgiven and received genuine atonement through animal sacrifice, the New Testament clearly states that during the Old Testament period God's justice was not served: "For it is not possible that the blood of bulls and goats could take away sins" (Heb. 10:4, NKJV). Atonement was possible "because in His forbearance God had passed over the sins that were previously committed" (Rom. 3:25, NKJV). However, God's justice was served in the death of Jesus Christ as a substitute: "Not with the blood of goats and calves, but with His own blood He entered the Most Holy Place once for all, having obtained eternal redemption" (Heb. 9:12, NKJV). "And for this reason He is the Mediator of the new covenant" (Heb. 9:15, NKJV).

Our Response
The Lord Jesus came according to God's will (Acts 2:23; 1 Pet. 1:20) "to give His life a ransom for many" (Mark 10:45, NKJV), or "for all" (1 Tim. 2:6, NKJV). Though God "laid on Him the iniquity of us all" (Isa. 53:6, NKJV; also 2 Cor. 5:21; Gal. 3:13), yet Christ "has loved us and given Himself for us, an offering and a sacrifice to God" (Eph. 5:2, NKJV), so that those who believe in him (Rom. 3:22) might receive atonement and "be saved from [God's] wrath" (Rom. 5:9, NKJV) through "the precious blood of Christ" (1 Pet. 1:19, NKJV).

No believer who truly understands the awesome holiness of God's wrath and the terrible hopelessness that comes from personal sin can fail to be overwhelmed by the deep love of Jesus for each of us, and the wonder of God's gracious gift of eternal atonement through Christ. Through Jesus, God will present us "faultless before the presence of His glory with exceeding joy" (Jude 1:24, NKJV).

(adapted from Ronald F. Youngblood, Ed., *Nelson's New Illustrated Bible Dictionary* [Nashville, TN: Thomas Nelson Publishers) 1997, c1995], CD-ROM)

7. The mood of Leviticus 16 is decidedly somber and serious. Is such a state of mind appropriate for modern-day saints who have been forgiven by the sacrifice of Christ? Why or why not?

_____

_____

_____

Day 2) *Forgiveness in the New Testament*

Read
Hebrews 9:11–28
11But Christ came as High Priest of the good things to come, with the greater and more perfect tabernacle not made with hands, that is, not of this creation.
12Not with the blood of goats and calves, but with His own blood He entered the Most Holy Place once for all, having obtained eternal redemption.
13For if the blood of bulls and goats and the ashes of a heifer, sprinkling the unclean, sanctifies for the purifying of the flesh,
14how much more shall the blood of Christ, who through the eternal Spirit offered Himself without spot to God, cleanse your conscience from dead works to serve the living God?
15And for this reason He is the Mediator of the new covenant, by means of death, for the redemption of the transgressions under the first covenant, that those who are called may receive the promise of the eternal inheritance.
16For where there is a testament, there must also of necessity be the death of the testator.
17For a testament is in force after men are dead, since it has no power at all while the testator lives.
18Therefore not even the first covenant was dedicated without blood.
19For when Moses had spoken every precept to all the people according to the law, he took the blood of calves and goats, with water, scarlet wool, and hyssop, and sprinkled both the book itself and all the people,

20saying, "This is the blood of the covenant which God has commanded you."
21Then likewise he sprinkled with blood both the tabernacle and all the vessels of the ministry.
22And according to the law almost all things are purified with blood, and without shedding of blood there is no remission.
23Therefore it was necessary that the copies of the things in the heavens should be purified with these, but the heavenly things themselves with better sacrifices than these.
24For Christ has not entered the holy places made with hands, which are copies of the true, but into heaven itself, now to appear in the presence of God for us;
25not that He should offer Himself often, as the high priest enters the Most Holy Place every year with blood of another—
26He then would have had to suffer often since the foundation of the world; but now, once at the end of the ages, He has appeared to put away sin by the sacrifice of Himself.
27And as it is appointed for men to die once, but after this the judgment,
28so Christ was offered once to bear the sins of many. To those who eagerly wait for Him He will appear a second time, apart from sin, for salvation. (NKJV)

Realize

1. With what did Christ enter the Most Holy Place to make his sacrifice?

_____

_____

_____

2. What phrases speak of the frequency of Christ's sacrifice for sin?

_____

_____

_____

3. In contrast to the Jewish high priests who went into the earthly tabernacle to offer their sacrifices, where did Christ go?

_____

_____

_____

> God says, "You wonder how long my love will last? Find your answer on a splintered cross, on a craggy hill. That's me you see up there, your maker, your God, nail-stabbed and bleeding. Covered in spit and sin-soaked.
> "That's your sin I'm feeling. That's your death I'm dying. That's your resurrection I'm living. That's how much I love you."
> Max Lucado[5]

4. Christ is called the Mediator of a new covenant. What does this mean?

_____

_____

_____

5. What are the blessings promised to those who are part of this new covenant? (See verse 15.)

_____

_____

_____

WordFocus

COVENANT (Gk. *diatheke*) (Heb. 9:15–18, 20; 13:20; Matt. 26:28; Gal. 3:17)
The word *diatheke* can refer either to an agreement or a will (or testament). In 9:15–20, the author of Hebrews explains why the second covenant (8:7) has succeeded the first one made at Mount Sinai. The explanation employs an analogy to a will. Thus the author used the word *diatheke* throughout the section, employing the two different meanings of the word and tying them together. Just as the stipulations of a will go into effect when a person dies, so Christ died to initiate the New Covenant, the covenant that frees us from bondage to the first covenant.

(adapted from *The Nelson Study Bible*, [Nashville, TN: Thomas Nelson Publishers, 1997], 2091)

Respond

6. What truth from this passage has had the deepest effect on you? Why?

_____

_____

_____

_____

7. In light of what Christ has done for you, how specifically do you want to alter your current attitudes and actions?

_____

_____

_____

Jesus Christ the Mediator

Thus it was that the human race was bound in a just doom and all men were children of wrath. Of this wrath it is written: For all our days are wasted; we are ruined in thy wrath; our years seem like a spider's web. Likewise Job spoke of this wrath: Man born of woman is of few days and full of trouble. And even the Lord Jesus said of it: He that believes in the Son has life everlasting, but he that believes not does not have life. Instead, the wrath of God abides in him. He does not say, It will come, but, It now abides. Indeed every man is born into this state. Wherefore the apostle says, For we too were by nature children of wrath even as the others. Since men are in this state of wrath through original sin—a condition made still graver and more pernicious as they compounded more and worse sins with it—a Mediator was required; that is to say, a Reconciler who by offering a unique sacrifice, of which all the sacrifices of the Law and the Prophets were shadows, should allay that wrath. Thus the apostle says, "For if, when we were enemies, we were reconciled to God by the death of his Son, even more now being reconciled by his blood we shall be saved from wrath through him."

It would take too long to say all that would be truly worthy of this Mediator. Indeed, men cannot speak properly of such matters.

(St. Augustine, _Enchiridion on Faith, Hope, and Love,_ Chapter X [Austin, TX: WORDsearch , NavPress Software ©1987-1996], Paragraphs 33-34, CD-ROM)

Day 3 _Forgiveness in No Other Name_

Read

John 10:9
(Jesus is speaking) "Yes, I am the gate. Those who come in through me will be saved. Wherever they go, they will find green pastures." (NLT)

John 14:6
Jesus answered, "I am the way and the truth and the life. No one comes to the Father except through me." (NIV)

Acts 4:12
(Peter is speaking) "Nor is there salvation in any other, for there is no other name under heaven given among men by which we must be saved." (NKJV)

Realize

1. Why in John 10:9 did Jesus refer to himself as the gate? What does this mean?

_____

_____

2. In that same verse what is the implication for those who do not come in by way of the gate?

_____

_____

3. In John 14:6, Christ called himself the way, the truth, and the life. What is significant about his choice of the word "the"?

_____

_____

_____

4. According to Jesus, what is the only path to the Father?

_____

_____

5. What did Peter state as the only source or means of salvation (Acts 4:12)?

_____

_____

Once while flying between cities on the African continent, I began to share my faith in Christ with some reporters who were accompanying me. None seemed interested in hearing the gospel. Suddenly the plane entered a very turbulent storm. The plane shook and began to bounce up and down.

After we successfully came through the storm, one of the reporters approached me and said, "What were you saying about life after death?"
Billy Graham[6]

Respond

6. How do you respond to those who claim there are many ways to God? to the claim that all religions are just different paths to the same goal?

_____

_____

_____

7. If salvation is found only in Christ, how should that change the way you live today?

_____

_____

_____

Only One Way

Many people react negatively to the claim that salvation is found in Christ alone (there is salvation in no one else!). How narrow-minded/exclusive/arrogant! is the common charge leveled against Christianity. But two facts are worth remembering. First, this is not something the church arbitrarily decided; it is the specific teaching of Jesus himself (John 14:6). Second, rather than obsessing over the phrase, . . . *in no one else*, people would be better served to focus on the wonderful promise, *there is salvation* . . . That is the good news of the Gospel! God has provided a way for sinners to be forgiven and granted entrance into heaven! To be sure, it is a narrow way (Luke 13:24), but it is a way nonetheless. If your cruise ship is sinking, it is foolish to remain on deck criticizing the emergency evacuation plan. The wiser course of action is to thankfully take a seat in the nearest lifeboat!

(adapted from Bruce B. Barton, et. al., *Life Application Bible Commentary: Acts* [Wheaton, IL: Tyndale House Publishers, 1999], 62)

Day 4) *Appreciating the Fact of Forgiveness*

Read
Luke 7:36–50
36Now one of the Pharisees invited Jesus to have dinner with him, so he went to the Pharisee's house and reclined at the table.
37When a woman who had lived a sinful life in that town learned that Jesus was eating at the Pharisee's house, she brought an alabaster jar of perfume,

38and as she stood behind him at his feet weeping, she began to wet his feet with her tears. Then she wiped them with her hair, kissed them and poured perfume on them.
39When the Pharisee who had invited him saw this, he said to himself, "If this man were a prophet, he would know who is touching him and what kind of woman she is—that she is a sinner."
40Jesus answered him, "Simon, I have something to tell you." "Tell me, teacher," he said.
41"Two men owed money to a certain moneylender. One owed him five hundred denarii, and the other fifty.
42Neither of them had the money to pay him back, so he canceled the debts of both. Now which of them will love him more?"
43Simon replied, "I suppose the one who had the bigger debt canceled." "You have judged correctly," Jesus said.
44Then he turned toward the woman and said to Simon, "Do you see this woman? I came into your house. You did not give me any water for my feet, but she wet my feet with her tears and wiped them with her hair.
45You did not give me a kiss, but this woman, from the time I entered, has not stopped kissing my feet.
46You did not put oil on my head, but she has poured perfume on my feet.
47Therefore, I tell you, her many sins have been forgiven—for she loved much. But he who has been forgiven little loves little."
48Then Jesus said to her, "Your sins are forgiven."
49The other guests began to say among themselves, "Who is this who even forgives sins?"
50Jesus said to the woman, "Your faith has saved you; go in peace." (NIV)

Realize

1. What is significant about the fact that Jesus' host was a Pharisee?

_____

_____

_____

2. Why did the sinful woman seek out Jesus?

_____

_____

_____

3. Why do you think the woman did what she did when she found Jesus?

_____

_____

_____

4. What did Jesus' religious host think when Jesus did not rebuke this sinful woman?

_____

_____

_____

5. In his parable, to what did Jesus compare sin?

_____

_____

_____

Respond

6. According to Jesus, if we fully appreciate the depths of God's forgiveness, what will we do?

_____

_____

_____

7. When was the last time Christ's sacrifice of love moved you deeply—perhaps even to tears?

_____

_____

Why Did Jesus Come?

Many people get confused as to the real purpose of Christ's coming into the world. He was not merely a good man, or a wise teacher, but he is, as this poem suggests, the Savior of the world.

Why did Jesus come?
To set a good example?
For purposes of teaching?
To give the Sermon on the Mount,
A masterpiece of preaching?

Or did he come to heal the sick?
To raise Lazarus from the dead?
To change the water into wine?
Or multiply the bread?

Perhaps all he really wanted
was to liberate his people?
Or found a new religion
marked by buildings, each with steeple?

No!
He came for greater purpose.
He came to claim a cross.
To seek and save a dying race,
He paid the highest cost.

(by Len Woods, original unpublished poem, 1998)

Day 5) Telling the Good News of Forgiveness

Read
Acts 2:21–38

²¹"And it shall come to pass that whoever calls on the name of the LORD shall be saved.'
²²Men of Israel, hear these words: Jesus of Nazareth, a Man attested by God to you by miracles, wonders, and signs which God did through Him in your midst, as you yourselves also know—
²³Him, being delivered by the determined purpose and foreknowledge of God, you have taken by lawless hands, have crucified, and put to death;
²⁴whom God raised up, having loosed the pains of death, because it was not possible that He should be held by it.
²⁵For David says concerning Him: 'I foresaw the LORD always before my face, for He is at my right hand, that I may not be shaken.
²⁶Therefore my heart rejoiced, and my tongue was glad; moreover my flesh also will rest in hope.
²⁷For You will not leave my soul in Hades, nor will You allow Your Holy One to see corruption.
²⁸You have made known to me the ways of life; You will make me full of joy in Your presence.'
²⁹Men and brethren, let me speak freely to you of the patriarch David, that he is both dead and buried, and his tomb is with us to this day.
³⁰Therefore, being a prophet, and knowing that God had sworn with an oath to him that of the fruit of his body, according to the flesh, He would raise up the Christ to sit on his throne,

31he, foreseeing this, spoke concerning the resurrection of the Christ, that His soul was not left in Hades, nor did His flesh see corruption.

32This Jesus God has raised up, of which we are all witnesses.

33Therefore being exalted to the right hand of God, and having received from the Father the promise of the Holy Spirit, He poured out this which you now see and hear.

34For David did not ascend into the heavens, but he says himself: 'The LORD said to my Lord, "Sit at My right hand,

35till I make Your enemies Your footstool."'

36Therefore let all the house of Israel know assuredly that God has made this Jesus, whom you crucified, both Lord and Christ."

37Now when they heard this, they were cut to the heart, and said to Peter and the rest of the apostles, "Men and brethren, what shall we do?"

38Then Peter said to them, "Repent, and let every one of you be baptized in the name of Jesus Christ for the remission of sins; and you shall receive the gift of the Holy Spirit." (NKJV)

Realize

1. How do Peter's actions here in his Pentecost sermon contrast with his behavior during the trial and crucifixion of Christ only weeks earlier? How do you account for this change?

_____

_____

2. How did Peter describe Jesus in verse 22?

_____

_____

_____

3. According to verse 23, was the death of Jesus the result of man's behavior or God's will? What is significant about this?

_____

_____

_____

> O the divine mystery of that cross! Weakness hangs on it, power is freed by it, evil is nailed to it and triumphal trophies are raised toward it. One saint said: "Pierce my flesh with nails for fear of Thee." He doesn't mean nails of iron, but of fear and faith. For the chains of righteousness are stronger than those of punishment. Peter's faith bound him when he followed the Lord as far as the high priest's hall. No person had bound him and punishment didn't free him since his faith bound him. Again, when Peter was bound by the Jews, prayer freed him. Punishment didn't hold him because he hadn't turned from Christ.
>
> *Ambrose*

4. What was the effect of Peter's sermon on the gathered crowd?

_____

_____

_____

_____

5. What did Peter tell his listeners they needed to do in order to experience forgiveness?

_____

_____

_____

Respond

6. Why are we quick to share good news (pregnancy, a raise, etc.), but often reluctant to share the good news of Christianity?

_____

_____

7. Peter boldly shared the good news of forgiveness in Christ. How often do you speak with others about your faith? If you do not do this often, why not?

_____

_____

Theological Insight
Forgiveness

Forgiveness involves pardoning another person for wrongs and offenses so as to restore a relationship. When God releases sinners from judgment and frees them from the divine penalty of their sin, this is a display of forgiveness. Since only God is holy and without sin, only God can forgive sin. That is why the Jewish leaders considered it blasphemous for Jesus to say that he could forgive sins (Mark 2:7; Luke 5:21). But since Jesus was and is God incarnate, he was expressing his deity when he told others that he forgave them their sins.

The greatest display of Jesus' forgiveness came at a most unusual time. While Jesus was being crucified, Jesus forgave those who were responsible for his death. He said, "Father, forgive them for they do not know what they are doing" (Luke 23:34). According to the immediate context, it would appear that Jesus was forgiving only the Roman soldiers who had been responsible for his crucifixion. However, the ultimate responsibility traced back to Pilate who was pushed—even coerced—by the Jewish leaders to crucify Jesus.

At first, Pilate was not about to crucify Jesus because Pilate knew that the Jewish leaders wanted to get rid of him due to envy, not due to the breaking of any law. Thus, Pilate told the Jewish leaders, "You take him and crucify him, for I find him not guilty" (John 19:6, NLT). Thus, Pilate dared the Jewish leaders to usurp the exclusive Roman authority of capital punishment by crucifying their "King" themselves. The Jewish leaders were too shrewd to fall into this trap. Their retort was, "By our laws he ought to die because he called himself the Son of God" (John 19:7, NLT). The irony here is that the Jews appealed to Pilate to punish Jesus with Roman crucifixion for violating a strictly Jewish law! But when Pilate heard this, he was the more afraid. Since Romans were inclined to believe in human deities, Pilate took this statement seriously—and perhaps he intuitively sensed that the man in his presence was more than just a human being. Driven by this sense, Pilate wanted to question Jesus even further. But Jesus made no reply. Frustrated, Pilate gave Jesus an ultimatum: "Don't you realize that I have the power to release you or to crucify you?" To which Jesus replied, "You would have no power over me at all unless it were given to you from above" (John 19:10–11, NLT).

In this one statement, Jesus revealed that a greater authority than Caesar's (who vested Pilate with the power of capital punishment) was at work in all of this. God was making all things work for the purpose of bringing Jesus to the cross. In this regard, Pilate was not completely guilty. The one who delivered Jesus over to Pilate was guilty of a greater sin. This person was Caiaphas, the high priest who had just handed Jesus over to the Romans. For a Jewish high priest to deliver the Jew's King and Messiah over to the Romans for execution was more a heinous sin than for the Roman governor to sentence him to death.

By this time Pilate was apparently convinced that Jesus was some kind of extra-special, supernatural person, so he tried still another time to let him go. But the Jews were not about to let Jesus escape at this point in the trial, so in a final desperate ploy they appealed to Pilate's friendship with Caesar: "If you release this man, you are not a friend of Caesar. Anyone who declares himself a king is a rebel against Caesar" (John 19:12, NLT). Since most Jews despised the Roman ruler, this was utter hypocrisy; but their hatred for Jesus led them to this lie. At any rate, their ploy worked—for Pilate was very likely afraid that he would be reported to Caesar as having released a man who had been charged with sedition. Ironically and symbolically, Pilate sentenced Jesus to death at the same time the Passover lambs were being slaughtered, which was on the day of the preparation for the Passover (that is, on Friday) some time before noon. Again, this points to Jesus as the Passover Lamb.

But it was not Pilate who was ultimately responsible for Jesus' death. Caiaphas and the Jewish leaders were. That is why John 19:16 (NLT) says, "Then Pilate gave Jesus to them to be crucified." According to the grammatical structure of the Greek text, the pronoun "them" refers to the "chief priests" in 19:15, even though it was the Roman soldiers who actually carried out the crucifixion. The ambiguity was intentional; John wanted his readers to realize that it was the Jewish leaders who were ultimately responsible for Jesus' death, even though the Romans performed the execution.

This said, we should marvel that Jesus offered forgiveness to his crucifiers. They did not know that Jesus had to die for the sins of the world. That he offered forgiveness does not mean that they necessarily accepted it. That is the responsibility of every person—to tell God, "I am a sinner. Thank you, God, that you forgave my sins when Christ died for me."

L E S S O N

"I Will Let You Choose"

God's Promise through the Two Crosses

LOOKING BACK

1. How would you now define the word "forgiveness"? What are its chief components?

_____

_____

_____

2. *Max writes:* "Jesus himself chose the nails. . . . Had the soldier hesitated, Jesus himself would have swung the mallet. He knew how; he was no stranger to the driving of nails. As a carpenter he knew what it took. And as a Savior he knew what it meant. He knew that the purpose of the nail was to place your sins where they could be hidden by his sacrifice and covered by his blood. So, Jesus himself swung the hammer."
   When in your life have you been most affected (spiritually, emotionally, etc.) by the fact that Jesus voluntarily went to the cross for you?

_____

_____

_____

3. What does it mean to you to know you are forgiven? Is forgiveness primarily a feeling? How has forgiveness changed your approach to life?

_____

_____

_____

4. As you worked through the Taking It Home lessons from the last lesson, what insights into forgiveness had the biggest impact on you personally? Why?

_____

_____

_____

GETTING STARTED

VIDEO—In video segment number 4, Max tells about when he and Denalyn were preparing to entertain a guest speaker in the early years of their marriage. (The video script is reprinted on page 224.)

5. Why do you think Max missed Denalyn's nonverbal signs?

_____

_____

_____

6. What nonverbal signs does Max say God has given us?

_____

_____

_____

7. What does the cross symbolize?

_____

_____

_____

8. How do you think the three crosses of Calvary symbolize the most important choice we must make?

_____

_____

_____

9. What factors most influence the choices you make? Desire for security? Desire for the approval of others? Love? Fear? Conscience? Sense of right and wrong?

_____

_____

_____

10. What are some issues on which you've undergone a major change of mind? What happened to make you change your mind? Was it humbling to do an "about face"? Was it liberating? Why?

_____

_____

_____

> *This is our work in creation: to decide. And what we decide is woven into the thread of time and being forever. Choose wisely, then, but you must choose.*
> Steven R. Lawhead[1]

11. An old favorite hymn is, "I Have Decided to Follow Jesus." What circumstances prompted you to decide to follow Jesus? Was this a hard decision for you or not? Why?

_____

_____

_____

DIGGING IN

12. *Max writes:* "In every age of history, on every page of Scripture, the truth is revealed: God allows us to make our own choices."

    Why do you think God allows us to make our own choices?

_____

_____

_____

13. What factors usually influence the choices that people make?

_____

_____

_____

14. What *big* choices are facing you right now? How do you intend to make them?

_____

_____

_____

GOING DEEPER

John 19:18
Here they crucified him, and with him two others—one on each side and Jesus in the middle. (NIV)

Theological Insight

The Gospel writers make a very simple, poignant statement about Jesus' death; they simply say, "They crucified him" (NIV). They do not provide any gruesome description of the crucifixion. Many have not followed the restraint of the divine record, and much has been said about the physical suffering of Jesus. That he suffered incredibly is undeniably so, but we should realize that the physical suffering was small compared to the fact that he suffered as the bearer of our sins. In fact, he was considered "unclean" and "unholy" as he took on the sins of the world—so much so that he had to die outside the city. In the book of Leviticus, God gave the pattern to Israel that on the Day of Atonement, the priest confessed his sins and the sins of the people over the head of the scapegoat. That goat was then taken outside the camp to die—because it was unclean (Lev. 16:10). Hebrews 13:12 states that Jesus suffered outside the city gates so that he might sanctify the people with his own blood.

Jesus not only suffered outside the city gate, he was crucified between two criminals. By an act of malice they executed Jesus among sinners, rebels, and lawless ones. The gospel of Luke (23:42) reveals that one of the criminals believed while the other scoffed at Jesus. That is the picture of how the world today is divided—for in God's sight the world is not divided among the rich and the poor, the great and the insignificant, the educated and the ignorant—but there are just two groups, those who reject him and those who believe in his name.

For those who believe in Christ, the cross has become a symbol of adoration instead of execution, for the cross represents Jesus' sacrificial death. The cross has meaning because of the significance of the person who was put to death on it and because of what his death accomplished. The message of the cross was central in the preaching of the early church (1 Cor. 2:2) because it was God's principal saving act in history. Though it was a past event, it has present significance for each and every believer. For example, the apostle Paul considered himself to have been co-crucified with Christ. In spiritual union, Paul died when Christ died. Paul said, "I have been crucified with Christ and I no longer live, but Christ lives in me" (Gal. 2:20, NIV). He considered this to be a spiritual reality that all the believers have participated in. Our old life of sin ended when Christ was crucified, for in his death he joined us with him (see Col. 2:20).

Isaiah 53:12b
And He was numbered with the transgressors, and He bore the sin of many, and made intercession for the transgressors. (NKJV)

Matthew 27:44a
Even the robbers who were crucified with Him reviled Him. (NKJV)

Luke 23:39–43
39One of the criminals who hung there hurled insults at him: "Aren't you the Christ? Save yourself and us!"
40But the other criminal rebuked him. "Don't you fear God," he said, "since you are under the same sentence?
41We are punished justly, for we are getting what our deeds deserve. But this man has done nothing wrong."
42Then he said, "Jesus, remember me when you come into your kingdom."
43Jesus answered him, "I tell you the truth, today you will be with me in paradise." (NIV)

15. What kind of men were crucified with Jesus? Describe them.

_____

_____

_____

_____

16. Why was Christ's execution between two thieves important in light of Isaiah 53:12?

_____

_____

_____

_____

17. How do we know that a change occurred in the heart of one of these two men? What do you think brought about this change?

_____

_____

_____

18. How did Jesus respond to this criminal's request? Why did he respond like this?

_____

_____

_____

> The penitent thief's prayer reflected his belief that the soul lives on after death; that Christ had a right to rule over a kingdom of the souls of human beings; and that he would soon enter that kingdom despite his impending death. His request to be remembered was a plea for mercy, which also reveals that the thief understood he had no hope but divine grace, and that the dispensing of that grace lay in Jesus' power. All of this demonstrates true faith on the part of the dying thief, and Christ graciously affirmed the man's salvation.
>
> (adapted from _The MacArthur Study Bible_ [Nashville, TN: Word Bibles, 1997], 1565)

Colossians 1:12–14
¹²Always thanking the Father, who has enabled you to share the inheritance that belongs to God's holy people, who live in the light.
¹³For he has rescued us from the one who rules in the kingdom of darkness, and he has brought us into the Kingdom of his dear Son.
¹⁴God has purchased our freedom with his blood and has forgiven all our sins. (NLT)

19. According to this passage, who took the initiative? What did he do?

_____

_____

_____

20. In what are we to "share"? How was this made possible?

_____

_____

_____

_____

21. From what were we rescued? To what were we "brought into"?

_____

_____

_____

_____

22. What have we been given in "his dear Son"?

_____

_____

_____

_____

Matthew 6:24
(Jesus is speaking) "No one can serve two masters; for either he will hate the one and love the other, or else he will be loyal to the one and despise the other. You cannot serve God and mammon." (NKJV)

Matthew 7:13–15

(Jesus is speaking) 13"Enter by the narrow gate; for wide is the gate and broad is the way that leads to destruction, and there are many who go in by it.

14Because narrow is the gate and difficult is the way which leads to life, and there are few who find it.

15Beware of false prophets, who come to you in sheep's clothing, but inwardly they are ravenous wolves." (NKJV)

Matthew 7:24–27

(Jesus is speaking) 24"Therefore whoever hears these sayings of Mine, and does them, I will liken him to a wise man who built his house on the rock:

25and the rain descended, the floods came, and the winds blew and beat on that house; and it did not fall, for it was founded on the rock.

26But everyone who hears these sayings of Mine, and does not do them, will be like a foolish man who built his house on the sand:

27and the rain descended, the floods came, and the winds blew and beat on that house; and it fell. And great was its fall." (NKJV)

Matthew 25:32–33

(Jesus is speaking) 32"All the nations will be gathered before Him, and He will separate them one from another, as a shepherd divides his sheep from the goats.

33And He will set the sheep on His right hand, but the goats on the left." (NKJV)

On the wood of the Cross the world was saved all at once, and whoever is lost loses himself, because he will not receive the Savior, because he falls again and repeats the fall of Adam.
Count Nicholas Ludwig von Zinzendorf[2]

23. What choices are we given in these sermons of Jesus?

_____

_____

_____

24. What choices have you made in each of these areas of your life? How did you make these choices?

_____

_____

_____

25. *Max writes:* "God gives eternal choices, and these choices have eternal consequences." What does Max mean by "eternal choices"?

_____

_____

26. Is it fair that some choices have eternal consequences? Explain.

_____

_____

Never forget that Jesus gives all that is needed for our salvation. It is very important that all seekers after mercy remember this. Faith is as much the gift of God as is the Savior upon whom that faith relies. Repentance of sin is as truly the work of grace as the making of an atonement by which sin is blotted out. Salvation, from first to last, is of grace alone.

Do not misunderstand me. It is not the Holy Spirit who repents. He has never done anything for which he should repent. If he could repent, it would not help us. We ourselves must repent of our own sin, or we are not saved from its power. It is not the Lord Jesus Christ who repents. What should he repent of? We ourselves repent with the full consent of every faculty of our mind. The will, the affections, and the emotions all work together most heartily in the blessed act of repentance for sin. And yet, at the back of all which is our personal act, there is a secret holy influence which melts the heart, gives contrition, and produces a complete change.

(Charles Spurgeon, *All of Grace* [30 Hunt Valley Circle, New Kensington, PA: Whitaker House © 1981. Used by permission of the publisher.] 105–106)

MAKING IT REAL

Max writes: "Think about the thief who repented. Though we know little about him, we know this. He made some bad mistakes in life. He chose the wrong crowd, the wrong morals, the wrong behavior. But would you consider his life a waste? Is he spending eternity reaping the fruit of all the bad choices he made? No, just the opposite. He is enjoying the fruit of the one good choice he made. In the end, all his bad choices were redeemed by a solitary good one.

"You've made some bad choices in life, haven't you? You've chosen the wrong friends, maybe the wrong career, even the wrong spouse. You look back over your life and say, 'If only . . . if only I could make up for those bad choices.' You can. One good choice for eternity offsets a thousand bad ones on earth.

"The choice is yours."

27. When did you become aware that you had this choice to make?

_____

_____

_____

Joshua 24:14–15
14Now fear the Lord and serve him with all faithfulness. Throw away the gods your forefathers worshiped beyond the River and in Egypt, and serve the Lord.
15But if serving the Lord seems undesirable to you, then choose for yourselves this day whom you will serve, whether the gods your forefathers served beyond the River, or the gods of the Amorites, in whose land you are living. But as for me and my household, we will serve the Lord. (NIV)

28. What choice did Joshua set before the people of Israel?

_____

_____

_____

Does this seem like a hard choice to you?

_____

_____

_____

> *The choice of ways at any crossroads may be more important than we think; and . . . shortcuts may lead to very nasty places.*
> C. S. Lewis[3]

29. What "gods" are we tempted to serve in our modern-day culture?

_____

_____

_____

30. How will a radical decision to serve Christ alone change your everyday life this week?

_____

_____

_____

31. Of what specific attitudes and actions do you need to repent?

_____

_____

_____

THINKING IT THROUGH

Take a few quiet moments to reflect on all you've just studied. God's gift, Christ's supreme sacrifice, the mind-boggling offer of salvation—all requires a human response. Thank God for the light he shed on your heart that opened your eyes to the truth of the gospel. Let the words of "Worthy Is the Lamb" by Twila Paris on the CD motivate your heart to praise.

PERSONAL NOTES

Memory Verse:
Romans 10:13
"Everyone who calls on the name of the Lord will be saved." (NIV)

For "whoever calls on the name of the LORD shall be saved." (NKJV)

For "Anyone who calls on the name of the Lord will be saved." (NLT)

During the next week, study the following passages.

Day 1) *We Are Chosen*

Read
Ephesians 1:1–14
¹Paul, an apostle of Jesus Christ by the will of God, to the saints who are in Ephesus, and faithful in Christ Jesus:
²Grace to you and peace from God our Father and the Lord Jesus Christ.
³Blessed be the God and Father of our Lord Jesus Christ, who has blessed us with every spiritual blessing in the heavenly places in Christ,
⁴just as He chose us in Him before the foundation of the world, that we should be holy and without blame before Him in love,
⁵having predestined us to adoption as sons by Jesus Christ to Himself, according to the good pleasure of His will,
⁶to the praise of the glory of His grace, by which He has made us accepted in the Beloved.
⁷In Him we have redemption through His blood, the forgiveness of sins, according to the riches of His grace
⁸which He made to abound toward us in all wisdom and prudence,
⁹having made known to us the mystery of His will, according to His good pleasure which He purposed in Himself,
¹⁰that in the dispensation of the fullness of the times He might gather together in one all things in Christ, both which are in heaven and which are on earth—in Him.
¹¹In Him also we have obtained an inheritance, being predestined according to the purpose of Him who works all things according to the counsel of His will,
¹²that we who first trusted in Christ should be to the praise of His glory.
¹³In Him you also trusted, after you heard the word of truth, the gospel of your salvation; in whom also, having believed, you were sealed with the Holy Spirit of promise,
¹⁴who is the guarantee of our inheritance until the redemption of the purchased possession, to the praise of His glory. (NKJV)

Realize
1. Paul begins his letter to the church at Ephesus with the statement that "He chose us in Him before the foundation of the world." What does this mean?

_____

_____

_____

_____

2. What was his plan for us from the beginning?

_____

_____

_____

_____

Of all the mysteries of the Christian faith, the doctrine of election has probably generated more heated debate than any other topic. Theologians through the ages have pondered the meaning of the words of Rom. 8:29, "For whom He foreknew, he also predestined to be conformed to the image of His Son" (NKJV). What did Paul mean when he wrote that God "foreknew" certain people? How are we to understand the notion of God having "predestined" the salvation/sanctification of certain individuals?

In attempting to resolve these profound questions, Bible students have typically aligned themselves in two camps. Arminians (those who embrace the position first espoused by the 17th century Dutch pastor Jacobus Arminius) understand "foreknowledge" to mean God's advance knowledge of those who would repent of their sin and believe the gospel. In other words, they portray God in eternity past as looking down the corridors of time and seeing all those individuals who would one day accept the offer of salvation through Christ.

In the Arminian view, these are the "elect." The fact of their eventual belief is the condition that prompted God to choose them "before the foundation of the world" (Eph. 1:4, NKJV) or "predestine" them to eternal life. To bolster their position Arminians point to verses that clearly state God's desire for all people to be saved (1 Tim. 2:3–4; 2 Peter 3:9). Furthermore they argue that God's universal call for sinners everywhere to repent and believe the gospel is meaningless if salvation is determined solely by God apart from the free will of humankind.

Calvinism is the name given to the other dominant viewpoint in this matter of election. Calvinists (named for the influential Swiss Reformer John Calvin) understand "foreknowledge" in a different way. They interpret it not in a "time" sense, but as a "relational" term. In other words, it refers to God's intimate knowledge of and love for his elect before they ever came into existence.

From the Calvinistic perspective, it is God's sovereign choice (not a person's exercised faith) that determines who the elect are. Put simply, Calvinists define election as "the unconditional choice of God that is the cause of our faith"; whereas Arminians would define it as "the conditional choice of God that is the result of our faith." Calvinists defend their position with passages like Romans 9:6–24. And they argue powerfully that depraved, spiritually dead people could never choose to believe and would never choose to believe.

This puzzling debate will no doubt continue until the end of time. But this much is clear: God is infinitely wise, powerful, and good. He cannot rightly be accused of being unfair in his dealings with people. Meanwhile, for those who have been saved by grace through faith, the job description is this: "to be conformed to the image of His Son."

(adapted from *The Prophecy Study Bible* [Nashville, TN: Thomas Nelson Publishers, 1997], CD-ROM)

3. Twice Paul says that believers are "predestined" (vv. 5, 11). How do most people understand this word?

_____
_____
_____
_____

4. How does the actual meaning of the word (see below) change your understanding?

_____
_____
_____
_____

WordFocus

PREDESTINED (Gk. *proorizo*) (Rom. 8:29–30; Acts 4:28; 1 Cor. 2:7; Eph. 1:5, 11)
To *predestine* means "to mark out beforehand," "to establish one's boundary, or one's limits, beforehand." Our English word "horizon" is a derivative of this Greek word. The Christian's ultimate destiny or horizon has been fixed by God from all eternity: to be made like his Son. Note how the words *presdestined, called, justified,* and especially *glorified* in Rom. 8:29–30 are in the past tense. That is because

God, from his eternal perspective, sees this process as having been completed already. From God's perspective, we have been glorified already because he sees us righteous because of the work of Jesus on the cross. But still, in the march of time, we must undergo the process of being conformed to the image of God's Son.

(adapted from *The Nelson Study Bible* [Nashville: Thomas Nelson Publishers, 1997], 1895)

5. In addition to being chosen, what other blessings does Paul cite in Ephesians 1?

_____

_____

_____

_____

The doctrine of election is emphasized throughout Scripture (Deut. 7:6; Is. 45:4; John 6:44; Acts 13:48; Rom. 8:29; 9:11; 1 Thess. 1:3–4; 2 Thess. 2:13; 2 Tim. 2:10). The form of the Greek verb behind "chose" indicates that God not only chose by himself but for himself to the praise of his own glory (vv. 6, 12, 14). God's election or predestination does not operate apart from or nullify man's responsibility to believe in Jesus as Lord and Savior (see Matt. 3:1–2; 4:17; John 5:40).

(adapted from *The MacArthur Study Bible* [Nashville, TN: Word Bibles, 1997], 1803)

6. Ephesians 1:13 mentions faith in Christ. What does this indicate about human responsibility?

_____

_____

_____

7. How does the Holy Spirit reward our belief in Christ (verses 13–14)?

_____

_____

_____

Though it is true that God has the right to do anything consistent with his nature, it is equally true that he has chosen to exercise his rights by including the responsible and relatively free actions of people. I say relatively free simply because no one has absolute freedom if for no other reason than the limitations of being fallen human creatures. He has made us responsible, and when we fail to act responsibly we are justly blamed.

An illustration: does God know the day you are going to die? The answer is yes, he does. Question: could you die a day sooner? The answer is no. Question: then why do you eat? Answer: to live. The means of eating is essential to the end of living to the preordained day of death. From this point on the illustration can easily and uselessly get into the realm of the hypothetical. Suppose I do not eat? Then I will die. Would that be the day God planned that I should die? These are questions that do not need to be asked or answered. Just eat.

Or to change the illustration. Has God planned the answers to my prayers? Yes. Then why pray? Because those answers come when I pray.

Or again. Does God know who are elect? Of course—he elected them. Can any of them be lost? No. Then why pray and witness? Because that is how they will be saved. Will any of them fail to believe? No. Then why do they have to believe? Because that is the only way they can be saved, and unless they do believe they will not be saved. Do not let your mind ask the theoretical and useless questions. Let your mind and your life concentrate on doing what is God's will and making sure you act responsibly.

(© 1986 Cook Communications Ministries. *Bible Knowledge Commentary* by Walvoord and Zuck. Reprinted with permission. May not be further reproduced. All rights reserved.)

Respond

8. How does it make you feel to realize that God chose you? Why?

_____

_____

_____

9. How does today's lesson motivate you to worship? to share your faith with others?

_____

_____

_____

Day 2) The Heart of God

Read

Ezekiel 18:31–32

³¹"Cast away from you all the transgressions which you have committed, and get yourselves a new heart and a new spirit. For why should you die, O house of Israel?
³²For I have no pleasure in the death of one who dies," says the Lord GoD. "Therefore turn and live!" (NKJV)

John 3:16

(Jesus is speaking) "For God loved the world so much that he gave his only Son, so that everyone who believes in him may not die but have eternal life." (TEV)

1 Timothy 2:3,6

³This is good and pleases God our Savior,
⁴for he wants everyone to be saved and to understand the truth.
⁵For there is only one God and one Mediator who can reconcile God and people. He is the man Christ Jesus.
⁶He gave his life to purchase freedom for everyone. This is the message that God gave to the world at the proper time. (NLT)

2 Peter 3:9

The Lord is not slow in keeping his promise, as some understand slowness. He is patient with you, not wanting anyone to perish, but everyone to come to repentance. (NIV)

Realize

1. How would you describe God's tone in Ezekiel 18?

_____

_____

_____

2. How does this passage deal a death blow to the common misconception that God enjoys punishing the unrepentant?

_____

_____

_____

_____

3. What is God's greatest demonstration of his desire to see people enjoy eternal life?

_____

_____

_____

4. Who does God desire to receive as repentant sinners? Who does God wish to save? How do you know? What are the implications of this for your neighbors, relatives, and colleagues?

_____

_____

_____

---

2 Peter 3:9

This text does not teach that God actually decrees that all will be saved (universalism). The reference here is not to God's decree, but to his desire. Obviously everything that a sovereign God decrees will occur. Here Peter is describing the sovereign God's desire that all people would turn to him and turn away from unprofitable lives.

(adapted from *The Nelson Study Bible* [Nashville, TN: Thomas Nelson Publishers, 1997], 2136)

Respond

5. How are Christ's "open arms" on the cross a fitting picture of what you have studied today?

_____

_____

6. If God's heart is to see us enjoy salvation, how should that affect your heart (and actions) today?

_____

_____

_____

Day 3 ⟩ A Look at Repentance

Read

Jeremiah 31:18–22a

18"I have surely heard Ephraim bemoaning himself: 'You have chastised me, and I was chastised, like an untrained bull; restore me, and I will return, For You are the LORD my God.
19Surely, after my turning, I repented; and after I was instructed, I struck myself on the thigh; I was ashamed, yes, even humiliated, because I bore the reproach of my youth.'
20Is Ephraim My dear son? Is he a pleasant child? For though I spoke against him, I earnestly remember him still; therefore My heart yearns for him; I will surely have mercy on him," says the LORD.
21Set up signposts, make landmarks; set your heart toward the highway, the way in which you went. Turn back, O virgin of Israel, turn back to these your cities.
22How long will you gad about, O you backsliding daughter?" (NKJV)

Ezekiel 18:30

"Therefore, O house of Israel, I will judge you, each one according to his ways, declares the Sovereign LORD. Repent! Turn away from all your offenses; then sin will not be your downfall." (NIV)

WordFocus

REPENT (Heb. *shub*) (Ezek. 14:6; 18:30; Gen. 8:3; Ps. 85:4)
This Hebrew word translated *repent* means "to turn back" or "turn around." The word refers to a reversal or change in direction, as when the word is used of the receding floodwaters (Gen. 8:3). The prophets commonly used this word to call the Israelites to a radical conscious rejection of their past

sin. A psalm writer used the word to describe God's restoration of a believer (see Ps. 85:4). When used as a theological term, repentance implies not only sorrow but a complete turnaround; to change one's mind about sin, receive God's provision of salvation, and return wholeheartedly to him.

(adapted from *The Nelson Study Bible* [Nashville, TN: Thomas Nelson Publishers, 1997], 1352)

Acts 3:19
(Peter is speaking) "Repent, then, and turn to God, so that your sins may be wiped out, that times of refreshing may come from the Lord." (NIV)

1 Thessalonians 1:9
All those people speak about how you received us when we visited you, and how you turned away from idols to God, to serve the true and living God. (TEV)

Revelation 3:19
(Jesus is speaking) "Those whom I love I rebuke and discipline. So be earnest, and repent." (NIV)

Realize
1. The Jeremiah 31 passage speaks of Ephraim (that is, Israel) realizing what truths?

_____

_____

_____

2. What was Israel's need at this point in history? What did God urge the nation to do?

_____

_____

The prison has been stormed, and the gates of the prison have been opened, but unless we leave our prison cells and go forward into the light of freedom, we are still unredeemed in actuality.
Donald Bloesch[4]

3. What role does God play in this process?

_____

_____

_____

4. What is "repentance"? What does it look like in a person's life? Give examples.

_____

_____

_____

_____

5. According to the passages you just read, what does God do when people repent?

_____

_____

_____

Respond
6. When in your life did repentance become more than just a theological idea? What happened?

_____

_____

_____

7. Is feeling bad about an action the same as repentance? How do you know? (Hint: See 1 Samuel 15:24–31 and Matthew 27:3–5.)

_____

_____

8. From what in your life right now do you need to turn? What would keep you from changing your mind about this attitude or action and turning away from it?

_____
_____
_____
_____

Day 4) *The Possibility of Real Change*

Read
2 Chronicles 33:1–20
¹Manasseh was twelve years old when he became king, and he reigned fifty-five years in Jerusalem.
²But he did evil in the sight of the Lord, according to the abominations of the nations whom the Lord had cast out before the children of Israel.
³For he rebuilt the high places which Hezekiah his father had broken down; he raised up altars for the Baals, and made wooden images; and he worshiped all the host of heaven and served them.
⁴He also built altars in the house of the Lord, of which the Lord had said, "In Jerusalem shall My name be forever."
⁵And he built altars for all the host of heaven in the two courts of the house of the Lord.
⁶Also he caused his sons to pass through the fire in the Valley of the Son of Hinnom; he practiced soothsaying, used witchcraft and sorcery, and consulted mediums and spiritists. He did much evil in the sight of the Lord, to provoke Him to anger.
⁷He even set a carved image, the idol which he had made, in the house of God, of which God had said to David and to Solomon his son, "In this house and in Jerusalem, which I have chosen out of all the tribes of Israel, I will put My name forever;
⁸"and I will not again remove the foot of Israel from the land which I have appointed for your fathers—only if they are careful to do all that I have commanded them, according to the whole law and the statutes and the ordinances by the hand of Moses."
⁹So Manasseh seduced Judah and the inhabitants of Jerusalem to do more evil than the nations whom the Lord had destroyed before the children of Israel.
¹⁰And the Lord spoke to Manasseh and his people, but they would not listen.
¹¹Therefore the Lord brought upon them the captains of the army of the king of Assyria, who took Manasseh with hooks, bound him with bronze fetters, and carried him off to Babylon.
¹²Now when he was in affliction, he implored the Lord his God, and humbled himself greatly before the God of his fathers,
¹³and prayed to Him; and He received his entreaty, heard his supplication, and brought him back to Jerusalem into his kingdom. Then Manasseh knew that the Lord was God.
¹⁴After this he built a wall outside the City of David on the west side of Gihon, in the valley, as far as the entrance of the Fish Gate; and it enclosed Ophel, and he raised it to a very great height. Then he put military captains in all the fortified cities of Judah.
¹⁵He took away the foreign gods and the idol from the house of the Lord, and all the altars that he had built in the mount of the house of the Lord and in Jerusalem; and he cast [them] out of the city.
¹⁶He also repaired the altar of the Lord, sacrificed peace offerings and thank offerings on it, and commanded Judah to serve the Lord God of Israel.
¹⁷Nevertheless the people still sacrificed on the high places, but only to the Lord their God.
¹⁸Now the rest of the acts of Manasseh, his prayer to his God, and the words of the seers who spoke to him in the name of the Lord God of Israel, indeed they are written in the book of the kings of Israel.
¹⁹Also his prayer and how God received his entreaty, and all his sin and trespass, and the sites where he built high places and set up wooden images and carved images, before he was humbled, indeed they are written among the sayings of Hozai.

[20]*So Manasseh rested with his fathers, and they buried him in his own house. Then his son Amon reigned in his place. (NKJV)*

2 Corinthians 5:17
What this means is that those who become Christians become new persons. They are not the same anymore, for the old life is gone. A new life has begun! (NLT)

Realize

1. How does the Scripture describe Manasseh's early life and reign?

_____

_____

_____

_____

2. What clear indications do you see of the grace and mercy of God in Manasseh's life?

_____

_____

_____

_____

> *We have the power to choose whom we will serve, but the alternative to choosing Christ brings certain destruction. Christ said that! The broad, wide, easy, popular way leads to death and destruction. Only the way of the Cross leads home.*
> Billy Graham[5]

3. What events precipitated a change in Manasseh's heart?

_____

_____

_____

_____

4. What evidence from this passage suggests to you that Manasseh's repentance was genuine?

_____

_____

_____

5. How were Manasseh's actions different following his change of heart?

_____

_____

_____

Respond

6. The change described in 2 Corinthians 5—is this figurative, symbolic, or actual? Why do you say this?

_____

_____

_____

7. If God can change the heart of someone like Manasseh, obviously he can change anyone! What people in your life or sphere of influence are candidates for major life change? (List them.)

_____

_____

_____

8. How can you make a difference today in the lives of those you listed above?

_____

_____

_____

The apostle John wrote such profound and stirring words about faith and love, it's easy to forget the facts of his early life:
• He was, by training, a professional fisherman—without formal education.
• He and his brother James once wanted to call down fire from heaven on some unfriendly Samaritans. (No wonder Jesus nicknamed them the "Sons of Thunder"!)
• On another occasion these sons of Zebedee shamelessly schemed (without success) to get special favors from Jesus.
• When Jesus was arrested, a frightened John scattered along with all the rest of the disciples.

Not the most glowing resume in the world. But then something revolutionary happened in John's life. The scared, inconsistent, self-centered, hot-tempered disciple of the Gospels is replaced in the book of Acts by a bold, devoted, unselfish apostle of love. So extreme was the transformation that even the Jewish leaders noticed. Their explanation? "The members of the council were amazed when they saw the boldness of Peter and John, for they could see that they were ordinary men who had had no special training. They also recognized them as men who had been with Jesus" (Acts 4:13, NLT).

That's the kind of change that is possible when we make the commitment to follow the Jewish carpenter. He's not that concerned with where we've been or even with what we are. Instead, he sees us as we can be. And when we give our lives to him, he changes us (for the better) in mind-boggling ways.

If you're not too excited about what you've accomplished or where you're headed, ask Jesus to take your life and make it everything he wants it to be. If you give him the go-ahead, God will revolutionize your life.

(adapted from Michael Kendrick & Daryl Lucas, Eds., *365 Life Lessons from Bible People* [Wheaton, IL: Tyndale House Publishers, 1996], 265)

Day 5) *Choosing to Walk with God*

Read
1 Kings 8:22–30, 54–62
22Then Solomon stood before the altar of the LORD in the presence of all the assembly of Israel, and spread out his hands toward heaven;
23and he said: "LORD God of Israel, there is no God in heaven above or on earth below like You, who keep Your covenant and mercy with Your servants who walk before You with all their hearts.
24You have kept what You promised Your servant David my father; You have both spoken with Your mouth and fulfilled it with Your hand, as it is this day.
25Therefore, LORD God of Israel, now keep what You promised Your servant David my father, saying, 'You shall not fail to have a man sit before Me on the throne of Israel, only if your sons take heed to their way, that they walk before Me as you have walked before Me.'
26And now I pray, O God of Israel, let Your word come true, which You have spoken to Your servant David my father.
27But will God indeed dwell on the earth? Behold, heaven and the heaven of heavens cannot contain You. How much less this temple which I have built!
28Yet regard the prayer of Your servant and his supplication, O LORD my God, and listen to the cry and the prayer which Your servant is praying before You today:
29that Your eyes may be open toward this temple night and day, toward the place of which You said, 'My name shall be there,' that You may hear the prayer which Your servant makes toward this place.
30And may You hear the supplication of Your servant and of Your people Israel, when they pray toward this place. Hear in heaven Your dwelling place; and when You hear, forgive."

54And so it was, when Solomon had finished praying all this prayer and supplication to the LORD, that he arose from before the altar of the LORD, from kneeling on his knees with his hands spread up to heaven.
55Then he stood and blessed all the assembly of Israel with a loud voice, saying:

⁵⁶"Blessed be the Lᴏʀᴅ, who has given rest to His people Israel, according to all that He prom- ised. There has not failed one word of all His good promise, which He promised through His servant Moses.
⁵⁷May the Lᴏʀᴅ our God be with us, as He was with our fathers. May He not leave us nor for- sake us,
⁵⁸that He may incline our hearts to Himself, to walk in all His ways, and to keep His com- mandments and His statutes and His judgments, which He commanded our fathers.
⁵⁹And may these words of mine, with which I have made supplication before the Lᴏʀᴅ, be near the Lᴏʀᴅ our God day and night, that He may maintain the cause of His servant and the cause of His people Israel, as each day may require,
⁶⁰that all the peoples of the earth may know that the Lᴏʀᴅ is God; there is no other.
⁶¹Let your heart therefore be loyal to the Lᴏʀᴅ our God, to walk in His statutes and keep His commandments, as at this day."
⁶²Then the king and all Israel with him offered sacrifices before the Lᴏʀᴅ. (NKJV)

Realize

1. Following the completion of the temple, what did Solomon do?

_____

_____

_____

2. How did Solomon describe God's character in his prayer? Why are these attributes sig- nificant?

_____

_____

_____

3. Upon what did Solomon understand God's continued blessing to be contingent?

_____

_____

_____

4. What is the solution when the people of God sin?

_____

_____

_____

Respond

5. What choices did Solomon suggest the people of God would face in their immediate future?

_____

_____

_____

6. What choices are you facing right now?

_____

_____

_____

_____

7. Someone has said that life is the sum total of the choices we make. Do you agree? Why or why not?

_____

_____

_____

8. What is the secret to making choices in your walk with God that will result in God's glory and your own happiness?

_____

_____

_____

_____

PERSONAL NOTES

L E S S O N

5

"I Will Not Abandon You"

God's Promise in the Path

LOOKING BACK

Lesson 4 focused on the biblical truth that God, without surrendering his sovereignty, presents his human creatures with the profound commands to repent of their sins and believe the gospel. And he also holds them responsible for the choices they make. How well do you remember our memory verse for that lesson? Try saying Romans 10:13 (and no peeking!).

Max, writing about the eternal decision facing each person, observes: "The thief who repented is enjoying the fruit of the one good choice he made. In the end, all his bad choices were redeemed by a solitary good one."

1. Is it fair that all of life's bad choices can be redeemed by a single good one? Why or why not?

    _____

    _____

    _____

2. How would you respond to someone who said, "Do you mean to tell me that if Adolf Hitler made a last-second decision to trust in Christ for forgiveness, he's now in heaven? If that's true, then I sure don't want to go there!"

    _____

    _____

    _____

3. Someone has attempted to explain the seeming contradiction between God's sovereignty and human free will by picturing a gate leading into heaven. Above the entryway on the *outside* is a sign that invites, "Whosoever will." Above the door on the *inside* is a sign that reads, "Chosen of God!"

    Do you think this is a good illustration of the truths you studied in lesson 4? Why or - why not?

    _____

    _____

    _____

    _____

GETTING STARTED

VIDEO—In video segment number 5, Max tells the touching story of Joe and Madeline. (The script is reprinted on page 225.)

4. What factors make people run away?

    _____

    _____

    _____

5. What issues often rupture relationships?

_____

_____

_____

6. How would you define "enemy"? What events or circumstances create "enemies"?

_____

_____

_____

7 Who would be the main enemies of:
   Dieters?

_____

   Homeowners?

_____

   Marriage?

_____

   Your country?

_____

   Contentment?

_____

   Financial health?

_____

   Children?

_____

8. During your childhood, who did you consider to be an enemy? Why?

_____

_____

_____

9. How did you ever become friends with an enemy? What happened to create peace?

_____

_____

_____

DIGGING IN

10. *Max writes:* "The most notorious road in the world is the *Via Dolorosa,* 'the Way of Sorrows.' According to tradition, it is the route Jesus took from Pilate's hall to Calvary. The path is marked by stations frequently used by Christians for their devotions. One station marks the passing of Pilate's verdict. Another the appearance of Simon to carry the cross. Two stations commemorate the stumble of Christ; another, the words of Christ. There are fourteen stations in all, each one a reminder of the events of Christ's final journey.

"Is the route accurate? Probably not. When Jerusalem was destroyed in 70 A.D. and again in 135 A.D., the streets of the city were destroyed. As a result, no one knows the exact route Christ followed that Friday.

"But we do know where the path actually began.

"The path began, not in the court of Pilate, but in the halls of heaven. The Father began his journey when he left his home in search of us. Armed with nothing more than a passion to win your heart, he came looking. His desire was singular, to bring his children home. The Bible has a word for this quest: 'reconciliation.'"

What's the most powerful example you've ever seen of reconciliation? Why?

11. *Max writes:* "Just look at Mom's face as she nurses her baby. Just watch Dad's eyes as he cradles his child. And just try to harm or speak evil of the infant. If you do, you'll encounter a mighty strength, for the love of a parent is a mighty force." Describe an incident in which you or someone you know has displayed this "mighty force" Max talks about.

12. Why is the love of a parent such a potent force?

13. *Max writes:* "If we humans who are sinful have such a love, how much more would God, the sinless and selfless father, love us? But what happens when the love isn't returned? What happens to the heart of the father when his child turns away?" How have you experienced the love of God? How has he expressed his fatherly love to you?

14. How would your parents react if one of their children were to turn away? How would you react? How do you think God reacts?

Going Deeper

John 19:17
Carrying his own cross, Jesus went out to a place called The Place of the Skull, which in the Jewish language is called Golgotha. (NCV)

Luke 23:26–27
26As they led Jesus away, Simon a man from Cyrene, was coming in from the fields. They forced him to carry Jesus' cross and to walk behind him.
27A large crowd of people was following Jesus, including some women who were sad and crying for him. (NCV)

15. Jesus was "carrying his own cross" (John 19), so why was Simon forced to carry it?

16. Perhaps you've seen this scene acted out in filmed versions of the life of Christ. What do you imagine this procession was like? What do you suppose Jesus was thinking and feeling as he walked this path?

1Therefore having been justified by faith, we have peace with God through our Lord Jesus Christ,

2through whom also we have obtained our introduction by faith into this grace in which we stand; and we exult in hope of the glory of God.

3And not only this, but we also exult in our tribulations, knowing that tribulation brings about perseverance;

4and perseverance, proven character; and proven character, hope;

5and hope does not disappoint, because the love of God has been poured out within our hearts through the Holy Spirit who was given to us.

6For while we were still helpless, at the right time Christ died for the ungodly.

7For one will hardly die for a righteous man; though perhaps for the good man someone would dare even to die.

8But God demonstrates His own love toward us, in that while we were yet sinners, Christ died for us.

9Much more then, having now been justified by His blood, we shall be saved from the wrath of God through Him.

10For if while we were enemies, we were reconciled to God through the death of His Son, much more, having been reconciled, we shall be saved by His life.

11And not only this, but we also exult in God through our Lord Jesus Christ, through whom we have now received the reconciliation. (NASB)

17. How does this passage suggest that we find peace with God?

_____

_____

_____

_____

18. What contrast does this passage use to demonstrate and magnify the love of God? What is so unusual about it?

_____

_____

_____

_____

19. What vivid words does this passage use to describe us?

_____

_____

_____

_____

20. Someone might say, "Why does this New Testament passage mention the 'wrath of God'? I thought that was only an Old Testament concept." How would you respond?

_____

_____

_____

_____

21. How can this passage talk simultaneously about God's love and God's wrath?

_____

_____

_____

_____

The doctrine of the atonement is, to my mind, one of the surest proofs of the divine inspiration of Holy Scripture. Who would or could have thought of the just Christ dying for the unjust rebel? This is no teaching of human mythology or dream of poetic imagination. This method of atonement is only known among men because it is a fact. Fiction could not have devised it. God himself ordained it; it is not a matter which could have been imagined. . . .

Jesus has borne the death penalty on our behalf. Behold the wonder! There he hangs upon the cross! This is the greatest sight you will ever see. Son of God and Son of man, there he hangs— bearing pains unutterable, the Just for the unjust—to bring us to God. Oh, the glory of that sight! The Innocent punished! The Holy One condemned! The ever-blessed One made a curse! The infinitely glorious One put to a shameful death! The more I look at the sufferings of the Son of God, the more I am sure that they must meet my case. Why did he suffer if not to take the penalty away from us? If, then, he took it away by his death, it is surely taken. . . .

God will spare the sinner because he did not spare his Son. God can pass by your transgressions because he laid them upon his only begotten Son nearly two thousand years ago. If you believe in Jesus (that is the point), then your sins were carried away by him who was the scapegoat for his people.

Charles Spurgeon[1]

72

22. What does "reconciliation" mean?

_____

_____

Reconciliation means a change of relationship from hostility to harmony and peace between two parties. People can be reconciled to each other (Matt. 5:24, *diallasso*; 1 Cor. 7:11, *katalasso*), and people have been reconciled to God (Rom. 5:1–11; 2 Cor. 5:18–21, *katallasso*; Eph. 2:16; Col. 1:20, *apokatallasso*).

Because of sin God and man are in a relationship of hostility and enmity. Though this is not mentioned in 2 Corinthians 5, it is clear in Romans 5. We were enemies of God (v. 10). Does this refer to humankind's enmity toward God or to God's enmity toward humans? The latter seems to be the sense; that is, God reckoned us to be his enemies. This is the sense of the same word in Romans 11:28 where God is said to reckon the people of Israel his enemies. Paul's mention of God's wrath in 5:9 supports the interpretation that the enemies were the objects of his wrath. Our state of estrangement could not have been more serious, nor the need for a change, a reconciliation, more urgent.

Clearly the testimony of the New Testament is that reconciliation comes about through the death of the Lord Jesus (v. 10). God made him to be sin for us that we might be made the righteousness of God in him. The death of Christ completely changed humanity's former state of enmity into one of righteousness and complete harmony with a righteous God.

(© 1986 Cook Communications Ministries. *Bible Knowledge Commentary* by Walvoord and Zuck. Reprinted with permission. May not be further reproduced. All rights reserved.)

2 Corinthians 5:10–21

10For we must all appear before the judgment seat of Christ, that each one may receive the things done in the body, according to what he has done, whether good or bad.
11Knowing, therefore, the terror of the Lord, we persuade men; but we are well known to God, and I also trust are well known in your consciences.
12For we do not commend ourselves again to you, but give you opportunity to boast on our behalf, that you may have an answer for those who boast in appearance and not in heart.
13For if we are beside ourselves, it is for God; or if we are of sound mind, it is for you.
14For the love of Christ compels us, because we judge thus: that if One died for all, then all died;
15and He died for all, that those who live should live no longer for themselves, but for Him who died for them and rose again.
16Therefore, from now on, we regard no one according to the flesh. Even though we have known Christ according to the flesh, yet now we know Him thus no longer.
17Therefore, if anyone is in Christ, he is a new creation; old things have passed away; behold, all things have become new.
18Now all things are of God, who has reconciled us to Himself through Jesus Christ, and has given us the ministry of reconciliation,
19that is, that God was in Christ reconciling the world to Himself, not imputing their trespasses to them, and has committed to us the word of reconciliation.
20Now then, we are ambassadors for Christ, as though God were pleading through us: we implore you on Christ's behalf, be reconciled to God.
21For He made Him who knew no sin to be sin for us, that we might become the righteousness of God in Him. (NKJV)

23. What motivated Paul to live and minister faithfully?

_____

_____

_____

24. What did Paul mean by "the terror of the Lord"?

_____

_____

25. What does Paul say here about reconciliation? What does it mean? What are its effects? Who is eligible? How does it come about?

_____

_____

_____

26. Why doesn't God count any sins against those who have been reconciled?

_____

_____

_____

27. *Max writes:* "The Greek word for *reconcile* means 'to render something otherwise.' Reconciliation restitches the unraveled, reverses the rebellion, rekindles the cold passion. Reconciliation touches the shoulder of the wayward and woos him homeward. The path to the cross tells us exactly how far God will go to call us back." What if God had taken no steps to repair our ruptured relationship with him?

_____

_____

_____

THINKING IT THROUGH

Carve out some time for reflecting on the truth you've been studying in this lesson. God will go to almost any length to find . . . and save . . . and bless . . . his wayward children. So often we underestimate just how much he has done to bring us back to him. The doctrine of reconciliation is a staggering truth expressed beautifully in "I Missed the Signs" by Kim Hill on the CD.

PERSONAL NOTES

Memory Verse
Romans 5:1

Therefore, since we have been justified through faith, we have peace with God through our Lord Jesus Christ. (NIV)

Therefore, having been justified by faith, we have peace with God through our Lord Jesus Christ. (NKJV)

Therefore, since we have been made right in God's sight by faith, we have peace with God because of what Jesus Christ our Lord has done for us. (NLT)

During the next week, study the following passages.

Day 1) The Rebelliousness of Sin

Read
Romans 1:18–32
¹⁸*For the wrath of God is revealed from heaven against all ungodliness and unrighteousness of men, who suppress the truth in unrighteousness,*
¹⁹*because what may be known of God is manifest in them, for God has shown it to them.*
²⁰*For since the creation of the world His invisible attributes are clearly seen, being understood by the things that are made, even His eternal power and Godhead, so that they are without excuse,*
²¹*because, although they knew God, they did not glorify Him as God, nor were thankful, but became futile in their thoughts, and their foolish hearts were darkened.*
²²*Professing to be wise, they became fools,*
²³*and changed the glory of the incorruptible God into an image made like corruptible man— and birds and four-footed animals and creeping things.*
²⁴*Therefore God also gave them up to uncleanness, in the lusts of their hearts, to dishonor their bodies among themselves,*
²⁵*who exchanged the truth of God for the lie, and worshiped and served the creature rather than the Creator, who is blessed forever. Amen.*
²⁶*For this reason God gave them up to vile passions. For even their women exchanged the natural use for what is against nature.*
²⁷*Likewise also the men, leaving the natural use of the woman, burned in their lust for one another, men with men committing what is shameful, and receiving in themselves the penalty of their error which was due.*
²⁸*And even as they did not like to retain God in their knowledge, God gave them over to a debased mind, to do those things which are not fitting;*
²⁹*being filled with all unrighteousness, sexual immorality, wickedness, covetousness, maliciousness; full of envy, murder, strife, deceit, evil-mindedness; they are whisperers,*
³⁰*backbiters, haters of God, violent, proud, boasters, inventors of evil things, disobedient to parents,*
³¹*undiscerning, untrustworthy, unloving, unforgiving, unmerciful;*
³²*who, knowing the righteous judgment of God, that those who practice such things are deserving of death, not only do the same but also approve of those who practice them. (NKJV)*

Ephesians 2:1–3
¹*In the past you were spiritually dead because of your sins and the things you did against God.*
²*Yes, in the past you lived the way the world lives, following the ruler of the evil powers that are above the earth. That same spirit is now working in those who refuse to obey God.*
³*In the past all of us lived like them, trying to please our sinful selves and doing all the things our bodies and minds wanted. We should have suffered God's anger because of the way we were. We were the same as all other people. (NCV)*

Ephesians 4:17b–19

17. . . the Gentiles . . . walk, in the futility of their mind,

18being darkened in their understanding, excluded from the life of God, because of the ignorance that is in them, because of the hardness of their heart;

19and they, having become callous, have given themselves over to sensuality, for the practice of every kind of impurity with greediness. (NASB)

Isaiah 53:6

We all, like sheep, have gone astray, each of us has turned to his own way; and the LORD has laid on him the iniquity of us all. (NIV)

Realize

1. What does Paul cite in Romans 1 as the root of sin?

_____

_____

_____

2. What are the results of continued rejection of God?

_____

_____

_____

_____

God's son had to be offered for our sins. But consider the price of this ransom carefully. Look at Christ who was captured and offered for you. He is infinitely greater than and superior to anything else in creation. How will you respond when you hear that such a priceless ransom was offered for you? Do you still want to bring God your own good works? What is it compared to Christ's work? He shed his most precious blood for your sins.

Martin Luther

3. What does it mean that "God gave them up/over" (verses 24, 26, 28)?

_____

_____

_____

4. How does Ephesians 2 describe those without Christ? What is their lifestyle? What are their priorities?

_____

_____

_____

_____

5. What picture does Isaiah paint of sinners? People who just "make mistakes"? Or people who deliberately go astray?

_____

_____

_____

6. C. S. Lewis once remarked that we are not just decent folks who need to improve our lives a bit, but "rebels who need to lay down our arms." How (if at all) do these passages confirm Lewis's observation?

_____

_____

_____

_____

Respond

7. How do you feel as you contemplate the depths of your rebellion against God?

_____

_____

_____

_____

_____

_____

Day 2) *The Wrath of God*

Read

Deuteronomy 29:24–29
24All the nations will ask: "Why has the LORD done this to this land? Why this fierce, burning anger?"
25And the answer will be: "It is because this people abandoned the covenant of the LORD, the God of their fathers, the covenant he made with them when he brought them out of Egypt.
26They went off and worshiped other gods and bowed down to them, gods they did not know, gods he had not given them.
27Therefore the LORD's anger burned against this land, so that he brought on it all the curses written in this book.
28In furious anger and in great wrath the LORD uprooted them from their land and thrust them into another land, as it is now."
29The secret things belong to the LORD our God, but the things revealed belong to us and to our children forever, that we may follow all the words of this law. (NIV)

2 Chronicles 36:11–21
11Zedekiah was twenty-one years old when he became king, and he reigned eleven years in Jerusalem.
12He did evil in the sight of the LORD his God, and did not humble himself before Jeremiah the prophet, who spoke from the mouth of the LORD.
13And he also rebelled against King Nebuchadnezzar, who had made him swear an oath by God; but he stiffened his neck and hardened his heart against turning to the LORD God of Israel.
14Moreover all the leaders of the priests and the people transgressed more and more, according to all the abominations of the nations, and defiled the house of the LORD which He had consecrated in Jerusalem.
15And the LORD God of their fathers sent warnings to them by His messengers, rising up early and sending them, because He had compassion on His people and on His dwelling place.
16But they mocked the messengers of God, despised His words, and scoffed at His prophets, until the wrath of the LORD arose against His people, till there was no remedy.
17Therefore He brought against them the king of the Chaldeans, who killed their young men with the sword in the house of their sanctuary, and had no compassion on young man or virgin, on the aged or the weak; He gave them all into his hand.
18And all the articles from the house of God, great and small, the treasures of the house of the LORD, and the treasures of the king and of his leaders, all these he took to Babylon.
19Then they burned the house of God, broke down the wall of Jerusalem, burned all its palaces with fire, and destroyed all its precious possessions.
20And those who escaped from the sword he carried away to Babylon, where they became servants to him and his sons until the rule of the kingdom of Persia,
21to fulfill the word of the LORD by the mouth of Jeremiah, until the land had enjoyed her Sabbaths. As long as she lay desolate she kept Sabbath, to fulfill seventy years. (NKJV)

Psalm 7:11
God judges by what is right, and God is always ready to punish the wicked. (NCV)

Romans 1:18
But God shows his anger from heaven against all sinful, wicked people who push the truth away from themselves. (NLT)

Realize

1. What did Moses say about God's wrath in his farewell address to the nation of Israel (Deuteronomy 29)?

_____

_____

_____

2. Why did the nation under King Zedekiah experience God's wrath? What was the result?

_____

_____

_____

3. Psalm 7 seems to indicate the reason God expresses wrath. What is that reason?

_____

_____

4. What kind of behavior elicits God's wrath, according to Romans 1?

_____

_____

_____

It seems most reasonable to suppose that 'wrath' is the negative aspect of God's righteousness. It does not express anger in the sense in which it is applied to man, that is, of an uncontrolled outburst of passion (which would certainly be an irrational concept), but it must express the revulsion of absolute holiness towards all that is unholy. This is in harmony with the context where 'wrath' is explicitly said to be against (*epi*) ungodliness and wickedness. The same may be said of Romans 5:9 where salvation is said to be from 'the wrath' which may well denote the wrath of God, as an expression of God's rejection of all that is sinful. Salvation of the sinner does not affect God's attitude towards sin.

(Donald Guthrie, *New Testament Theology* [Leicester, England: InterVarsity Press, 1981] 102)

Respond

5. What would you say to the person who argues that divine love and divine wrath are incompatible?

_____

_____

_____

6. How do you feel as you study the idea of God's wrath?

_____

_____

_____

7. Why are Christians often tempted to downplay this attribute of God's character?

_____

_____

_____

Day 3) *The Meaning of "Propitiation"*

Read
1 John 2:2
He is the atoning sacrifice for our sins, and not only for ours but also for the sins of the whole world. (NIV)

This is love: not that we loved God, but that he loved us and sent his Son as an atoning sacrifice for our sin. (NIV)

Hebrews 10:1–14

¹For the law, having a shadow of the good things to come, and not the very image of the things, can never with these same sacrifices, which they offer continually year by year, make those who approach perfect.

²For then would they not have ceased to be offered? For the worshipers, once purified, would have had no more consciousness of sins.

³But in those sacrifices there is a reminder of sins every year.

⁴For it is not possible that the blood of bulls and goats could take away sins.

⁵Therefore, when He came into the world, He said: "Sacrifice and offering You did not desire, But a body You have prepared for Me.

⁶In burnt offerings and sacrifices for sin You had no pleasure.

⁷Then I said, 'Behold, I have come—In the volume of the book it is written of Me—to do Your will, O God.'"

⁸Previously saying, "Sacrifice and offering, burnt offerings, and offerings for sin You did not desire, nor had pleasure in them" (which are offered according to the law),

⁹then He said, "Behold, I have come to do Your will, O God." He takes away the first that He may establish the second.

¹⁰By that will we have been sanctified through the offering of the body of Jesus Christ once for all.

¹¹And every priest stands ministering daily and offering repeatedly the same sacrifices, which can never take away sins.

¹²But this Man, after He had offered one sacrifice for sins forever, sat down at the right hand of God,

¹³from that time waiting till His enemies are made His footstool.

¹⁴For by one offering He has perfected forever those who are being sanctified. (NKJV)

Reconciliation is something that God has already effected through the death of Christ, and people are called upon to accept it, to enter into the good of it, to be at peace with God.

This peace carries with it free access to God; the former rebels are not merely forgiven in the sense that their due punishment has been remitted, but they are brought into a place of high favor with God—"this grace wherein we stand." It is through Christ that they have entered into this state of grace, and through him, too, that they "rejoice in hope of the glory of God." Peace and joy are twin blessings of the gospel; as an old Scots preacher put it, "peace is joy resting; joy is peace dancing."

(F.F. Bruce, *The Epistle of Paul to the Romans, Tyndale New Testament Commentary* [Grand Rapids, MI: Wm. B. Eerdmans Publishing Company, June 1963, reprinted October 1978], 120)

Realize

1. What does it mean that John called Christ "the atoning sacrifice for our sins"? What is significant about this description?

_____

_____

_____

2. What was the scope of Christ's sacrifice (that is, for whom was it made, and is it valid)?

_____

_____

_____

3. What was the motive behind Christ's sacrifice (see 1 John 4:10)?

_____

_____

_____

4. What was the purpose of the Old Testament sacrificial system?

_____

_____

_____

5. How was Christ's sacrifice for sins different than the Old Testament sacrifices made for sin?

_____

_____

_____

WordFocus

RECONCILIATION (Gk. *katallage*) (Romans 5:11; 11:15; 2 Cor. 5:18–19)
The Greek word basically means "change" or "exchange." In the context of relationships between people, the term implies a change in attitude on the part of both individuals, a change from enmity to friendship. When used to describe the relationship existing between God and a person, the term implies the change of attitude on the part of both a person and God. The need to change the sinful ways of a human being is obvious; but some argue that no change is needed on the part of God. But inherent in the doctrine of justification is the changed attitude of God toward the sinner. God declares a person who was formerly his enemy to be righteous before him.

(adapted from *The Nelson Study Bible* [Nashville, TN: Thomas Nelson Publishers, 1997], 1887)

Respond

6. In truth, the doctrine of reconciliation/atonement says that Christ willingly endured God's full, terrible, and holy displeasure for the sin of the world—including your sin. How does this affect you?

_____

_____

_____

Right here on this earth there are two worlds: a world dominated by evil and a world dominated by Christ. We have to live in this world, but we are not part of it. We have to be willing to be different. We have to be willing to be laughed at, sneered at, made fun of. We have to be willing to go to the cross and take a stand for Christ where we live, where we work, where we study. Everyone must know that we are of Christ.
Billy Graham[2]

7. What are you learning about the lengths to which God pursues his wayward creatures?

_____

_____

_____

8. How does the truth of God's immeasurable love motivate you to want to live?

_____

_____

_____

_____

Day 4) *A Portrait of Reconciliation*

Read
Luke 15:11–32
11Then Jesus said: "A certain man had two sons.
12And the younger of them said to his father, 'Father, give me the portion of goods that falls to me.' So he divided to them his livelihood.
13And not many days after, the younger son gathered all together, journeyed to a far country,

and there wasted his possessions with prodigal living.
¹⁴*But when he had spent all, there arose a severe famine in that land, and he began to be in want.*
¹⁵*Then he went and joined himself to a citizen of that country, and he sent him into his fields to feed swine.*
¹⁶*And he would gladly have filled his stomach with the pods that the swine ate, and no one gave him anything.*
¹⁷*But when he came to himself, he said, 'How many of my father's hired servants have bread enough and to spare, and I perish with hunger!*
¹⁸*I will arise and go to my father, and will say to him, "Father, I have sinned against heaven and before you,*
¹⁹*and I am no longer worthy to be called your son. Make me like one of your hired servants."'*
²⁰*And he arose and came to his father. But when he was still a great way off, his father saw him and had compassion, and ran and fell on his neck and kissed him.*
²¹*And the son said to him, 'Father, I have sinned against heaven and in your sight, and am no longer worthy to be called your son.'*
²²*But the father said to his servants, 'Bring out the best robe and put it on him, and put a ring on his hand and sandals on his feet.*
²³*And bring the fatted calf here and kill it, and let us eat and be merry;*
²⁴*for this my son was dead and is alive again; he was lost and is found.' And they began to be merry.*
²⁵*Now his older son was in the field. And as he came and drew near to the house, he heard music and dancing.*
²⁶*So he called one of the servants and asked what these things meant.*
²⁷*And he said to him, 'Your brother has come, and because he has received him safe and sound, your father has killed the fatted calf.'*
²⁸*But he was angry and would not go in. Therefore his father came out and pleaded with him.*
²⁹*So he answered and said to his father, 'Lo, these many years I have been serving you; I never transgressed your commandment at any time; and yet you never gave me a young goat, that I might make merry with my friends.*
³⁰*But as soon as this son of yours came, who has devoured your livelihood with harlots, you killed the fatted calf for him.'*
³¹*And he said to him, 'Son, you are always with me, and all that I have is yours.*
³²*It was right that we should make merry and be glad, for your brother was dead and is alive again, and was lost and is found.'" (NKJV)*

Realize

1. How and why is the story of the prodigal son a good illustration of reconciliation?

_____

_____

_____

2. What strikes you about the actions of the son?

_____

_____

_____

3. What stands out to you about the response of the father?

_____

_____

_____

4. How would the story be different if the father had set out in pursuit of the son?

_____

_____

_____

5. What needed to happen in the boy's heart before true reconciliation could take place?

_____

_____

_____

6. Which son's behavior was the more deplorable—the younger or older? Why?

_____

_____

_____

Children of God (1 John 3:1–2)

If there is a richer, more wonderful biblical image than the concept of being a "child of God," it's hard to know what that would be. How does this miracle happen? What does it mean?
• It is a privilege reserved only for those who have "received" (that is, believed in) Christ (John 1:12).
• It becomes a reality the moment we are "born again" (that is, spiritually regenerated—John 3:3; 1 Pet. 1:23).
• It involves our being adopted by God (Eph. 1:5).
• It means were are the recipients of God's infinite, lavish love (1 John 3:1).
• It means that we are heirs of God and co-heirs with Christ (Rom. 8:17).
• It means that we are expected to live up to our identity as God's children (Eph. 5:8).
• It means we will be disciplined if we go astray (Heb. 12:5–11).

(adapted from the *Life Application Bible Commentary: 1, 2 & 3 John* [Wheaton, IL: Tyndale House Publishers, 1998], 63)

Respond

7. In what areas of your life are you running away from your heavenly Father? Why?

_____

_____

_____

8. What emotions, attitudes, circumstances, fears, etc., keep people from returning to the ones (or One) who love (loves) them best?

_____

_____

_____

9. List some folks you know who need to experience the open arms of the Father and his joy at their return "home."

_____

_____

_____

Day 5 ⟩ The Ministry of Reconciliation

Read

2 Corinthians 5:16–21

16Therefore, from now on, we regard no one according to the flesh. Even though we have known Christ according to the flesh, yet now we know Him thus no longer.
17Therefore, if anyone is in Christ, he is a new creation; old things have passed away; behold, all things have become new.

18Now all things are of God, who has reconciled us to Himself through Jesus Christ, and has given us the ministry of reconciliation,
19that is, that God was in Christ reconciling the world to Himself, not imputing their trespasses to them, and has committed to us the word of reconciliation.
20Now then, we are ambassadors for Christ, as though God were pleading through us: we implore you on Christ's behalf, be reconciled to God.
21For He made Him who knew no sin to be sin for us, that we might become the righteousness of God in Him. (NKJV)

Realize

1. What are the radical implications of verse 17?

_____

_____

_____

2. What has God given to those who are his children?

_____

_____

_____

3. What is the "ministry of reconciliation"? How does Paul describe it?

_____

_____

_____

4. What is an ambassador? Why is this term important?

_____

_____

_____

> *If God had a refrigerator, your picture would be on it. If he had a wallet, your photo would be in it. He sends you flowers every spring and a sunrise every morning.*
> *Whenever you want to talk, he'll listen. He can live anywhere in the universe, and he chose your heart. . . . Face it, friend, He's crazy about you.*
> Max Lucado[3]

5. What part do people play in being reconciled to God?

_____

_____

_____

Theological Insight

Reconciliation presupposes a separation or alienation that needs to be overcome if two parties are to resume friendship. In the case of the broken relationship between people and God, it is God who took the initiative in providing for reconciliation because sinners cannot bridge the gap between themselves and God. All of Scripture (cited below from the RSV) declares the thoroughness of that sinfulness. The prophet Isaiah said, "All we like sheep have gone astray" (Isa. 53:6). According to another prophet, Jeremiah, "The heart is deceitful above all things, and desperately corrupt; who can understand it?" (Jer. 17:9). David the psalmist cried, "There is none that does good, no, not one" (Ps. 14:3). Paul described the complete sinfulness of humanity as follows: "All have sinned and fall short of the glory of God" (Rom. 3:23). Elsewhere Paul described people as being "enemies of God" (Rom. 5:10) and "hostile to God" (Rom. 8:7).

The problem of the sinfulness of humanity is compounded by the holiness of God, who cannot look upon sin. Not only are people terribly sinful, but God is fearfully holy. Consequently, people dread God and can do nothing to change their situation, as they stand helpless before God. The possibility of reconciliation, then, rests entirely with God.

In Old Testament times, reconciliation occurred between God and his people by means of the atoning sacrifices. Atonement was accomplished by the sacrifice and offering up of the blood of a victim. The shedding of blood was the central act. Since life is in the blood (Lev. 17:11), life is sacrificed when the blood is poured out. According to the New Testament, God provided for complete reconciliation when he sent his Son to die on the cross for the sins of the world. By the shedding of his blood for the sins of the world, Jesus took away the sin-problem that alienated people from God. The reconciliation Christ provided is complete and perfect, covering humankind both extensively and intensively—that is, all sinners and all sin. The cause of rupture between God and sinners has now been healed. The way has been opened for people to come to God and fellowship with him.

The gospel is the message that informs the sinner of God's reconciliation with sinners through Christ. The gospel urges sinners to accept this truth in faith. This is wonderfully described by the apostle Paul, who said: "For God was in Christ, reconciling the world to himself, no longer counting people's sins against them. This is the wonderful message he has given us to tell others. We are Christ's ambassadors, and God is using us to speak to you. We urge you, as though Christ himself were here pleading with you, 'Be reconciled to God!'" (2 Cor. 5:18–19).

Respond

6. As an "ambassador," where do you have embassies set up from which you can represent your sovereign Lord?

_____

_____

_____

7. How effective (and attractive!) an ambassador are you?

_____

_____

_____

8. For whom can (and should) you be praying—that they might be reconciled to God?

_____

_____

_____

9. With whom can (and should) you be talking—that they might be reconciled to God? What effective means have you found for doing this?

_____

_____

_____

Couples often debate about "who loved whom first," but John (1 John 4:10) makes it clear that when it comes to our relationship with God, there's no question about who made the first move. God loved us first. He initiated. Not in response to our overtures, not because we were lovable or deserving. In fact, the opposite is true. The apostle Paul observed that while we were still sinners, Christ died for us (Rom. 5:8). This is the mystery of mercy, the miracle of grace: God chose to love a race of rebels and prodigals. And it is this kind of love we are called to share with the world. Imagine the impact we Christians could have today by letting God fill us with this kind of unconditional, redemptive love—a love that actually pursues evildoers until they stop running, and then blesses them! Trust God for the wisdom and courage to love someone who is not a believer, and then take a step of faith to do something concrete for that person.

(adapted from Bruce B. Barton, et. al. , *Life Application Bible Commentary: 1, 2 & 3, John* [Wheaton, IL, Tyndale House Publishing, 1998], 95)

Scripture makes clear that there is indeed a way to God, but that it is not based on anything human beings themselves can do to achieve or merit it. A person can be made right with God, but not on his or her own terms or in his or her own power. In that basic regard Christianity is distinct from every other religion. As far as the way of salvation is concerned, there are therefore only two religions the world has ever known or will ever know—the religion of divine accomplishment, which is biblical Christianity, and the religion of human achievement, which includes all other kinds of religion, by whatever names they may go under.

(adapted from John MacArthur, *Romans, MacArthur Bible Study Series* [Nashville, TN: Word Bibles, 2000])

L E S S O N

6

"I Will Give You My Robe"

God's Promise in the Garment

LOOKING BACK

The last lesson focused on the doctrine of reconciliation as we looked at the path to the cross. See if you can say our memory verse for that lesson, Romans 5:1.

1. What does the word "reconciliation" mean?

_____

_____

_____

2. Why is reconciliation to God so important?

_____

_____

_____

3. During your daily study, what did you learn about God's love and our response to that love?

_____

_____

_____

GETTING STARTED

4. Take a few moments to look around. What different types of garments do you see in the room?

_____

_____

_____

5. What's the most expensive garment you've ever owned?

_____

6. What is your preferred outfit (you'd wear it all the time if you could get away with it)?

_____

7. Why do we wear the following clothes:
   • overcoat?_____
   • dress or slacks? _____
   • bathrobe? _____
   • tie? _____

DIGGING IN

VIDEO—In video segment number 6, Max tells of a time in a restaurant when he was given a jacket to wear. (The video script has been reprinted on page 227.)

_____

_____

_____

Theological Insight

Imputation

There are two aspects to imputation (which means ascription or attribution), both of which are summed up in Paul's statement, "For He made Him who knew no sin to be sin for us, that we might become the righteousness of God in Him" (2 Cor. 5:21, NKJV). The first part of the verse indicates that the sinless one, Christ, became sin for us—this means that sin was imputed to him, sin was attributed to him, even though he was not a sinner. The second part of the verse indicates that we, who were not righteous, were imputed with Christ's righteousness. Let us look at each of these aspects.

The trial scenes prior to Jesus' crucifixion make it abundantly clear that Jesus was sinless and blameless. The high priest Annas interrogated Jesus but couldn't find anything to blame Jesus for (see John 18:23). So Jesus was sent on to Caiaphas and then on to Pilate. When Pilate asked Jesus if he were the king of the Jews, Jesus said, "My kingdom does not belong to this world. If it belonged to this world, my servants would fight so that I would not be given over to the Jews. But my kingdom is from another place" (18:36, NCV). To which, Pilate responded, "So you are a king!" Yes, but not the kind Herod was or Pilate wished he was. Jesus replied, "You are the one saying I am a king. This is why I was born and came into this world: to tell people the truth. And everyone who belongs to the truth listens to me" (18:37, NCV).

Pilate, unable to comprehend the meaning of "truth," was still capable of seeing that Jesus was truly not guilty of any crime. Pilate's intention was to teach Jesus a lesson by scourging him and then to release him (see John 19:1; Luke 23:16, 22). He thought the scourging would appease the Jews, but the Jewish leaders were adamant—they demanded Jesus' death. But Pilate countered: "Crucify him yourselves, because I find nothing against him" (19:6, NCV). After Jesus' beating and the display of mockery, Pilate, for a second time (see 18:38 for the first occasion), declared Jesus "not guilty"—that is, not guilty of a crime warranting death.

Even a Gentile ruler, Pilate, could see that Jesus was blameless. Jesus was more than just blameless, however; he was sinless. Jesus had never sinned; therefore, he was the perfect sin offering. Paul's statement that Christ became "sin for us" means that he assumed the full obligations of the Law, perfectly fulfilling it and fully bearing the guilt and punishment. All of our sins were laid on him, and he bore them on our behalf. This is why Paul said that he became sin for us—or, on our behalf. He was our substitutionary sacrifice.

Having taken care of the sin problem, Christ could then impute to us God's righteousness. The reformer Martin Luther defined the *righteousness of God* as a "righteousness valid before God, which a man may possess through faith." The *righteousness of God* is the righteousness that comes from God; it is God's way of making a sinner justified. Luther said that this righteousness is the first and last need of any sinful individual. This righteousness is a gift from God, imputed (attributed) to the believer (Rom. 3:21—5:21). God declares people to be righteous when they put their trust in his Son (Rom. 8:33—34; 2 Cor. 3:8; 11:15).

9. *Max writes:* "Garments can symbolize character, and like his garment, Jesus' character was seamless. Coordinated. Unified. He was like his robe: uninterrupted perfection." Why was it crucial that Jesus' character be seamless?

_____

_____

_____

GOING DEEPER

John 19:23–24

²³ *When the soldiers had crucified Jesus, they divided his clothes among the four of them. They*

also took his robe, but it was seamless, woven in one piece from the top.
²⁴So they said, "Let's not tear it but throw dice to see who gets it." This fulfilled the Scripture that says, "They divided my clothes among themselves and threw dice for my robe." (NLT)

10. What did the soldiers do with Jesus' clothes?

_____

_____

_____

11. Why didn't they tear his robe?

_____

_____

Roman law as later codified in their legal digests granted the soldiers the right to the clothes the executed man was wearing; it was customary to execute the condemned man naked. The basic unit of the Roman army was the *contubernium*, composed of eight soldiers who shared a tent; half-units of four soldiers each were sometimes assigned to special tasks, such as execution quads.

John's mention that the soldiers did not want to "tear" it might allude to the high priest's garment in the Old Testament (Lev. 21:10), which Josephus mentions was also seamless; but this interpretation probably reads too much into the text. John finds two very distinct acts in Psalm 22:18 (a very Jewish method of interpretation), as Matthew does in Zechariah 9:9.

(adapted from Craig S. Keener, *IVP Bible Backgrounds Commentary New Testament* [Downers Grove, IL: InterVarsity Press, 1993], 313)

John cites Psalm 22:18. In the psalm, David, beset by physical distress and mockery by his opponents, used the symbolism of the common practice in an execution scene in which the executioner divided the victim's clothes to portray the depth of his trouble. It is notable that David precisely described a form of execution that he had never seen. The passage was typologically prophetic of Jesus, David's heir to the messianic throne (see Matt. 27:46; Mark 15:34).

(adapted from *The MacArthur Study Bible* [Nashville, TN: Word Bibles, 1997], 1624)

2 Corinthians 5:21
For He made Him who knew no sin to be sin for us, that we might become the righteousness of God in Him. (NKJV)

1 Peter 2:24
He himself bore our sins in his body on the tree, so that we might die to sins and live to righteousness. (CEV)

The perfect surrender and humiliation were undergone by Christ: perfect because he was God, surrender and humiliation because he was man. Now the Christian belief is that if we somehow share the humility and suffering of Christ, we shall also share in his conquest of death and find a new life after we have died and in it become perfect, and perfectly happy, creatures. This means something much more than our trying to follow his teaching. People often ask when the next step in evolution—the step to something beyond man—will happen. But on the Christian view, it has happened already. In Christ a new kind of man appeared: and the new kind of life which began in him is to be put into us.
C.S. Lewis[1]

12. What did Jesus do with our sins on the cross?

_____

_____

_____

13. What was the purpose of Jesus becoming sin for us?

_____

_____

_____

14. Why did this have to happen for us to be made right in God's sight?

_____

_____

15. What is the significance of the phrase, "once for all"?

The doctrine of imputation is an important revelation of divine dealing with humanity. It is frequently mentioned in the Old Testament (Lev. 7:18; 17:4; 2 Sam. 19:19; Psa. 32:2) as expressed by the Hebrew *hasab,* translated variously as impute, reckon, esteem, purpose, account, be counted, devise, think, etc., appearing over one hundred times in the Hebrew text. The doctrine of imputation is an important element in the sacrificial system of the Old Testament. In the New Testament the doctrine is given extensive revelation in Romans (4:6–25; 5:13) and is mentioned in 2 Corinthians 5:19 and James 2:23, using the verb *logizomai* in all passages except in Romans 5:13 where *ellogeo* is found. The book of Philemon is a biblical illustration of imputation, "Put that on my account" (v. 18, NKJV), where Paul assumed the debt of Onesimus.

In its principal meaning of "reckoning to the account of another," it is found in three theological connections in Scripture.

I. Imputation of Adam's Sin to All People
According to the argument of Romans 5:12–21, the one sin of Adam was imputed to the race to the extent that "death reigned" (v. 14), all were condemned in Adam (v. 18), and all were made sinners (v. 19). The judgment "all have sinned" (Rom. 3:23, Greek aorist tense) is based not on the individual experience of sin but on the imputation of Adam's sin to the race. Adam as the fountain of human life was representative of the race, and his sin is the basis of divine reckoning of all people as sinning in Adam.

II. Imputation of the People's Sin to Christ
In contrast to the imputation of Adam's sin to the race, often considered a real imputation, the imputation of the sin of human beings to Christ is considered judicial and related to the death of Christ on the cross. Christ "has borne our griefs, and carried our sorrows. . . . But He was wounded for our transgressions, . . . and the Lord has laid on Him the iniquity of us all" (Isa. 53:4–6, NKJV). "God made him who had no sin to be sin for us, so that in him we might become the righteousness of God" (2 Cor. 5:21, NIV). "He himself bore our sins in his body on the tree. . . ." (1 Peter 2:24, NIV). Though the word "impute" is not actually used to express this idea in the New Testament, the idea is clearly stated in other words.

III. Imputation of the Righteousness of God to the Believer
Embodied in the doctrine of justification by faith is the imputation of the righteousness of God to the believer in Christ (see Romans 3:21–5:21). The righteous work of Christ manifested in his death on the cross is reckoned to the account of the believer as a gift of righteousness apart from human merit or works. The imputation of righteousness is a judicial act by which the believer is declared righteous before a holy God. Though this is accompanied by experimental sanctification, conversion, and other spiritual manifestations, in itself it is not an experience but a fact of divine reckoning. Believers are declared "justified by faith" (Romans 5:1), and Abraham and David are cited as examples in the Old Testament (Romans 4:1–22).

The imputation of righteousness to believers in Christ is one of the most important doctrines of the New Testament and rests at the heart of the doctrine of salvation. It is related to the believer's identification with Christ, his or her position in Christ, and his or her participation theologically in the substitutionary work of Christ. Though it is not the believer's antecedently, it is reckoned to the believer at the moment of faith and becomes his or hers forever by judicial declaration of God. The righteousness thus imputed meets completely the demands of righteous God and is the sole basis for our acceptance by God.

(adapted from John F. Walvoord, *Baker Dictionary of Theology* [Grand Rapids, MI: Baker Book House, 1960], 281-282)

16. *Max writes:* "When Christ was nailed to the cross, he took off his robe of seamless perfection and assumed a different wardrobe, the wardrobe of indignity.

"The indignity of nakedness. Stripped before his own mother and loved ones. Shamed before his family.

"The indignity of failure. For a few pain-filled hours, the religious leaders were the victors, and Christ appeared the loser. Shamed before his accusers.

"Worst of all, he wore the *indignity* of sin."

What does it mean to you that Jesus bore your sin?

_____

_____

_____

_____

MAKING IT REAL

Max says: "It wasn't enough for him to prepare you a feast.

"It wasn't enough for him to reserve you a seat.

"It wasn't enough for him to cover the cost and provide the transportation to the banquet.

"He did something more. He let you wear his own clothes, so that you would be properly dressed.

"He did that . . . just for you."

Jesus took our sins and then gave us his righteousness. Romans 13:14 says, *Rather, clothe yourselves with the Lord Jesus Christ, and do not think about how to gratify the desires of the sinful nature. (NIV)*

On our own and through our own efforts, we could never have freed ourselves. He sent his only Son into the world. He put all the sin of all the people on his Son and said, "You will be Peter, who denied me; Paul, who persecuted, blasphemed, and acted violently; David, who committed adultery; the sinner who ate the apple in paradise; the thief on the cross. In summary, you will be the one who committed all the sins of all the people. Make sure you pay for these sins and make atonement for them."

At this point the law said, "I find Christ to be a sinner—the one who has taken the sins of all the people upon himself. I don't see sin on anyone else except him. Therefore, he must die on the cross." Then the law grabbed him and killed him.

Martin Luther

17. Why is it important to clothe ourselves "with the Lord Jesus Christ"?

_____

_____

_____

18. How can this happen?

_____

_____

_____

19. What will you do this week to "clothe yourself with Christ"?

_____

_____

_____

THINKING IT THROUGH

Spend a few moments in quiet reflection. Thank God for placing your sin on his sinless Son, taking away your filthy clothes of unrighteousness and clothing you in righteousness.

TAKING IT HOME

Memory Verse

1 Peter 3:18

For Christ died for sins once for all, the righteous for the unrighteous, to bring you to God. (NIV)

For Christ also suffered once for sins, the just for the unjust, that He might bring us to God. (NKJV)

Christ also suffered when he died for our sins once for all time. He never sinned, but he died for sinners that he might bring us safely home to God. (NLT)

During the next week, study the following passages.

Day 1) *Imputation in the Old Testament*

Read

Leviticus 7:15–18

¹⁵ The flesh of the sacrifice of his peace offering for thanksgiving shall be eaten the same day it is offered. He shall not leave any of it until morning.

¹⁶ But if the sacrifice of his offering is a vow or a voluntary offering, it shall be eaten the same day that he offers his sacrifice; but on the next day the remainder of it also may be eaten;

¹⁷ the remainder of the flesh of the sacrifice on the third day must be burned with fire.

¹⁸ And if any of the flesh of the sacrifice of his peace offering is eaten at all on the third day, it shall not be accepted, nor shall it be imputed to him; it shall be an abomination to him who offers it, and the person who eats of it shall bear guilt. (NKJV)

Leviticus 17:2–18:5

²"Speak to Aaron and his sons and to all the Israelites and say to them: 'This is what the Lᴏʀᴅ has commanded:

³Any Israelite who sacrifices an ox, a lamb or a goat in the camp or outside of it

⁴instead of bringing it to the entrance to the Tent of Meeting to present it as an offering to the Lᴏʀᴅ in front of the tabernacle of the Lᴏʀᴅ—that man shall be considered guilty of bloodshed; he has shed blood and must be cut off from his people.

⁵This is so the Israelites will bring to the Lᴏʀᴅ the sacrifices they are now making in the open fields. They must bring them to the priest, that is, to the Lᴏʀᴅ, at the entrance to the Tent of Meeting and sacrifice them as fellowship offerings.

⁶The priest is to sprinkle the blood against the altar of the Lᴏʀᴅ at the entrance to the Tent of Meeting and burn the fat as an aroma pleasing to the Lᴏʀᴅ.

⁷They must no longer offer any of their sacrifices to the goat idols to whom they prostitute themselves. This is to be a lasting ordinance for them and for the generations to come.'

⁸"Say to them: 'Any Israelite or any alien living among them who offers a burnt offering or sacrifice

⁹and does not bring it to the entrance to the Tent of Meeting to sacrifice it to the Lᴏʀᴅ—that man must be cut off from his people.

¹⁰"'Any Israelite or any alien living among them who eats any blood—I will set my face against that person who eats blood and will cut him off from his people.

¹¹For the life of a creature is in the blood, and I have given it to you to make atonement for yourselves on the altar; it is the blood that makes atonement for one's life.

¹²Therefore I say to the Israelites, "None of you may eat blood, nor may an alien living among you eat blood."

¹³"'Any Israelite or any alien living among you who hunts any animal or bird that may be eaten must drain out the blood and cover it with earth,

¹⁴because the life of every creature is its blood. That is why I have said to the Israelites, "You must not eat the blood of any creature, because the life of every creature is its blood; anyone who eats it must be cut off."

¹⁵"'Anyone, whether native-born or alien, who eats anything found dead or torn by wild animals must wash his clothes and bathe with water, and he will be ceremonially unclean till evening; then he will be clean.

16But if he does not wash his clothes and bathe himself, he will be held responsible."
18:1The LORD said to Moses,
2"Speak to the Israelites and say to them: 'I am the LORD your God. 3You must not do as they do in Egypt, where you used to live, and you must not do as they do in the land of Canaan, where I am bringing you. Do not follow their practices.
4You must obey my laws and be careful to follow my decrees. I am the LORD your God.
5Keep my decrees and laws, for the man who obeys them will live by them. I am the LORD.'"
(NIV)

Realize

1. When was the "peace offering" to be eaten? (see Leviticus 17:15).

_____

_____

> *The good news is that we do not need to live with a spirit of inadequacy. God says that in Christ Jesus, we are adequate! We are covered with his identity, and in accepting Jesus as our personal Savior and Lord, we take on his image so that when the Father looks at us, he no longer sees our weaknesses, our faults, and our frailties. Instead, he sees the person of Jesus. He sees his strengths, his perfection, and his uncompromising goodness.*
> *Charles Stanley²*

2. God said that if the offering were eaten at the wrong time, "it shall not be accepted, nor shall it be imputed to him." Why would that be bad?

_____

_____

_____

3. The word "imputation" means the act of laying responsibility of blame or credit upon someone. What did "imputation" mean for the Jews as they presented their sacrifices?

_____

_____

_____

4. The Leviticus 17 passage says a lot about blood. Why is blood so important?

_____

_____

_____

5. What evidence do you find in these passages to indicate that God took these sacrifices very seriously?

_____

_____

_____

Burnt Offering—Leviticus 1; voluntary. The purpose of the Burnt Offering was to make payment for sins in general. It showed a person's devotion to God.

Grain Offering—Leviticus 2; voluntary. The purpose of the Grain Offering was to show honor and respect to God in worship. It acknowledged that all we have belongs to God.

Peace Offering—Leviticus 3; required. The purpose of the Peace Offering was to express gratitude to God. It symbolized peace and fellowship with God.

Sin Offering—Leviticus 4; required. The purpose of the Sin Offering was to make payment for unintentional sins of uncleanness, neglect, or thoughtlessness. It restored the sinner to fellowship with God and showed the seriousness of sin.

Guilt Offering—Leviticus 5; required. The purpose of the Guilt Offering was to make payment for sins against God and others. A sacrifice was made to God and the injured person repaid or compensated. It provided compensation for injured parties.

(adapted from the *Life Application Bible/NLT* [Wheaton, IL, Tyndale House Publishers, Inc., 1995], 159)

Respond

6. Why did God give the Jews these sacrifices to observe?

_____

_____

_____

_____

7. What do you think a child would learn about God from watching his parents make these sacrifices?

_____

_____

_____

8. What have *you* learned about God from the Old Testament sacrifices?

_____

_____

_____

_____

We shall never understand the extent of God's love in Christ at the cross until we understand that we shall never have to stand before the judgment of God for our sins. Christ took our sins. He finished the work of redemption. I am not saved through any works or merit of my own. I have preached to thousands of people on every continent, but I shall not go to heaven because I am a preacher. I am going to heaven entirely on the merit of the work of Christ. I shall never stand at God's judgment bar. That is all past.
Billy Graham[3]

Day 2) *Imputation in the Old Testament*

Read

Isaiah 53:1–12

[1]Who has believed our message? To whom will the Lord reveal his saving power?

[2]My servant grew up in the Lord's presence like a tender green shoot, sprouting from a root in dry and sterile ground. There was nothing beautiful or majestic about his appearance, nothing to attract us to him.

[3]He was despised and rejected—a man of sorrows, acquainted with bitterest grief. We turned our backs on him and looked the other way when he went by. He was despised, and we did not care.

[4]Yet it was our weaknesses he carried; it was our sorrows that weighed him down. And we thought his troubles were a punishment from God for his own sins!

[5]But he was wounded and crushed for our sins. He was beaten that we might have peace. He was whipped, and we were healed!

[6]All of us have strayed away like sheep. We have left God's paths to follow our own. Yet the Lord laid on him the guilt and sins of us all.

[7]He was oppressed and treated harshly, yet he never said a word. He was led as a lamb to the slaughter. And as a sheep is silent before the shearers, he did not open his mouth.

[8]From prison and trial they led him away to his death. But who among the people realized that he was dying for their sins—that he was suffering their punishment?

[9]He had done no wrong, and he never deceived anyone. But he was buried like a criminal; he was put in a rich man's grave.

[10]But it was the Lord's good plan to crush him and fill him with grief. Yet when his life is made an offering for sin, he will have a multitude of children, many heirs. He will enjoy a long life, and the Lord's plan will prosper in his hands.

[11]When he sees all that is accomplished by his anguish, he will be satisfied. And because of what he has experienced, my righteous servant will make it possible for many to be counted righteous, for he will bear all their sins.

[12]I will give him the honors of one who is mighty and great, because he exposed himself to death. He was counted among those who were sinners. He bore the sins of many and interceded for sinners. (NLT)

Realize

1. About whom is this passage speaking?

_____

_____

_____

> It wasn't the Romans who nailed Jesus to the cross. It wasn't spikes that held Jesus to the cross. What held him to that cross was his conviction that it was necessary that he become sin- that he who is pure become sin and that the wrath of God be poured down, not upon creation, but upon the Creator.
>
> Max Lucado[4]

2. Why is this person called "a man of sorrows"?

_____

_____

_____

3. Isaiah wrote: "But who among the people realized that he was dying for their sins—that he was suffering their punishment?" (verse 8). What does this mean?

_____

_____

_____

4. To what do you think Isaiah's original audience thought Isaiah was referring?

_____

_____

53:3 _despised, rejected_—The Hebrew words used here occur together also in 2:22. _sorrows_—The Hebrew for this word is used of both physical and mental pain.

(adapted from _The NIV Study Bible_ [Grand Rapids, MI: Zondervan Publishing House, 1985], 1095)

The prophet foresees the hatred and rejection by humankind toward the Messiah/Servant, who suffered not only external abuse, but also internal grief over the lack of response from those he came to save (see Matt. 23:37; Luke 13:34).

53:4 _carried . . . weighed down_—Isaiah was saying that the Messiah would bear the consequences of the sins of people, namely the griefs and sorrows of life, though incredibly the Jews who watched him die thought he was being punished by God for his own sins.

(adapted from _The MacArthur Study Bible_ [Nashville, TN: Word Bibles, 1997], 1772)

53:4–5 How could an Old Testament person understand the idea of Christ dying for our sins—actually taking our sins as his own? The sacrifices suggested this idea, but it is one thing to kill a lamb and something quite different to think of God's Chosen Servant as that Lamb. God was pulling aside the curtain of time to let the people of Isaiah's day look ahead to the suffering of the future Messiah and the resulting forgiveness made available to all of humankind.

(adapted from the _Life Application Bible/NIV_ [Wheaton, IL: Tyndale House Publishing, 1995], 1105)

5. In what ways was Christ the ultimate and final sacrifice? (see Hebrews 9:11–15; 10:1–10).

_____

_____

_____

Respond

6. We have the privilege of having the whole Bible and of being able to look back and see how Christ fulfilled Old Testament prophecies. As you consider Christ's sacrifice on the cross, what do you learn about God?

_____

_____

Read
Romans 5:12–21

¹²*Therefore, just as through one man sin entered the world, and death through sin, and thus death spread to all men, because all sinned—*

¹³*(For until the law sin was in the world, but sin is not imputed when there is no law.*

¹⁴*Nevertheless death reigned from Adam to Moses, even over those who had not sinned according to the likeness of the transgression of Adam, who is a type of Him who was to come.*

¹⁵*But the free gift is not like the offense. For if by the one man's offense many died, much more the grace of God and the gift by the grace of the one Man, Jesus Christ, abounded to many.*

¹⁶ *And the gift is not like that which came through the one who sinned. For the judgment which came from one offense resulted in condemnation, but the free gift which came from many offenses resulted in justification.*

¹⁷*For if by the one man's offense death reigned through the one, much more those who receive abundance of grace and of the gift of righteousness will reign in life through the One, Jesus Christ.)*

¹⁸*Therefore, as through one man's offense judgment came to all men, resulting in condemnation, even so through one Man's righteous act the free gift came to all men, resulting in justification of life.*

¹⁹*For as by one man's disobedience many were made sinners, so also by one Man's obedience many will be made righteous.*

²⁰*Moreover the law entered that the offense might abound. But where sin abounded, grace abounded much more,*

²¹*so that as sin reigned in death, even so grace might reign through righteousness to eternal life through Jesus Christ our Lord. (NKJV)*

Realize

1. How did sin enter the world?

_____

_____

_____

2. Why are all people sinners?

_____

_____

_____

3. What is the result of sin?

_____

_____

_____

4. *Paul wrote*: "For as by one man's disobedience many were made sinners, so also by one Man's obedience many will be made righteous." What was "one Man's obedience"?

_____

_____

_____

> *The Holy Scripture, in contrast, says that the sins of the world aren't laid on the world. John's sins weren't laid on John, and Peter's sins weren't laid on Peter, for no one can bear his own sins. Rather, the sins of the world were laid on Christ. He is the Lamb of God. He stepped forward to become a sinner for us, to even become sin itself, and to act as though he had committed the sins of the entire world from the beginning of its creation (2 Corinthians 5:21) . The Lamb's mission, role, and function were to take away the sins of the world. The Lamb carried them all.*
> *Martin Luther*

5. How can "many" be "made righteous"?

_____

_____

_____

Romans 5:12 How can we be declared guilty for something Adam did thousands of years ago? Many feel it isn't right for God to judge us because of Adam's sin. Yet each of us confirms our solidarity with Adam by our own sins each day. We are made of the same stuff and are prone to rebel, and we are judged for the sins we commit. Because we are sinners, it isn't fairness we need—it's mercy.

5:13–14 Paul has shown that keeping the law does not bring salvation. Here he adds that breaking the law is not what brings death. Death is the result of Adam's sin and of the sins we all commit, even if they don't resemble Adam's. Paul reminds his readers that for thousands of years the law had not yet been explicitly given, and yet people died. The law was added, he explains in Romans 5:20, to help people see their sinfulness, to show them the seriousness of their offenses, and to drive them to God for mercy and pardon.

5:14 Adam is a *pattern;* he is the counterpart of Christ. Just as Adam was a representative of created humanity, so is Christ the representative of a new spiritual humanity.

5:15–19 We were all born into Adam's physical family—the family line that leads to certain death. All of us have reaped the results of Adam's sin. We have inherited his guilt, a sinful nature (the tendency to sin), and God's punishment. Because of Jesus, however, we can trade judgment for forgiveness. We can trade our sin for Jesus' righteousness. Christ offers us the opportunity to be born into his spiritual family—the family line that begins with forgiveness and leads to eternal life. If we do nothing, we have death through Adam; but if we come to God by faith, we have life through Christ.

5:17 What a promise this is to those who love Christ! We can reign over sin's power, over death's threats, and over Satan's attacks. Eternal life is ours now and forever. In the power and protection of Jesus Christ, we can overcome temptation. See Romans 8:17 for more on our privileged position in Christ.

5:20 As a sinner, separated from God, you see his law from below, as a ladder to be climbed to get to God. Perhaps you have repeatedly tried to climb it, only to fall to the ground every time you have advanced one or two rungs. Or perhaps the sheer height of the ladder seems so overwhelming that you have never even started up. In either case, what relief you should feel to see Jesus offering with open arms to lift you above the ladder of the law, to take you directly to God! Once Jesus lifts you into God's presence, you are free to obey—out of love, not necessity, and through God's power, not your own, You know that if you stumble, you will not fall back to the ground. Instead, you will be caught and held in Christ's loving arms.

(adapted from the *Life Application Bible/NLT* [Wheaton, IL: Tyndale House Publishing, 1996], 1776)

Respond

6. Where would we stand before God if Adam were our only representative?

_____

_____

_____

7. What has Christ done about our sin?

_____

_____

_____

Day 4) *Imputation to Christ*

Read
Isaiah 53:4–6
⁴Yet it was our weaknesses he carried; it was our sorrows that weighed him down. And we thought his troubles were a punishment from God for his own sins!
⁵But he was wounded and crushed for our sins. He was beaten that we might have peace. He was whipped, and we were healed!

⁶All of us have strayed away like sheep. We have left God's paths to follow our own. Yet the Lord laid on him the guilt and sins of us all. (NLT)

2 Corinthians 5:21
God made him who had no sin to be sin for us, so that in him we might become the righteousness of God. (NIV)

1 Peter 2:21–25
²¹To this you were called, because Christ suffered for you, leaving you an example, that you should follow in his steps.
²²"He committed no sin, and no deceit was found in his mouth."
²³When they hurled their insults at him, he did not retaliate; when he suffered, he made no threats. Instead, he entrusted himself to him who judges justly.
²⁴He himself bore our sins in his body on the tree, so that we might die to sins and live for righteousness; by his wounds you have been healed.
²⁵For you were like sheep going astray, but now you have returned to the Shepherd and Overseer of your souls. (NIV)

Realize

1. According to Isaiah, what weighed down the Messiah?

2. Why was he "wounded" and "crushed"?

3. According to 2 Corinthians 5:21, what happened to our sins as a result of what Christ did for us on the cross?

4. How does Peter describe what happened to Jesus on the cross?

If you try to deal with sin in your conscience, let it remain there, and continue to look at it in your heart, your sins will become too strong for you. They will seem to live forever. But when you think of your sins as being on Christ and boldly believe that he conquered them through his resurrection, then they are dead and gone. Sin can't remain on Christ. His resurrection swallowed sin up.
Martin Luther

5. Why do you think this event is called "the great transaction"?

2 Corinthians 5:21

Here Paul summarized the heart of the gospel, explaining how sinners can be reconciled to God through Jesus Christ. These fifteen Greek words express the doctrines of imputation and substitution like no other single verse.

who had no sin—Jesus Christ, the sinless Son of God

sin for us—God the Father, using the principle of imputation, treated Christ as if he were a sinner though he was not, and had him die as a substitute to pay the penalty for the sins of those who believe in him. On the cross, he did not become a sinner, but remained as holy as ever. He was treated as if he were guilty of all the sins ever committed by all who would ever believe, though he committed none.

The wrath of God was exhausted on him, and the just requirement of God's law met for those for whom he died.

the righteousness of God—another reference to justification and imputation. The righteousness that is credited to the believer's account is the righteousness of Jesus Christ, God's Son. As Christ was not a sinner but was treated as if he were, so believers who have not yet been made righteous (until glorification) are treated as if they were righteous. He bore their sins so that they could bear his righteousness. God treated him as if he committed believers' sins and treats believers as if they did only the righteous deeds of the sinless Son of God.

(adapted from *The MacArthur Study Bible* [Nashville, TN: Word Bibles, 1997], 1772)

1 Peter 2:21–25 Peter had learned about suffering from Jesus. He knew that Jesus' suffering was part of God's plan (Matt. 16:21–23; Luke 24:25–27, 44–47) and was intended to save us (Matt. 20:28; 26:28). He also knew that all who follow Jesus must be prepared to suffer (Mark 8:34–35). Peter learned these truths from Jesus and passed them on to us.

2:24 Christ died for *our* sins, in *our* place, so we would not have to suffer the punishment we deserve. This is called *substitutionary atonement*.

(adapted from the *Life Application Bible/NLT* [Wheaton, IL: Tyndale House Publishers, 1996], 2001)

Respond

6. Why is what Christ did on the cross important for you?

_____

_____

_____

7. Where would you be without Christ?

_____

_____

_____

Day 5) *Imputation from Christ*

Read
Romans 3:21–28; 5:1–21

21But now God has shown us a different way of being right in his sight—not by obeying the law but by the way promised in the Scriptures long ago.
22We are made right in God's sight when we trust in Jesus Christ to take away our sins. And we all can be saved in this same way, no matter who we are or what we have done.
23For all have sinned; all fall short of God's glorious standard.
24Yet now God in his gracious kindness declares us not guilty. He has done this through Christ Jesus, who has freed us by taking away our sins.
25For God sent Jesus to take the punishment for our sins and to satisfy God's anger against us. We are made right with God when we believe that Jesus shed his blood, sacrificing his life for us. God was being entirely fair and just when he did not punish those who sinned in former times.
26And he is entirely fair and just in this present time when he declares sinners to be right in his sight because they believe in Jesus.
27Can we boast, then, that we have done anything to be accepted by God? No, because our acquittal is not based on our good deeds. It is based on our faith.
28So we are made right with God through faith and not by obeying the law.
5:1Therefore, since we have been made right in God's sight by faith, we have peace with God because of what Jesus Christ our Lord has done for us.
2Because of our faith, Christ has brought us into this place of highest privilege where we now stand, and we confidently and joyfully look forward to sharing God's glory.

³*We can rejoice, too, when we run into problems and trials, for we know that they are good for us—they help us learn to endure.*
⁴*And endurance develops strength of character in us, and character strengthens our confident expectation of salvation.*
⁵*And this expectation will not disappoint us. For we know how dearly God loves us, because he has given us the Holy Spirit to fill our hearts with his love.*
⁶*When we were utterly helpless, Christ came at just the right time and died for us sinners.*
⁷*Now, no one is likely to die for a good person, though someone might be willing to die for a person who is especially good.*
⁸*But God showed his great love for us by sending Christ to die for us while we were still sinners.*
⁹*And since we have been made right in God's sight by the blood of Christ, he will certainly save us from God's judgment.*
¹⁰*For since we were restored to friendship with God by the death of his Son while we were still his enemies, we will certainly be delivered from eternal punishment by his life.*
¹¹*So now we can rejoice in our wonderful new relationship with God—all because of what our Lord Jesus Christ has done for us in making us friends of God.*
¹²*When Adam sinned, sin entered the entire human race. Adam's sin brought death, so death spread to everyone, for everyone sinned.*
¹³*Yes, people sinned even before the law was given. And though there was no law to break, since it had not yet been given,*
¹⁴*they all died anyway—even though they did not disobey an explicit commandment of God, as Adam did. What a contrast between Adam and Christ, who was yet to come!*
¹⁵*And what a difference between our sin and God's generous gift of forgiveness. For this one man, Adam, brought death to many through his sin. But this other man, Jesus Christ, brought forgiveness to many through God's bountiful gift.*
¹⁶*And the result of God's gracious gift is very different from the result of that one man's sin. For Adam's sin led to condemnation, but we have the free gift of being accepted by God, even though we are guilty of many sins.*
¹⁷*The sin of this one man, Adam, caused death to rule over us, but all who receive God's wonderful, gracious gift of righteousness will live in triumph over sin and death through this one man, Jesus Christ.*
¹⁸*Yes, Adam's one sin brought condemnation upon everyone, but Christ's one act of righteousness makes all people right in God's sight and gives them life.*
¹⁹*Because one person disobeyed God, many people became sinners. But because one other person obeyed God, many people will be made right in God's sight.*
²⁰*God's law was given so that all people could see how sinful they were. But as people sinned more and more, God's wonderful kindness became more abundant.*
²¹*So just as sin ruled over all people and brought them to death, now God's wonderful kindness rules instead, giving us right standing with God and resulting in eternal life through Jesus Christ our Lord. (NLT)*

Realize
1. How can a person be "saved," declared "not guilty" (3:21–24)?

_____

_____

_____

2. Why are sinners declared "right" in God's sight (3:26)?

_____

_____

_____

_____

3. What do we have because of what Christ has done for us (5:1)?

_____

_____

_____

4. On the cross Christ took all our sins. What does he give us?

_____

_____

_____

RIGHTEOUSNESS

The New Testament uses "righteousness" in the sense of conformity to the demands and obligations of the will of God. . . . This righteousness is proclaimed by Jesus as a gift to those who are granted the kingdom of God. By faith in Jesus Christ and his work of atonement, human beings, unrighteous sinners though they are, receive God's righteousness (that is, they are given a true relationship with God which involves the forgiveness of all sin and a new moral standing with God in union with Christ "the Righteous One"). By dealing with all the consequences of human sin and unrighteousness (both Godward and humanward) in the cross, God at once maintains the moral order in which alone he can have fellowship with people and in grace delivers the needy.

(adapted from B.A. Milne, *New Bible Dictionary*, second edition [Downers Grove, IL: InterVarsity Press, 1962], 1031)

Respond

5. What does it mean to be "righteous"?

_____

_____

_____

6. How does what Christ did for you on the cross affect your relationship with God?

_____

_____

_____

7. How should it affect your relationship with others?

_____

_____

_____

"I Invite You into My Presence"

God's Promise through the Torn Flesh

LOOKING BACK

The previous lesson concentrated on the doctrine of imputation—that amazing truth that Jesus Christ not only took our sin upon himself, but he also gave us his perfect righteousness. Check yourself on the memory verse for that lesson, 1 Peter 3:18.

1. What is significant about the seamless garment Christ wore before going to the cross? Explain its symbolism.

   _____

   _____

   _____

2. On the cross, what did Jesus' battered, naked body represent?

   _____

   _____

   _____

3. *Max writes:* "While on the cross, Jesus felt the indignity and disgrace of a criminal. No, he was not guilty. No, he had not committed a sin. And no, he did not deserve to be sentenced. But you and I were, we had, and we did." Why is it that most people today definitely do not feel as if they are "criminals"?

   _____

   _____

   _____

   _____

4. Why is it necessary for a person to believe that he or she really is a criminal before that person can come to faith in Christ?

   _____

   _____

   _____

5. *Max writes:* "Jesus offers a robe of seamless purity and dons my patchwork coat of pride, greed, and selfishness." How can we accept Jesus' offer of a robe of seamless purity?

   _____

   _____

   _____

   _____

6. What passages, principles, or insights had the biggest impact on you during your daily study of the previous lesson? Why?

   _____

   _____

   _____

   _____

GETTING STARTED

VIDEO—In video segment number 7, Max imagines trying to get an appointment with the president. (The script is reprinted on page 228.)

7. Have you ever met a U.S. president or high-ranking government official? What was the experience like?

8. How do you think you'd react if you got an invitation to the White House or a Hollywood party or to be a guest on a popular talk show? Why?

9. Who is the most famous person you've ever encountered personally?

10. What is "name-dropping"? Do you do this much? Why or why not?

11. Why do you think we get so impressed (and intimidated) by prominent people (celebrities, politicians, athletes)?

So reach out to him and say, "Lord Christ, I know of no other Advocate, Comforter, and Mediator than you alone. I do not doubt that you are all this to me. I cling firmly to it, and I believe it." Christ was born for us. He suffered for us. He ascended into heaven for our sake, sits at the right hand of the Father, and prays for us. Satan tries with all his might to blind our hearts so we will not believe what the Holy Spirit says in this passage [1 John 2:1]. A Christian's condition is wonderful! For a Christian is both sinful and righteous. He's a sinful person because of the corrupt nature he carries with him that is contaminated by sin. He's a righteous person because the Spirit pulls him back from sin.
Martin Luther

12. Why doesn't the fact of "access to God" move us or amaze us more than it does?

DIGGING IN

13. *Max says:* "You and I both know when it comes to the president, don't hold your breath—no invitation will come. But when it comes to God, pick up your cookies and walk in, because it already has. . . . Nothing remains between you and God but an open door." Is this accessibility of God, this "invitation" into his very presence difficult for you to grasp or not? Why?

14. In what ways is it easier to visualize/imagine a trip to the White House than a real trip into the throne room of heaven?

15. *Max writes:* "What happened? In a word, someone opened the curtain. Someone tore down the veil. Something happened in the death of Christ that opened the door for you and me . . . in the horror of his torn flesh, we find the splendor of the open door."

Think about times in your life when you faced gigantic barriers that seemed impossible to break through (physical, relational, marital, occupational, etc.). Now, think of any occasions when events happened to remove those obstacles or to make a way through them. How did it feel to overcome or break through those barriers?

_____

_____

_____

GOING DEEPER

Matthew 27:50–51

50And Jesus cried out again with a loud voice, and yielded up His spirit.
51Then, behold, the veil of the temple was torn in two from top to bottom; and the earth quaked, and the rocks were split. (NKJV)

16. Are you surprised that Jesus cried out? Do you see a particular significance to this occurrance?

_____

_____

_____

17. In what specific way was the temple veil torn?

_____

_____

_____

18. What natural and supernatural phenomena accompanied the death of Christ and the tearing of the temple veil inside the Holy of Holies?

_____

_____

_____

No mean miracle was wrought in the rending of so strong and thick a veil; but it was not intended merely as a display of power—many lessons were herein taught us. The old law of ordinances was put away and, like a worn-out vesture, rent and laid aside. When Jesus died, the sacrifices were all finished because all were fulfilled in him, and therefore the place of their presentation was marked with an evident token of decay. The rent also revealed all the hidden things of the old dispensation: the mercy-seat could now be seen, and the glory of God gleamed forth above it. By the death of our Lord Jesus we have a clear revelation of God, for he was "not as Moses, who put a veil over his face." Life and immortality are now brought to light, and things which have been hidden since the foundation of the world are manifest in him. The annual ceremony of atonement was thus abolished. The atoning blood that was once every year sprinkled within the veil, was now offered once for all by the great High Priest, and therefore the place of the symbolical rite was broken up. No blood of bullocks or of lambs is needed now, for Jesus has entered within the veil with his own blood. Hence access to God is now permitted, and is the privilege of every believer in Christ Jesus. There is no small space laid open through which we may peer at the mercy-seat, but the rent reaches from the top to the bottom. We may come with boldness to the throne of the heavenly grace. Shall we err if we say that the opening of the Holy of Holies in this marvelous manner by our Lord's expiring cry was the type of the opening of the gates of paradise to all the saints by virtue of the Passion? Our bleeding Lord has the key of heaven; he opens and no man shuts; let us enter in with him into the heavenly places, and sit with him there till our common enemies shall be made his footstool.

(adapted from Charles Spurgeon, *Morning and Evening,* Morning April 20 Reading [30 Hunt Valley Circle, New Kensington, PA: Whitaker House © 1997. Used by permission of the publisher.], 224)

The rending of the veil signified that Christ, by his death, opened a way to God. We have an open way through Christ to the throne of grace, or mercy-seat now, and to the throne of glory hereafter. When we duly consider Christ's death, our hard and rocky hearts should be rent; the heart, and not the garments. That heart is harder than a rock that will not yield, that will not melt, where Jesus Christ is plainly set forth crucified. The graves were opened, and many bodies of saints that slept, arose. To whom they appeared, in what manner, and how they disappeared, we are not told; and we must not desire to be wise above what is written. The dreadful appearances of God in his providence sometimes work strangely for the conviction and awakening of sinners. This was expressed in the terror that fell upon the centurion and the Roman soldiers. We may reflect with comfort on the abundant testimonies given to the character of Jesus; and, seeking to give no just cause of offense, we may leave it to the Lord to clear our characters, if we live to him. Let us, with an eye of faith, behold Christ and him crucified, and be affected with that great love wherewith he loved us. But his friends could give no more than a look; they beheld him, but could not help him. Never were the horrid nature and effects of sin so tremendously displayed, as on that day when the beloved Son of the Father hung upon the cross, suffering for sin, the Just for the unjust, that he might bring us to God.

(adapted from *Matthew Henry's Concise Commentary* [Austin, TX: NavPress Software, *Bible Knowledge Library*, WORDsearch, 1996])

Hebrews 10:19–22
19Therefore, brothers, since we have confidence to enter the Most Holy Place by the blood of Jesus,
20by a new and living way opened for us through the curtain, that is, his body,
21and since we have a great priest over the house of God,
22let us draw near to God with a sincere heart in full assurance of faith, having our hearts sprinkled to cleanse us from a guilty conscience and having our bodies washed with pure water. (NIV)

19. Where does the writer of Hebrews say we can enter? By what means are we granted access?

_____

_____

_____

20. What does it mean that the writer identifies the curtain as "his body"?

_____

_____

_____

Hebrews 10:19 The Most Holy Place in the temple was sealed from view by a curtain (Heb. 10:20). Only the high priest could enter this holy room, and he did so only once a year on the Day of Atonement when he offered the sacrifice for the nation's sins. But Jesus' death removed the curtain, and all believers may walk into God's presence at any time (see also Heb. 6:19–20).

(adapted from *The Life Application Bible/NLT* [Wheaton, IL: Tyndale House Publishers, 1995], 1974)

Hebrews 10:19–22 The central assertion of these verses is in the words, "*Therefore, brothers* [see 3:1, 12] . . . *let us draw near to God.*" The intervening material, beginning with the word "since," gives the basis for the author's call to approach God. The readers are New-Covenant people ("brothers") who should *have confidence* . . . to come into the very presence of God. This idea is enriched by the use of Old-Covenant imagery. God's presence *in the most holy place* and *the curtain* that once was a barrier to people is now no longer so. It symbolized Christ's body, so the writer may have had in mind the rending of the temple curtain at the time of Christ's death (Matt. 27:51). At any rate his death gave believers the needed access and route to God, aptly described as new . . . *and living*, that is, partaking of the fresh and vitalizing realities of the New Covenant.

. . . There ought to be no wavering in regard to these superlative realities. Rather each New-Covenant worshiper should approach God in the conscious enjoyment of freedom from guilt *(having our hearts sprinkled to cleanse us from a guilty conscience)* and with a sense of the personal holiness that Christ's sacrifice makes possible *(having our bodies washed with pure water)*. The writer's words are probably an exhortation to lay hold consciously of the cleansing benefits of Christ's Cross and to draw near to God in enjoying them, putting away inward guilt and outward impurity.

(© 1986 Cook Communications Ministries. *Bible Knowledge Commentary* by Walvoord and Zuck. Reprinted with permission. May not be further reproduced. All rights reserved.)

Hebrews 4:16
So let us come boldly to the throne of our gracious God. There we will receive his mercy, and we will find grace to help us when we need it. (NLT)

21. How is God described in this verse? What does he offer us?

_____

_____

_____

22. How are we urged to approach God? Why?

_____

_____

_____

In a book filled with lovely and captivating turns of expression, few excel the memorable phrase "throne of our gracious God" (also translated "throne of grace"). Such a conception of the presence of God into which beleaguered Christians may come at any time, suggests both the sovereignty of the One they approach (since they come to a 'throne') and his benevolence. At a point of contact with God like this Christians can fully expect to *receive his mercy and . . . find grace to help us when we need it.*

(© 1986 Cook Communications Ministries. *Bible Knowledge Commentary* by Walvoord and Zuck. Reprinted with permission. May not be further reproduced. All rights reserved.)

WordFocus

MERCY (Gk. *eleos*) (Heb. 4:16; Rom. 15:9; Eph. 2:4; Titus 3:5; Jude 21)
The Greek word for "mercy" denotes an outward demonstration of pity, a sympathy that expresses itself in helping a person in need instead of remaining completely passive. The word *eleos* is often used in conjunction with the Greek word *charis,* usually translated grace (Eph. 2:4, 5; 1 Tim. 1:2; 1 Pet. 1:2,3). A similar idea is expressed by the Hebrew word *chesed,* often translated "lovingkindness" or "good-ness." It is the "loyal love" that God freely showed the Israelites because of his covenant with them. The ultimate expression of God's mercy is his voluntary offering of his only Son for our sins, even when we were still his enemies (Eph. 2:4–5). Since Jesus, our Intercessor at the right hand of God (Heb. 7:25), has experienced every kind of temptation we endure (Heb. 4:15), we can approach him with boldness, knowing that we will find sympathy and mercy. We who have experienced God's mercy and forgive-ness should, in turn, show mercy to others (Col. 3:12).

(adapted from *The Nelson Study Bible,* [Nashville, TN: Thomas Nelson Publishers, 1997], 2083)

23. *Max writes:* "We are welcome to enter God's presence—any day, any time. God has removed the barrier that separates us from him. The barrier of sin? Down. He has removed the curtain." In what way are we not only able to enter God's presence, but welcome there? What difference does this make?

_____

_____

_____

24. What is this "curtain" that has been removed? How was it removed?

_____
_____
_____

MAKING IT REAL

25. *Max continues:* "We have a tendency to put the barrier back up. Though there is no curtain in a temple, there is a curtain in the heart. Like the ticks on the clock are the mistakes of the heart. And sometimes, no, oftentimes, we allow those mistakes to keep us from God. Our guilty conscience becomes a curtain that separates us from God."
    When are you tempted to "put the barrier back up"? How does that usually work?

_____
_____
_____

26. How can we prevent a guilty conscience from erecting a curtain that separates us from God?

_____
_____
_____

THINKING IT THROUGH

Christ's work on the cross not only demonstrates his love and mercy, it is ultimately a reminder of his great power over sin and his decisive victory over Satan. He is Lord! He reigns! Let the truth of this lesson sink in and move you to worship as you listen to "He Reigns" by Glenn Wagner, Bernie Herms, and Bryan Lenox on the CD.

TAKING IT HOME

Memory Verse
1 Timothy 2:5, 6
For there is one God and one mediator between God and men, the man Christ Jesus, who gave himself as a ransom for all men—the testimony given in its proper time. (NIV)

For [there is] one God and one Mediator between God and men, [the] Man Christ Jesus, who gave Himself a ransom for all, to be testified in due time. (NKJV)

For there is only one God and one Mediator who can reconcile God and people. He is the man Christ Jesus. He gave his life to purchase freedom for everyone. This is the message that God gave to the world at the proper time. (NLT)

During the next week, study the following passages.

Day 1) *Sin Separates*

Read
Genesis 3:1–10
¹Now the serpent was more cunning than any beast of the field which the LORD God had made. And he said to the woman, "Has God indeed said, 'You shall not eat of every tree of the garden'?"
²And the woman said to the serpent, "We may eat the fruit of the trees of the garden;
³"but of the fruit of the tree which is in the midst of the garden, God has said, 'You shall not eat it, nor shall you touch it, lest you die.'"
⁴Then the serpent said to the woman, "You will not surely die.
⁵"For God knows that in the day you eat of it your eyes will be opened, and you will be like God, knowing good and evil."
⁶So when the woman saw that the tree was good for food, that it was pleasant to the eyes, and a tree desirable to make one wise, she took of its fruit and ate. She also gave to her husband with her, and he ate.
⁷Then the eyes of both of them were opened, and they knew that they were naked; and they sewed fig leaves together and made themselves coverings.
⁸And they heard the sound of the LORD God walking in the garden in the cool of the day, and Adam and his wife hid themselves from the presence of the LORD God among the trees of the garden.
⁹Then the LORD God called to Adam and said to him, "Where are you?"
¹⁰So he said, "I heard Your voice in the garden, and I was afraid because I was naked; and I hid myself." (NKJV)

Isaiah 59:1, 2
¹Surely the arm of the LORD is not too short to save, nor his ear too dull to hear.
²But your iniquities have separated you from your God; your sins have hidden his face from you, so that he will not hear. (NIV)

Realize
1. What happened when Adam and Eve ate the "forbidden fruit"?

_____

_____

_____

2. What did the first couple do when they heard the Lord in the garden? Why?

_____

_____

_____

3. What does Genesis 3:9–10 reveal about the consequences of sin?

_____

_____

_____

> **3:8** The scene is pathetic and sad. Here comes the Lord for an evening walk and a cozy chat. But Adam and Eve, who have "become wise," cower in the trees to avoid being seen by the Creator of the universe. What had been a perfect, shameless fellowship has turned into dreadful fear of God—not fear in the sense of true piety, as with Abraham, Moses, David, and Solomon—but the raw terror of being discovered in the wrong.
>
> (adapted from _The Nelson Study Bible_ [Nashville, TN: Thomas Nelson Publishers, 1997], 10)

4. What does Isaiah 59 declare about the effects of sin?

_____

_____

_____

5. Look up Isaiah 1:15. What does this verse suggest about human sinfulness and divine holiness?

_____

_____

_____

6. How is prayer impeded by sinful attitudes and actions?

_____

_____

_____

Respond

7. Describe a time in your life when you tried to avoid God. How did you work through this crisis?

_____

_____

_____

8. Evaluate your relationship with God right now. Are you are close to him and living obediently? Or do you sense a distance due to wrong choices you have made or are making?

_____

_____

_____

9. What specifically do you need to start doing or stop doing today to move towards God and a life that is honoring to him?

_____

_____

_____

Day 2) _The Danger of a Holy God_

Read
Exodus 19:10–12
¹⁰And the Lord said to Moses, "Go to the people and consecrate them today and tomorrow.

Have them wash their clothes
11and be ready by the third day, because on that day the LORD will come down on Mount Sinai in the sight of all the people.
12Put limits for the people around the mountain and tell them, 'Be careful that you do not go up the mountain or touch the foot of it. Whoever touches the mountain shall surely be put to death.'" (NIV)

Leviticus 10:1–3
1Then Nadab and Abihu, the sons of Aaron, each took his censer and put fire in it, put incense on it, and offered profane fire before the LORD, which He had not commanded them.
2So fire went out from the LORD and devoured them, and they died before the LORD.
3And Moses said to Aaron, "This is what the LORD spoke, saying: 'By those who come near Me I must be regarded as holy; and before all the people I must be glorified.'" So Aaron held his peace. (NKJV)

2 Samuel 6:1–7
1David again brought together out of Israel chosen men, thirty thousand in all.
2He and all his men set out from Baalah of Judah to bring up from there the ark of God, which is called by the Name, the name of the LORD Almighty, who is enthroned between the cherubim that are on the ark.
3They set the ark of God on a new cart and brought it from the house of Abinadab, which was on the hill. Uzzah and Ahio, sons of Abinadab, were guiding the new cart
4with the ark of God on it, and Ahio was walking in front of it.
5David and the whole house of Israel were celebrating with all their might before the LORD, with songs and with harps, lyres, tambourines, sistrums and cymbals.
6When they came to the threshing floor of Nacon, Uzzah reached out and took hold of the ark of God, because the oxen stumbled.
7The LORD's anger burned against Uzzah because of his irreverent act; therefore God struck him down and he died there beside the ark of God. (NIV)

Realize
1. In Exodus, what command did the Lord give Moses for the people of Israel at Sinai?

_____

_____

_____

2. What were the consequences for anyone who dared approach the Lord?

_____

_____

_____

3. What happened to Nadab and Abihu when they did not follow the strict commandments of God in worship?

_____

_____

_____

4. Who did the killing?

_____

_____

_____

5. What had Nadab and Abihu failed to do?

_____

_____

_____

Nadab and Abihu were Aaron's eldest sons. With Aaron and seventy elders of Israel, they had accompanied Moses part-way up Mount Sinai and had seen God (see Exod. 24:1, 9–11). They had participated with their father in the inaugural sacrifices recorded in chapter 9. They had obeyed, and God had accepted all that had been done on that day. . . . Nadab and Abihu violated God's holiness in some way the author does not spell out. *Profane* is literally "strange." "*Which He had not commanded them*" is in striking contrast with the careful obedience to God's commands recorded in chapters 8 and 9. Whatever the details, their act was clearly disobedient, and they knew it. . . . Their deaths were a result of their own rebellious action. God is a jealous God, unwilling to allow his people to be unfaithful to him.

(adapted from *The Nelson Study Bible* [Nashville, TN: Thomas Nelson Publishers, 1997], 189)

Leviticus 10:1–3. The two eldest *sons of Aaron* (see Exod. 6:23; 28:1; 1 Chron. 6:3), either through ignorance or presumption, offered "profane fire" *before the LORD, which He had not commanded them*. This incident interrupted the regular pattern of the previous two chapters in which everything was done in accord with the commands of the Lord (see Lev. 8:36). It is not stated what made their offering of incense "profane" ("strange," KJV). Perhaps they used coals in their *censers* that came from elsewhere than the altar (see 16:12) or they may have offered at the wrong time of day (Exod. 30:7–9). It may even be that they sought to go into the most holy place, and so usurped the prerogative of the high priest on the Day of Atonement (see Lev. 16:12–13). The command prohibiting the priests from drinking "wine or other fermented drink" (10:9) may suggest that drunkenness was a possible factor in their sin. In any event, they acted contrary to God's will, and their immediate judgment by God was a dramatic example of what it meant to be "cut off from his people" (see Num. 15:30). The moral of the story, as summarized by Moses, is that those who have the privilege of being nearest to God must bear special responsibility to exemplify his holiness and glory.

(© 1986 Cook Communications Ministries. *Bible Knowledge Commentary Old Testament* by Walvoord and Zuck. Reprinted with permission. May not be further reproduced. All rights reserved.)

6. What means did David use to bring the ark of God to Jerusalem? Why was this significant? (See Exod. 25:14, 15; Num. 3:30, 31.)

7. What were the consequences for Uzzah?

No matter how innocently it was done, touching the ark was in direct violation of God's law and was to result in death (see Num. 4:15). This was a means of preserving the sense of God's holiness and the fear of drawing near to him without appropriate preparation.

(adapted from *The MacArthur Study Bible* [Nashville, TN: Word Bibles, 1997], 435)

Respond
8. What do the deaths of Aaron's sons and Uzzah teach us?

9. What does the word "holy" mean? How would you define it to someone who has never heard of the word?

10. Why is God so intent on communicating to us his holiness? Why is this so vital?

_____

_____

_____

11. How reverently do you treat God? In what ways yesterday did you fail to honor God? What do you need to change today?

_____

_____

_____

Day 3) A Look Back at Atonement

Read
Leviticus 16:1–34

¹Now the LORD spoke to Moses after the death of the two sons of Aaron, when they offered profane fire before the LORD, and died;

²and the LORD said to Moses: "Tell Aaron your brother not to come at just any time into the Holy Place inside the veil, before the mercy seat which is on the ark, lest he die; for I will appear in the cloud above the mercy seat.

³Thus Aaron shall come into the Holy Place: with the blood of a young bull as a sin offering, and of a ram as a burnt offering.

⁴He shall put the holy linen tunic and the linen trousers on his body; he shall be girded with a linen sash, and with the linen turban he shall be attired. These are holy garments. Therefore he shall wash his body in water, and put them on.

⁵And he shall take from the congregation of the children of Israel two kids of the goats as a sin offering, and one ram as a burnt offering.

⁶"Aaron shall offer the bull as a sin offering, which is for himself, and make atonement for himself and for his house.

⁷He shall take the two goats and present them before the LORD at the door of the tabernacle of meeting.

⁸Then Aaron shall cast lots for the two goats: one lot for the LORD and the other lot for the scapegoat.

⁹And Aaron shall bring the goat on which the LORD's lot fell, and offer it as a sin offering.

¹⁰But the goat on which the lot fell to be the scapegoat shall be presented alive before the LORD, to make atonement upon it, and to let it go as the scapegoat into the wilderness.

¹¹And Aaron shall bring the bull of the sin offering, which is for himself, and make atonement for himself and for his house, and shall kill the bull as the sin offering which is for himself.

¹²Then he shall take a censer full of burning coals of fire from the altar before the LORD, with his hands full of sweet incense beaten fine, and bring it inside the veil.

¹³And he shall put the incense on the fire before the LORD, that the cloud of incense may cover the mercy seat that is on the Testimony, lest he die.

¹⁴He shall take some of the blood of the bull and sprinkle it with his finger on the mercy seat on the east side; and before the mercy seat he shall sprinkle some of the blood with his finger seven times.

¹⁵Then he shall kill the goat of the sin offering, which is for the people, bring its blood inside the veil, do with that blood as he did with the blood of the bull, and sprinkle it on the mercy seat and before the mercy seat.

¹⁶So he shall make atonement for the Holy Place, because of the uncleanness of the children of Israel, and because of their transgressions, for all their sins; and so he shall do for the tabernacle of meeting which remains among them in the midst of their uncleanness.

¹⁷There shall be no man in the tabernacle of meeting when he goes in to make atonement in the Holy Place, until he comes out, that he may make atonement for himself, for his household, and for all the assembly of Israel.

¹⁸And he shall go out to the altar that is before the Lᴏʀᴅ, and make atonement for it, and shall take some of the blood of the bull and some of the blood of the goat, and put it on the horns of the altar all around.

¹⁹Then he shall sprinkle some of the blood on it with his finger seven times, cleanse it, and consecrate it from the uncleanness of the children of Israel.

²⁰And when he has made an end of atoning for the Holy Place, the tabernacle of meeting, and the altar, he shall bring the live goat.

²¹Aaron shall lay both his hands on the head of the live goat, confess over it all the iniquities of the children of Israel, and all their transgressions, concerning all their sins, putting them on the head of the goat, and shall send it away into the wilderness by the hand of a suitable man.

²²The goat shall bear on itself all their iniquities to an uninhabited land; and he shall release the goat in the wilderness.

²³Then Aaron shall come into the tabernacle of meeting, shall take off the linen garments which he put on when he went into the Holy Place, and shall leave them there.

²⁴And he shall wash his body with water in a holy place, put on his garments, come out and offer his burnt offering and the burnt offering of the people, and make atonement for himself and for the people.

²⁵The fat of the sin offering he shall burn on the altar.

²⁶And he who released the goat as the scapegoat shall wash his clothes and bathe his body in water, and afterward he may come into the camp.

²⁷The bull for the sin offering and the goat for the sin offering, whose blood was brought in to make atonement in the Holy Place, shall be carried outside the camp. And they shall burn in the fire their skins, their flesh, and their offal.

²⁸Then he who burns them shall wash his clothes and bathe his body in water, and afterward he may come into the camp.

²⁹This shall be a statute forever for you: In the seventh month, on the tenth day of the month, you shall afflict your souls, and do no work at all, whether a native of your own country or a stranger who dwells among you.

³⁰For on that day the priest shall make atonement for you, to cleanse you, that you may be clean from all your sins before the Lᴏʀᴅ.

³¹It is a sabbath of solemn rest for you, and you shall afflict your souls. It is a statute forever.

³²And the priest, who is anointed and consecrated to minister as priest in his father's place, shall make atonement, and put on the linen clothes, the holy garments;

³³then he shall make atonement for the Holy Sanctuary, and he shall make atonement for the tabernacle of meeting and for the altar, and he shall make atonement for the priests and for all the people of the assembly.

³⁴This shall be an everlasting statute for you, to make atonement for the children of Israel, for all their sins, once a year." And he did as the Lᴏʀᴅ commanded Moses.

Realize

1. What were God's instructions to Aaron about coming "inside the veil"?

_____

_____

_____

2. What personal preparations was Aaron to make before entering the Holy Place?

_____

_____

_____

3. What was Aaron required to bring with him into the Holy Place? Why?

_____

_____

_____

4. What animals were required for this annual act of atonement?

_____

5. Why two goats? What was the fate of each goat?

_____

_____

_____

The annual Day of Atonement was the one fast day (see Acts 27:9) among Israel's annual feasts (see Lev. 23). Additional instructions are given in other passages (Exod. 30:10; Lev. 23:26–32; 25:9; Num. 29:7–11), but Leviticus 16 contains the fullest explanation of its ritual. . . . The main purpose of the Day of Atonement ceremonies is to cleanse the sanctuary from the pollution introduced into it by the unclean worshipers (see 16:16, 19) . . . so as to make possible God's continued presence among his people. It is true that the cleansing of "the most holy place, the Tent of Meeting, and the altar" (v. 20) was a theologically significant feature of the Day of Atonement that appeared to be accomplished by the blood manipulation ritual of the slain goat for the people (vv. 15–19). But the completion of the sin offering with the live goat ritual involved a substitutionary carrying away of the people's sins (v. 22) which were identified as "all the iniquities of the children of Israel and all their transgressions" (v. 21), so that they "will be clean from all [their] sins" (v. 30). Of course Aaron and his household were the initial objects of the atoning sacrifice's special rituals (vv. 6, 11–14). So the special atonement ritual averted the wrath of God for all the sins of the people for the past year.

The comprehensiveness of the sins atoned for by the Day of Atonement ritual was staggering. One might expect that certain sins would be excluded—either those already expiated by individual sacrifices or those defiant sins for which there was no individual sacrifice and for which the prescribed punishment was capital or "cutting off" from the people. . . . But no such limitation is evident in chapter 16. The one apparently limiting factor to the efficacy of this national Day of Atonement for the individual was a proper heart attitude of penitence and faith, which was also true of the individual sacrifices.

(© 1986 Cook Communications Ministries. *Bible Knowledge Commentary Old Testament* by Walvoord and Zuck. Reprinted with permission. May not be further reproduced. All rights reserved.)

The Day of Atonement was the greatest day of the year for Israel. The Hebrew word for atone means "to cover." Old Testament sacrifices could not actually remove sins, only "cover" them. On this day, the people confessed their sins as a nation, and the high priest went into the Most Holy Place to make atonement for them. Sacrifices were made and blood was shed so that the people's sins could be "covered" until Christ's sacrifice on the cross would give people the opportunity to have their sin removed forever.

(adapted from the *Life Application Bible/NLT* [Wheaton, IL: Tyndale House Publishers, 1996], 178)

Respond

6. What in chapter 16 indicates the severity of sin and solemnity of the process of atonement?

_____

_____

_____

7. How might it change you if you could be transported back in time to ancient Israel to personally witness the events described in Leviticus 16?

_____

_____

_____

8. How can Christ's sacrifice for your sins motivate you today to live a pure and holy life?

_____

_____

Read
1 Timothy 2:5–6
⁵For there is only one God and one Mediator who can reconcile God and people. He is the man Christ Jesus.
⁶He gave his life to purchase freedom for everyone. This is the message that God gave to the world at the proper time. (NLT)

1 John 2:1
My dear children, I write this to you so that you will not sin. But if anybody does sin, we have one who speaks to the Father in our defense—Jesus Christ, the Righteous One. (NIV)

Romans 8:34
Christ Jesus, who died—more than that, who was raised to life—is at the right hand of God and is also interceding for us. (NIV)

Realize
1. What is a mediator?

_____

_____

_____

2. Who is the mediator between God and man? Is there more than one? Why is this significant?

_____

_____

_____

_____

Theological Insight

The word *mediator* literally means "a go-between"; it connotes an intermediary between two parties. Christ is the mediator between God and humanity because he provides the access for people to come to God. Christ made it clear that he was this mediator when he said, "I am the way and the truth and the life; no one comes to the Father except through me" (John 14:6, NIV). The destination is not a place but a person. God is the destination, and the Son is the way to him. Through his death, resurrection, and ascension, Christ prepared the way for believers to come to God and live in God. In short, he prepared the way for disciples to have spiritual access (that is, access through the Spirit) to the Father. At the same time, he opened the way for the Triune God to be able to live in the disciples. In context, this has to be included in what Jesus was talking about when he told his disciples a few verses earlier: "In my Father's house are many rooms. If it were not so, I would have told you. I am going there to prepare a place for you. And if I go and prepare a place for you, I come back and take you to be with me" (John 14:2–3, NIV).

When Jesus said that he was going to prepare a place for the disciples in the Father's house, could he not have been suggesting that he himself was that house? Did not the Father dwell in him and he in the Father? Then, the way for the disciples to dwell in the Father would be for them to come and abide in the Son. In other words, by coming into the One who was indwelt by the Father, the believers would come simultaneously into the Indweller, the Father. Clearly, this was the Lord's desire and design (see John 14:20; 17:21–24). Therefore, when he said he was going to prepare a place for them, does it not mean that he, through the process of death and resurrection, was going to make himself ready to be inhabited by his disciples?

This is the true work of the mediator—to provide the way and even be the place where God and humanity can peacefully co-inhabit.

The book of Hebrews also speaks of Christ's mediation. This book opens with the assertion that Christ surpasses all other mediators—angels, Moses, and all the priests in Aaron's line. His is a timeless

116

priesthood, like Melchizedek's. Christ's mediation so far excels all others that it can never be super-seded. Hebrews tells us that, after Christ offered himself on the cross as the sacrifice for sins, he ascended to the Father and entered the heavenly sanctuary where he now represents his people. When his flesh was torn, the veil before the Holy of Holies was torn—thereby revealing that Christ's death had opened the way to the Father. With this open access, Christ "is able to save completely those who come to God through him, because he always lives to intercede for them" (Heb. 7:25, NIV). Further, Christ has "entered heaven itself, now to appear for us in God's presence" (Heb. 9:24, NIV). He is depict-ed as a priest engaged in his continuing ministry of intercession. As such, Christ's heavenly interces-sion is a sequel to his earthly sacrifice accomplished once for all (Heb. 10:10–18).

This heavenly intercession is explicitly affirmed in two other New Testament texts. The apostle Paul spoke of Christ "at the right hand of God . . . interceding for us" (Rom. 8:34, NIV). The apostle John also described that ministry: "But if anybody does sin, we have one who speaks to the Father in our defense—Jesus Christ the Righteous One" (1 John 2:1, NIV). The Greek word for "advocate" (translated in the NIV "one who speaks . . . in our defense") meant a legal counselor who appeared before a mag-istrate to plead a client's cause. John thus pictured the ascended Lord as appearing before God on behalf of his people.

3. What act of Christ served as the basis for this mediation?

_____

_____

_____

4. According to 1 John 2:1, what happens when a believer sins?

_____

_____

_____

5. What qualifies Christ to do this?

_____

_____

_____

For the Christian who wants to make progress in the spiritual life, nothing is as demoralizing as sin. "Why did I give in to that temptation again?" we lament. "I knew better!" we cry. "How could God for-give me for this?" we moan. Our enemy, Satan, is quite adept at using our failures to accuse us, to fill us with guilt, and to cause us to wallow in despair. The answer for such miserable moments? Remembering that Jesus Christ, the Righteous One, "speaks to the Father in our defense." The idea con-veyed by John is that Christ acts as our defense attorney. Having paid for all our sins and purchased our complete forgiveness, he is well able to represent us before a holy God. We need not fear judgment. Because of what Christ has done, we are "not guilty"; furthermore, we possess the very righteousness of Christ (2 Cor. 5:21)!

(adapted from the *Life Application Bible Commentary: 1, 2, & 3 John* [Wheaton, IL: Tyndale House Publishers, 1998], 29)

6. In addition to atoning for sin, what does Christ do for Christians in his role of mediator? (See Romans 8:34.)

_____

_____

_____

Respond

7. Why did Jesus have to die?

_____

_____

8. What would be the result if he hadn't died?

_____

_____

_____

9. How can you express gratitude to God today for the existence of a worthy mediator for sinful men?

_____

_____

_____

Day 5) *The Blessing of Nearness*

Read
Ephesians 2:13–19
¹³But now in Christ Jesus you who once were far away have been brought near through the blood of Christ.
¹⁴For he himself is our peace, who has made the two one and has destroyed the barrier, the dividing wall of hostility,
¹⁵by abolishing in his flesh the law with its commandments and regulations. His purpose was to create in himself one new man out of the two, thus making peace,
¹⁶and in this one body to reconcile both of them to God through the cross, by which he put to death their hostility.
¹⁷He came and preached peace to you who were far away and peace to those who were near.
¹⁸For through him we both have access to the Father by one Spirit.
¹⁹Consequently, you are no longer foreigners and aliens, but fellow citizens with God's people and members of God's household. (NIV)

Realize
1. How were we brought near to God?

_____

_____

_____

2. How did Jesus break down the barrier?

_____

_____

_____

3. What demonstrates the power of the cross?

_____

_____

_____

4. How do we have access to the Father?

_____

_____

5. How did our faith in Christ's person and work change our very identity?

_____

_____

Respond

6. When have you been "brought near" to God? What were the circumstances?

_____

_____

_____

7. Who do you know who needs to know about the tearing of the curtain—that there is a way right into the very presence of God?

_____

_____

_____

8. What can you do to communicate this truth effectively and compassionately?

_____

_____

_____

Every person who trusts in Christ alone for salvation, Jew or Gentile, is brought into spiritual union and intimacy with God. This is the reconciliation of 2 Corinthians 5:18–21. The atoning work accomplished by Christ's death on the cross washes away the penalty of sin and ultimately even its presence.

(adapted from _The MacArthur Study Bible_ [Nashville, TN: Word Bibles, 1997], 1805)

L E S S O N

"I Understand Your Pain"

God's Promise in the Wine-Soaked Sponge

LOOKING BACK

Lesson 7 focused on the theological concept of mediation—the profound truth that Jesus is the sinless high priest who offered himself as a perfect, final, and acceptable sacrifice for our sin, thus making it possible for us to have access into an eternal relationship with God.

Try to say our memory verses from that study, 1 Timothy 2:5, 6.

1. Other than the invitation to come into a relationship with God as a fully forgiven child, what's the greatest invitation you've ever received?

   _____

   _____

2. *Max writes:* "What did fifteen hundred years of a curtain-draped Holy of Holies communicate? Simple. God is holy . . . separate from us and unapproachable." What does the word "holy" mean to you? How would you define it to someone who had never heard of the word?

   _____

   _____

3. Why is God so intent on communicating to us his holiness? Why is this so vital?

   _____

   _____

   _____

4. *Max concludes:* "The message of the torn flesh is . . . God welcomes you. God is not avoiding you. God is not resisting you. The curtain is down, the door is open, and God invites you in." What did you learn in your daily studies for lesson 7 about how Jesus has made God approachable?

   _____

   _____

   _____

GETTING STARTED

VIDEO—In video segment number 8, Max tells the story of the mouse. (The script has been reprinted on page 229.)

5. A recent U.S. presidential candidate contributed the slogan "I feel your pain" to contemporary pop culture. To many this statement eventually became less of a noble declaration and more of a national punch line. Why do you think? Is it difficult for you to conceive of a powerful leader who is truly able to understand and sympathize with the struggles of the people whom he or she governs?

   _____

   _____

6. If you were appointed by your government as ambassador to another nation, what sort of actions would help you identify with your new neighbors? Why?

_____

_____

_____

_____

7. Who is the most sympathetic person in your immediate circle of family and friends? What makes him or her so understanding?

_____

_____

_____

_____

8. A friend complains: "I quit. I've tried praying and reading the Bible. I really have. But God just seems so distant, so remote, so elusive. How can I possibly relate to a God who is invisible, who is the exact opposite of me in every way?" What would you say?

_____

_____

_____

_____

Digging In

9. *Max writes:* "Why did Jesus live on the earth as long as he did? Couldn't his life have been much shorter? Why not step into our world just long enough to die for our sins and then leave? Why not a sinless year, or week? Why did he have to live a life?" What would be your answer to these questions?

_____

_____

_____

10. If Jesus had been killed as an infant, perhaps during Herod's paranoid and murderous plot (see Matthew 2:16–18) and raised to life three days later, what questions of ours might have gone unanswered? How would such an event change the nature of our faith?

The Son of God became a man to enable men to become sons of God.
C.S. Lewis[1]

_____

_____

_____

_____

11. *Max writes:* "Even his final act on earth was intended to win your trust. . . . In the concluding measure of his earthly composition, we hear the sounds of a thirsty man. And through his thirst—through a sponge and a jar of cheap wine—he leaves a final appeal. 'You can trust me.'" What message does Christ's thirst on the cross send to you? Why? What is Max driving at here? What's the deeper meaning?

_____

_____

_____

Going Deeper

Mark 15:22–23
²²*They led Jesus to the place called Golgotha, which means the Place of the Skull.*
²³*The soldiers tried to give Jesus wine mixed with myrrh to drink, but he refused. (NCV)*

12. Before crucifying Jesus, what did his captors offer him?

_____

_____

_____

13. With what was the wine mixed?

_____

_____

_____

14. What was Jesus' response? Why do you think?

_____

_____

_____

To temporarily deaden the pain, the Romans allowed this drink to be administered to victims of crucifixion, probably not out of compassion, but to keep them from struggling while being crucified.

Tasting what it was, Christ, though thirsty, would not drink, lest it dull his senses before he completed his work. The lessening of physical pain would probably not have diminished the efficacy of his atoning work. . . . But he needed his full mental faculties for the hours yet to come. It was necessary for him to be awake and fully conscious, for example, to minister to the dying thief (Luke 23:43).

(adapted from *The MacArthur Study Bible* [Nashville, TN: Word Bibles, 1997], 1500, 1449)

John 19:28–30
28After this, Jesus, knowing that all things were now accomplished, that the Scripture might be fulfilled, said, "I thirst!"
29Now a vessel full of sour wine was sitting there; and they filled a sponge with sour wine, put it on hyssop, and put it to His mouth.
30So when Jesus had received the sour wine, He said, "It is finished!" And bowing His head, He gave up His spirit. (NKJV)

15. How does this scene at the conclusion of Christ's time on the cross differ from the pre-crucifixion offer of wine?

_____

_____

_____

16. Why, according to John, did Jesus proclaim his thirst?

_____

_____

_____

17. What happened after Jesus accepted the "sour wine"?

_____

_____

_____

18. What's the significance of Jesus' cry, "It is finished!"?

_____

_____

Hyssop—A species of marjoram and a member of the mint family

Hyssop was an aromatic shrub under one meter (three feet) tall with clusters of yellow flowers. It grew in rocky crevices and was cultivated on terraced walls. "From the cedar tree of Lebanon even to the hyssop that springs out of the wall" (1 Kings 4:33, NKJV). Bunches of hyssop were used to sprinkle blood on the doorposts in Egypt (Exod. 12:22) and in purification ceremonies (Lev. 14:4, 6, 51–52). David mentioned it as an instrument of inner cleansing (Ps. 51:7). It was used at the crucifixion to relieve Jesus' thirst (John 19:29).

Myrrh—An extract from a stiff-branched tree with white flowers and plumlike fruit

After myrrh was extracted from the wood, it soon hardened and was valued as an article of trade. It was an ingredient used in anointing oil (Exod. 30:23) and was used as perfume (Ps. 45:8; Prov. 7:17; Song of Sol. 3:6), in purification rites for women (Esther 2:12), as a gift for the infant Jesus (Matt. 2:11), and in embalming (John 19:39). According to the gospel of Mark (15:23), the drink offered to Jesus before his crucifixion was "wine mingled with myrrh."

(adapted from Ronald F. Youngblood, Ed., *Nelson's New Illustrated Bible Dictionary* [Nashville, TN: Thomas Nelson Publishers, 1997, c1995], CD-ROM)

Sour wine was not the same as the drugged wine that had been offered to Jesus earlier (wine mixed with myrrh; see Mark 15:23). Jesus did not take that wine because he wanted to die fully conscious. He did take a sip of this wine; one of the agonies of crucifixion was incredible thirst, added to the terrible pain.

(adapted from *The Nelson Study Bible* [Nashville, TN: Thomas Nelson Publishers, 1997], 1805)

The purpose of this drink (see Mark 15:36) was to prolong life and increase the torture and pain.

(from *The MacArthur Study Bible* [Nashville, TN: Word Bibles, 1997], 1625)

Psalm 22:15
My strength is dried up like a potsherd, and my tongue cleaves to my jaws; and Thou dost lay me in the dust of death. (NASB)

Psalm 69:21
They also gave me gall for my food, and for my thirst they gave me vinegar to drink. (NASB)

19. What do these statements (from two of the "messianic psalms") have to do with the events of John 19?

_____

_____

_____

_____

Psalm 22 speaks of David's own distress and the Lord's deliverance of him, and it also prophetically describes in remarkable detail Jesus' crucifixion and resurrection.

Whereas Psalm 22 describes Jesus' physical sufferings, Psalm 69 focuses more on his emotional and spiritual suffering. Both psalms begin with the sufferings of David but have their full meaning in the sufferings of Jesus.

(adapted from *The Nelson Study Bible* [Nashville, TN: Thomas Nelson Publishers, 1997], 896, 947)

20. *Max writes:* "Why, in his final moments, was Jesus determined to fulfill prophecy? He knew we would doubt. He knew we would question. And since he did not want our heads to keep his love from our hearts, he used his final moments to offer proof that he was the Messiah." How does fulfilled prophecy help us to trust God?

_____

_____

_____

21. What fulfilled prophecies are most helpful to you?

_____

_____

_____

MAKING IT REAL

Jesus came to earth and identified totally with humanity. Fully God, yet fully human, Christ subjected himself to everything that we face—physical limitations, emotional turmoil, spiritual stress. As a result, because he utterly understands us, our world, and our plight, we can trust him without reserve.

Hebrews 4:15, 16

15For our high priest is able to understand our weaknesses. When he lived on earth, he was tempted in every way that we are, but he did not sin.
16Let us, then, feel very sure that we can come before God's throne where there is grace. There we can receive mercy and grace to help us when we need it. (NCV)

22. Why is Jesus called our "high priest"?

_____

_____

_____

23. How is Jesus able to sympathize with our weaknesses?

_____

_____

_____

24. What one area of life did Jesus not share with us? Why is this important?

_____

_____

_____

25. Because of who Jesus is and what he has done, what does the writer of Hebrews say that we may do?

_____

_____

_____

Theological Insight

The Son of God identified with humanity when he became a man and suffered in the flesh (Heb. 2:14). Peter tells us that Jesus bore the griefs and sorrows of humanity when he suffered for the sins of the world (1 Pet. 2:24). This is called Jesus' "passion"—a derivative from Latin, meaning "suffering." Each of the four Gospels has a passion-narrative, which is the section recording the sufferings of Jesus on the night of his arrest and the following day leading up to his death. These passages describe Jesus' agonizing prayer in the garden of Gethsemane, his arrest, his trials, his scourgings, and his crucifixion. In all of these sufferings, he completely identified with the worst of human experience.

The second chapter of Hebrews reveals that the Son of God joined the human race in order to participate in humanity, to feel our sufferings, and even to taste death on our behalf. In so doing, he became the pioneer, the captain of our salvation. He, as man, pioneered the way for all the other believers to follow. He, who was the express image of God's substance and the effulgence of his glory (Heb. 1:3), relinquished that place of glory and took a human body for the sake of accomplishing the Father's will. In that body he would suffer and die for our salvation (see Heb. 10:5–10). He did this because he loved the Father and because he anticipated the joy set before him (Heb. 12:2). His joy would be to return— via resurrection and ascension—to his Father. He would again be in glory, but now as a man!

Jesus is the one who pioneered the way for all other believers to follow. Hebrews 2:10 calls him "the captain of our salvation," or this could as easily be rendered "the pioneer of our salvation" or "the leader of our salvation." The Greek word underlying "captain," "pioneer," or "leader" designates "the first one to lead the way" (archegon, from arche "the first" and ago "to lead"). Hebrews 2:10 tells us that this Leader is the one who is leading the believers into glory.

Jesus himself entered into glory, but he did not just stay there, awaiting our arrival. No, after having entered into glory, he returned to the many sons so as to be with them and then lead them into glory. The verses following Hebrews 2:10 explain that Jesus is in the midst of the church; he is dwelling with all those whom he is not ashamed to call his brothers and sisters. It is impossible for our finite minds to comprehend how Jesus can both be on the throne in heaven and in the midst of the church simultaneously. But it is the truth—verified by the Scriptures and by our experience. Before Jesus left this world to return to the Father, he repeatedly told the disciples that he himself would be with them: "For where two or three are gathered together in my name, there am I in their midst" (Matt. 18.20); "Lo, I am with you always, even until the end of the age" (Matt. 28:20, NRSV); and "I will not leave you orphaned. I am coming to you" (John 14:18, NRSV).

Jesus, the one in our midst, is leading us to where he has already gone—into the glorious presence of the Father. The path to that glorious destiny cannot be different than the one the Lord himself traversed. He left a pattern for us to follow, a mold to which we are to be conformed. Each believer, to grow and mature, must be conformed to the image of God's Son. The Father wills it because he desires all his children to reach maturity and so bear the image of his beloved Son. The Son of God became like us so that we eventually can become like him. As 1 John says, "We will be like him, for we will see him as he is." (3:2, NRSV)

THINKING IT THROUGH

Spend a few moments in quiet, musical reflection, pondering all that you have just studied, as you listen to "Worthy Is the Lamb" by Twila Paris on the CD. Thank God for taking the initiative to come to you, and worship him for his remarkable gift of Jesus, the very Son of God.

INCARNATION—a theological term for the coming of God's Son into the world as a human being

The term itself is not used in the Bible, but it is based on clear references in the New Testament to Jesus as a person "in the flesh" (Rom. 8:3; Eph. 2:15; Col. 1:22).

Jesus participated fully in all that it means to live a human life. But if Jesus were merely a man, no matter how great, there would be no significance in drawing attention to his bodily existence. The marvelous thing is that in Jesus, God himself began to live a fully human life. The capacity of Jesus to reveal God to us and to bring salvation depends upon his being fully God and fully man at the same time (Col. 2:9).

Our human minds cannot understand how Jesus can be both fully God and fully man. But the Bible gives clear indication of how this works out in practice.

No person may see God and live (Exod. 33:20). He dwells in unapproachable light (1 Tim. 6:16). Can we, therefore, only know him from a distance? No, because God has come near in the person of Jesus (Matt. 1:23). He has taken on a form in which he can be seen, experienced, and understood by us as human beings (John 1:14, 18). Jesus reveals God to us perfectly since in his human life he is the image of God (2 Cor. 4:4), exhibiting full likeness with the Father (John 1:14). Jesus' godhood in his manhood is the key to our intimate knowledge of God.

This does not mean, however, that Jesus' humanity is only a display case for his divinity. Jesus lived out his human life by experiencing all the pressures, temptations, and limitations that we experience (Heb. 2:18; 4:15; 5:2, 7–8). That is why Jesus' life really is the supreme human success story (Heb. 5:8). Jesus was a "pioneer" (Heb. 2:10, NRSV), showing in practical terms the full meaning and possibility of human life, lived in obedience to God. In this respect, Jesus is a kind of second Adam (Rom. 5:14–15), marking a new beginning for the human race.

Jesus would have performed a great work if he had done no more than set a perfect example. But his full humanity is also the basis on which it is possible for him to represent us—indeed, take our place—in dying for us. The Bible makes this clear when it speaks of "one Mediator between God and men, the Man Christ Jesus, who gave Himself a ransom for all" (1 Tim. 2:5–6).

When he ascended to his Father after his resurrection, Jesus left behind some of the human restrictions experienced during his earthly life. He received at that time his original divine glory (John 17:5). But the joining together of deity and humanity that marks his incarnation did not come to an end with his ascension. Jesus took his resurrected body with him back to heaven (Luke 24:51; Acts 1:9). In heaven now he is our divine Lord, our human leader, and the great High Priest who serves as a mediator between God and humankind (Heb. 3:1).

(adapted from Ronald F. Youngblood, Ed., *Nelson's New Illustrated Bible* Dictionary [Nashville, TN: Thomas Nelson Publishers, 1997], CD-ROM)

Memory Verse:
Hebrews 4:15

For we do not have a high priest who is unable to sympathize with our weaknesses, but we have one who has been tempted in every way, just as we are—yet was without sin. (NIV)

For we do not have a High Priest who cannot sympathize with our weaknesses, but was in all points tempted as we are, yet without sin. (NKJV)

This High Priest of ours understands our weaknesses, for he faced all of the same temptations we do, yet he did not sin. (NLT)

During the next week, study the following passages.

Day 1) *The Incarnation*

Read
John 1:1–18
¹In the beginning was the Word, and the Word was with God, and the Word was God.
²He was in the beginning with God.
³All things were made through Him, and without Him nothing was made that was made.
⁴In Him was life, and the life was the light of men.
⁵And the light shines in the darkness, and the darkness did not comprehend it.
⁶There was a man sent from God, whose name was John.
⁷This man came for a witness, to bear witness of the Light, that all through him might believe.
⁸He was not that Light, but was sent to bear witness of that Light.
⁹That was the true Light which gives light to every man coming into the world.
¹⁰He was in the world, and the world was made through Him, and the world did not know Him.
¹¹He came to His own, and His own did not receive Him.
¹²But as many as received Him, to them He gave the right to become children of God, to those who believe in His name:
¹³who were born, not of blood, nor of the will of the flesh, nor of the will of man, but of God.
¹⁴And the Word became flesh and dwelt among us, and we beheld His glory, the glory as of the only begotten of the Father, full of grace and truth.
¹⁵John bore witness of Him and cried out, saying, "This was He of whom I said, 'He who comes after me is preferred before me, for He was before me'."
¹⁶And of His fullness we have all received, and grace for grace.
¹⁷For the law was given through Moses, but grace and truth came through Jesus Christ.
¹⁸No one has seen God at any time. The only begotten Son, who is in the bosom of the Father, He has declared Him. (NKJV)

Realize
1. What is the meaning of "the Word"?

_____
_____
_____

2. How is "the Word" described in the opening four verses of John's gospel? What is significant about this description?

_____
_____
_____
_____

Hark! The Herald Angels Sing

Christ, by highest heaven adored, Christ the everlasting Lord:
Long desired, behold him come, Finding here his humble home.
Veiled in flesh the Godhead see, Hail th' incarnate Deity!
Pleased as man with men to dwell, Jesus our Immanuel.
Hark! the herald angels sing, 'Glory to the newborn King.'

(Charles Wesley, 1739)

3. What is the meaning of "the Light" (verses 7–9)?

    _____

    _____

    _____

4. How would you put verse 14 in your own words? Why is this considered a major theological statement?

    _____

    _____

    _____

My trials are merely a fraction of the spitting and blows Christ endured. We face these dangers for Him and with His help. Even taken altogether, these dangers don't deserve the crown of thorns which robbed our Conqueror of His crown. Yet for His sake I am crowned for a hard life. I don't consider these trails even worth…the gall or vinegar alone. But by these we were cured of the bitter taste of life. My struggles aren't worthy of the gentleness He showed in His passion.
Gregory Nazianzen

5. What does verse 18 say about God? About the Son? About why the Son came?

    _____

    _____

    _____

6. What does it mean to "receive" the Word/Light/Son (verse 12)?

    _____

    _____

    _____

7. What happens to those who "receive" him?

    _____

    _____

    _____

Respond

8. Why do you think John began his Gospel in this manner rather than with a genealogy or birth narrative like the other Gospel writers?

    _____

    _____

    _____

9. What is ironic (and sad) about verse 10?

    _____

    _____

    _____

10. When did you "receive" Christ? What events led up to this decision?

    _____

    _____

    _____

INCARNATION

Though the word "incarnation" does not appear in Scripture, its components ("in" and "flesh") do. John wrote that the Word became flesh (John 1:14). He also wrote of Jesus coming in the flesh (1 John 4:2; 2 John 7). By this he meant that the eternal second Person of the Trinity took on himself humanity. He did not possess humanity until the birth, since the Lord became flesh (*egeneto,* John 1:14, in contrast to the four occurrences of *en* in verses 1 and 2. His humanity, however, was sinless, a fact guarded by writing that he came "in the likeness of sinful flesh" (Rom. 8:3).

Why did God send his Son in the likeness of human flesh? . . . Though God reveals himself in various ways including the magnificence of nature, only the Incarnation revealed the essence of God, though veiled (John 1:18; 14:7–11). The only way a person can see the Father is to know about the Son. . . . Because he became a man, the revelation of God was personalized; because he is God, that revelation is completely truthful.

The Incarnation has ramifications in relation to our knowledge of God, to our salvation, to our daily living, to our pressing needs, and to the future. It truly is the central fact of history.

The statement on the person of Christ incarnate formulated at the Council at Chalcedon (A.D. 451) has been considered definitive by orthodox Christianity. It reads as follows: "Therefore, following the holy fathers, we all with one accord teach men to acknowledge one and the same Son, our Lord Jesus Christ, at once complete in Godhead and complete in manhood, truly God and truly man, consisting also of a reasonable soul and body; of one substance with the Father as regards his Godhead, and at the same time of one substance with us as regards his manhood; like us in all respects apart from sin; as regards his Godhead, begotten of the Father before the ages, but yet as regards his manhood, begotten, for us men and for our salvation, of Mary the virgin, the God-bearer; one and the same Christ, Son, Lord, Only-Begotten, recognized in two natures, without confusion, without change, without division, without separation; the distinction of natures being in no way annulled by the union, but rather the characteristics of each nature being preserved and coming together to form one Person and subsistence, not as parted or separated into two Persons, but one and the same Son and only-begotten God the Word, Lord Jesus Christ; even as the prophets from earliest times spoke of him, and our Lord Jesus Christ himself taught us, and the creed of the fathers has been handed down to us."

More concisely one may describe the person of Christ incarnate as being full Deity and perfect humanity united without mixture, change, division, or separation in one Person forever.

(© 1986 Cook Communications Ministries. *Bible Knowledge Commentary* by Walvoord and Zuck. Reprinted with permission. May not be further reproduced. All rights reserved.)

Day 2) *The Humanity of Christ*

Read
Note what each passage says about the nature and actions of Christ.

John 11:35
Jesus wept. (NIV)

John 4:6
Jacob's well was there, and Jesus, tired out by the trip, sat down by the well. It was about noon. (TEV)

Mark 3:5
Jesus was angry as he looked at the people, and he felt very sad because they were stubborn. Then he said to the man, "Hold out your hand." The man held out his hand and it was healed. (NCV)

Mark 6:6
And he was amazed at their lack of faith. Then Jesus went around teaching from village to village. (NIV)

The importance of Jesus' humanity cannot be overestimated, for the issue in the incarnation is soteriological, that is, it pertains to our salvation. The problem for human beings is the gap between themselves and God. The gap is, to be sure, ontological. God is high above humanity, so much so that he cannot be known by unaided human reason. If he is to be known, God must take some initiative to make himself known to human beings. But the problem is not merely ontological. There also is a spiritual and moral gap between the two, a gap created by human sin. People are unable by their own moral effort to counter their sin, to elevate themselves to the level of God. If there is to be fellowship between the two, they have to be united in some other way. This, it is traditionally understood, has been accomplished by the incarnation, in which deity and humanity were united in one person. If, however, Jesus was not really one of us, humanity has not been united with deity, and we cannot be saved. For the validity of the work accomplished in Christ's death, or at least its applicability to us as human beings, depends upon the reality of his humanity, just as the efficacy of it depends upon the genuineness of his deity.

(adapted from Millard J. Erickson, *Christian Theology*, [Grand Rapids, MI: Baker Book House, 1983], 706)

Mark 4:38
Jesus was sleeping at the back of the boat with his head on a cushion (NLT).

Matthew 4:1–2
[1]Next Jesus was taken into the wild by the Spirit for the Test. The Devil was ready to give it. [2]Jesus prepared for the Test by fasting forty days and forty nights. That left him, of course, in a state of extreme hunger. (The Message)

Realize

1. What happened at Lazarus's funeral (see John 11:35)? Why do you think Jesus responded in this way?

_____

_____

_____

_____

> In the suffering of Jesus we have the participation of God in the act of atonement. Sin pierced God's heart. God felt every searing nail and spear. God felt the burning sun. God felt the scorn of His tormentors and the body blows. In the cross is the suffering of God bearing the guilt of man's sin. This love alone is able to melt the sinner's heart and bring him to repentance for salvation.
> Billy Graham[2]

2. If God is all powerful how do we explain the statement of John 4:6?

_____

_____

_____

_____

3. Mark 3:5 and 6:6 speak of what specific emotions of Jesus?

_____

_____

_____

4. Some skeptics cite accounts like these as evidence that Jesus sinned. How do you respond?

_____

_____

_____

_____

5. What strikes you about Mark 4:38? What in the passage tells you just how weary Jesus really was?

_____

_____

_____

6. Why did Jesus fast for such a long time (Matt. 4:1, 2)? What was the predictable result of the fast?

_____

_____

_____

Respond

7. What do all these everyday glimpses from the life of Christ reveal about his humanity?

_____

_____

_____

8. How do they increase your feeling that Christ really does understand your life circumstances?

_____

_____

_____

This man we are talking about either was (and is) just what he said or else a lunatic, or something worse. Now it seems to me obvious that he was neither lunatic nor a fiend: and consequently, however strange or terrifying or unlikely it may seem, I have to accept the view that he was and is God. God has landed on this enemy-occupied world in human form.

And now, what was the purpose of it all? What did he come to do? Well, to teach, of course; but as soon as you look into the New Testament or any other Christian writing you will find they are constantly talking about something different—about his death and his coming to life again. It is obvious that Christians think the chief point of the story lies here. They think the main thing he came to earth to do was to suffer and be killed.

(C. S. Lewis, _Mere Christianity_ [New York, NY: Collier Books, MacMillan Publishing Company, 1952], 43)

Day 3) _Worthy of Our Trust_

Read

Psalm 22:1–7, 8, 16–18

¹My God, my God, why have you forsaken me? Why are you so far from saving me, so far from the words of my groaning?
⁷All who see me mock me; they hurl insults, shaking their heads:
⁸"He trusts in the LORD; let the LORD rescue him. Let him deliver him, since he delights in him."
¹⁶Dogs have surrounded me; a band of evil men has encircled me, they have pierced my hands and my feet.
¹⁷I can count all my bones; people stare and gloat over me.
¹⁸They divide my garments among them and cast lots for my clothing. (NIV)

Psalm 41:9

My best and truest friend, who ate at my table, has even turned against me. (NCV)

Isaiah 53:1–12

Who has believed our report? And to whom has the arm of the LORD been revealed?
²For He shall grow up before Him as a tender plant, and as a root out of dry ground. He has no form or comeliness; and when we see Him, there is no beauty that we should desire Him.
³He is despised and rejected by men, a Man of sorrows and acquainted with grief. And we hid, as it were, our faces from Him; He was despised, and we did not esteem Him.

4Surely He has borne our griefs and carried our sorrows; yet we esteemed Him stricken, smitten by God, and afflicted.

5But He was wounded for our transgressions, He was bruised for our iniquities; The chastisement for our peace was upon Him, and by His stripes we are healed.

6All we like sheep have gone astray; we have turned, every one, to his own way; and the LORD has laid on Him the iniquity of us all.

7He was oppressed and He was afflicted, yet He opened not His mouth; He was led as a lamb to the slaughter, and as a sheep before its shearers is silent, so He opened not His mouth.

8He was taken from prison and from judgment, and who will declare His generation? For He was cut off from the land of the living; for the transgressions of My people He was stricken.

9And they made His grave with the wicked—but with the rich at His death, because He had done no violence, nor was any deceit in His mouth.

10Yet it pleased the LORD to bruise Him; He has put Him to grief. When You make His soul an offering for sin, He shall see His seed, He shall prolong His days, and the pleasure of the LORD shall prosper in His hand.

11He shall see the labor of His soul, and be satisfied. By His knowledge My righteous Servant shall justify many, for He shall bear their iniquities.

12Therefore I will divide Him a portion with the great, and He shall divide the spoil with the strong, because He poured out His soul unto death, and He was numbered with the transgressors, and He bore the sin of many, and made intercession for the transgressors. (NKJV)

Realize

1. In what specific ways does Psalm 22 mirror the events of the crucifixion?

_____

_____

_____

_____

2. What specific event does Psalm 41 predict?

_____

_____

_____

3. How does Isaiah 53:9 describe the Messiah's behavior before his accusers?

_____

_____

_____

4. What does verse 9 prophesy about Christ's burial place?

_____

_____

_____

5. What does Verse 12 say about transgressors? Why should this concern us?

_____

_____

_____

_____

Respond

6. Scholars have counted more than 330 Old Testament prophecies fulfilled by Christ. What is significant about this?

_____

_____

_____

_____

7. How would it affect your faith if there had been no prophecies made in Old Testament times about the Messiah?

_____

_____

_____

8. What would it mean to Christianity if it could be established that Jesus failed to fulfill even a handful of the Old Testament prophecies about the Messiah?

_____

_____

_____

9. What promises has God kept in your life for which you frequently feel especially grateful?

_____

_____

_____

Spend some time today thanking God for his faithfulness.

MESSIANIC PROPHECIES AND FULFILLMENTS

For the Gospel writers, one of the main reasons for believing in Jesus was the way his life fulfilled the Old Testament prophecies about the Messiah. Following is a list of some of the main prophecies.

	Old Testament Prophecies	New Testament Fulfillment
1. Messiah was to be born in Bethlehem	Micah 5:2	Matthew 2:1–6 Luke 2:1–20
2. Messiah was to be born of a virgin	Isaiah 7:14	Matthew 1:18–25 Luke 1:26–38
3. Messiah was to be a prophet like Moses	Deuteronomy 18:15, 18, 19	John 7:40
4. Messiah was to enter Jerusalem in triumph	Zechariah 9:9	Matthew 21:1–9 John 12:12–16
5. Messiah was to be rejected by his own people	Isaiah 53:1, 3 Psalm 118:22	Matthew 26:3, 4 John 12:37–43 Acts 4:1–12
6. Messiah was to be betrayed by one of his followers	Psalm 41:9	Matthew 26:14–16, 47–50 Luke 22:19–23
7. Messiah was to be tried and condemned	Isaiah 53:8	Luke 23:1–25 Matthew 27:1, 2
8. Messiah was to be silent before his accusers	Isaiah 53:7	Matthew 27:12–14 Mark 15:3–4 Luke 23:8–10
9. Messiah was to be struck and spat on by his enemies	Isaiah 50:6	Matthew 26:67; 27:30 Mark 14:65
10. Messiah was to be mocked and insulted	Psalm 22:7, 8	Matthew 27:39–44 Luke 23:11, 35
11. Messiah was to die by crucifixion	Psalm 22:14, 16, 17	Matthew 27:31 Mark 15:20, 25
12. Messiah was to suffer with criminals and pray for his enemies	Isaiah 53:12	Matthew 27:38 Mark 15:27, 28 Luke 23:32–34
13. Messiah was to be given vinegar	Psalm 69:21	Matthew 27:34 John 19:28–30

14. Others were to cast lots for Messiah's garments	Psalm 22:18	Matthew 27:35 John 19:23, 24
15. Messiah's bones were not to be broken	Exodus 12:46	John 19:31–36
16. Messiah was to die as a sacrifice for sin	Isaiah 53:5, 6, 8, 10, 11, 12	John 1:29; 11:49–52 Acts 10:43; 13:38–39
17. Messiah was to be raised from the dead	Psalm 16:10	Matthew 28:1–10 Acts 2:22–32
18. Messiah is now at God's right hand	Psalm 110:1	Mark 16:19 Luke 24:50, 51

(from the *Life Application Bible/NLT* [Wheaton IL: Tyndale House Publishers, 1998], 1682)

Day 4) *The Comfort and Compassion of Christ*

Read
Isaiah 49:13
Heavens and earth, be happy. Mountains, shout with joy, because the LORD comforts his people and will have pity on those who suffer. (NCV)

John 14:1–20
(Jesus is speaking) ¹Let not your heart be troubled; you believe in God, believe also in Me.
²In My Father's house are many mansions; if it were not so, I would have told you. I go to prepare a place for you.
³And if I go and prepare a place for you, I will come again and receive you to Myself; that where I am, there you may be also.
⁴And where I go you know, and the way you know."
⁵Thomas said to Him, "Lord, we do not know where You are going, and how can we know the way?"
⁶Jesus said to him, "I am the way, the truth, and the life. No one comes to the Father except through Me.
⁷If you had known Me, you would have known My Father also; and from now on you know Him and have seen Him."
⁸Philip said to Him, "Lord, show us the Father, and it is sufficient for us."
⁹Jesus said to him, "Have I been with you so long, and yet you have not known Me, Philip? He who has seen Me has seen the Father; so how can you say, 'Show us the Father'?
¹⁰Do you not believe that I am in the Father, and the Father in Me? The words that I speak to you I do not speak on My own authority; but the Father who dwells in Me does the works.
¹¹Believe Me that I am in the Father and the Father in Me, or else believe Me for the sake of the works themselves.
¹²Most assuredly, I say to you, he who believes in Me, the works that I do he will do also; and greater works than these he will do, because I go to My Father.
¹³And whatever you ask in My name, that I will do, that the Father may be glorified in the Son.
¹⁴If you ask anything in My name, I will do it.
¹⁵If you love Me, keep My commandments.
¹⁶And I will pray the Father, and He will give you another Helper, that He may abide with you forever—
¹⁷the Spirit of truth, whom the world cannot receive, because it neither sees Him nor knows Him; but you know Him, for He dwells with you and will be in you.
¹⁸I will not leave you orphans; I will come to you.
¹⁹A little while longer and the world will see Me no more, but you will see Me. Because I live, you will live also.
²⁰At that day you will know that I am in My Father, and you in Me, and I in you. (NKJV)

2 Corinthians 1:3–5
³Blessed be the God and Father of our Lord Jesus Christ, the Father of mercies and God of all comfort;

4who comforts us in all our affliction so that we may be able to comfort those who are in any affliction with the comfort with which we ourselves are comforted by God.
5For just as the sufferings of Christ are ours in abundance, so also our comfort is abundant through Christ. (NASB)

Realize

1. What does Isaiah 49:13 say about God's care and concern for his people?

_____

_____

_____

2. What is the setting of John 14?

_____

_____

_____

3. What is the mood of the disciples? (See verse 1.)

_____

_____

_____

4. With what assurances does Jesus attempt to bolster the faith of the disciples?

_____

_____

_____

5. What's the promise of verse 18?

_____

_____

_____

6. How would you summarize verses 3–5 of 2 Corinthians?

_____

_____

_____

Respond

7. How do the verses from today's study suggest that God understands our pain and is able to sympathize with us?

_____

_____

_____

_____

8. In what specific situation of your life do you sense the need for divine understanding?

_____

_____

_____

9. How do we experience God's comfort and reassurance?

_____

_____

_____

Day 5) *Friend of Sinners*

Read
Luke 5:27–32
²⁷*After this, Jesus went out and saw a tax collector named Levi sitting in the tax collector's booth. Jesus said to him, "Follow me!"*
²⁸*So Levi got up, left everything, and followed him.*
²⁹*Then Levi gave a big dinner for Jesus at his house. Many tax collectors and other people were eating there, too.*
³⁰*But the Pharisees and the men who taught the law for the Pharisees began to complain to Jesus' followers, "Why do you eat and drink with tax collectors and sinners?"*
³¹*Jesus answered them, "It is not the healthy people who need a doctor, but the sick.*
³²*I have not come to invite good people but sinners to change their hearts and lives." (NCV)*

Luke 7:34–50
(Jesus is speaking) ³⁴*"The Son of Man has come eating and drinking, and you say, 'Look, a glutton and a winebibber, a friend of tax collectors and sinners!'*
³⁵*But wisdom is justified by all her children."*
³⁶*Then one of the Pharisees asked Him to eat with him. And He went to the Pharisee's house, and sat down to eat.*
³⁷*And behold, a woman in the city who was a sinner, when she knew that Jesus sat at the table in the Pharisee's house, brought an alabaster flask of fragrant oil,*
³⁸*and stood at His feet behind Him weeping; and she began to wash His feet with her tears, and wiped them with the hair of her head; and she kissed His feet and anointed them with the fragrant oil.*
³⁹*Now when the Pharisee who had invited Him saw this, he spoke to himself, saying, "This man, if He were a prophet, would know who and what manner of woman this is who is touching Him, for she is a sinner."*
⁴⁰*And Jesus answered and said to him, "Simon, I have something to say to you." So he said, "Teacher, say it."*
⁴¹*There was a certain creditor who had two debtors. One owed five hundred denarii, and the other fifty.*
⁴²*And when they had nothing with which to repay, he freely forgave them both. Tell Me, therefore, which of them will love him more?"*
⁴³*Simon answered and said, "I suppose the one whom he forgave more." And He said to him, "You have rightly judged."*
⁴⁴*Then He turned to the woman and said to Simon, "Do you see this woman? I entered your house; you gave Me no water for My feet, but she has washed My feet with her tears and wiped them with the hair of her head.*
⁴⁵*You gave Me no kiss, but this woman has not ceased to kiss My feet since the time I came in.*
⁴⁶*"You did not anoint My head with oil, but this woman has anointed My feet with fragrant oil.*
⁴⁷*Therefore I say to you, her sins, which are many, are forgiven, for she loved much. But to whom little is forgiven, the same loves little."*
⁴⁸*Then He said to her, "Your sins are forgiven."*
⁴⁹*And those who sat at the table with Him began to say to themselves, "Who is this who even forgives sins?"*
⁵⁰*Then He said to the woman, "Your faith has saved you. Go in peace." (NKJV)*

Realize
1. After Jesus called Levi (Matthew) to follow him, what did Levi do?

_____

_____

2. Who participated in this social gathering?

_____

_____

3. How did the religious establishment respond to this turn of events?

_____

_____

_____

4. What did Jesus state about his purpose or mission?

_____

_____

_____

5. According to Luke 7, what was Jesus' reputation?

_____

_____

_____

6. What happened when Jesus was invited to eat at Simon the Pharisee's home?

_____

_____

_____

7. What lesson did Jesus try to teach Simon?

_____

_____

_____

Respond

8. Who seemed to be more comfortable around Jesus—the respected and religious elements of society or the lowlife? Why?

_____

_____

_____

9. Do you get the sense that the woman who anointed Jesus' feet was afraid of him? Why or why not?

_____

_____

_____

10. How do you approach Jesus? Do you typically view him as hostile and angry over your sin or willing to forgive and accept you? Why?

_____

_____

_____

11. How effectively does the modern-day church model the love and acceptance of Christ? How well do you reflect this to a sinful world?

_____

_____

_____

LESSON

9

"I Have Redeemed You and I Will Keep You"

God's Promise in the Blood and Water

LOOKING BACK

Lesson 8 was a rich and fascinating study of the incarnation. Christ, without being diminished in his divinity, took on full humanity. He was the God-Man who lived for thirty-three years immersed a sinful world, and yet he never sinned. At the time of his crucifixion his great thirst (and his refusal to quench it with a narcotic-like mixture) was a final example of the loving lengths to which God would go in order to fully identify with and reach our rebel race.

Our theme verse from the lesson was Hebrews 4:15. Can you say it from memory?

1. How does it affect you to stop and ponder the fact that had you lived in Israel early in the first century you might have actually witnessed the Creator, in human form, walking and talking with people?

_____

_____

_____

2. *Max writes:* "Jesus has been where you are and can relate to how you feel. And if his life on earth doesn't convince you, his death on the cross should. He understands what you are going through." How would it change our attitudes if we really became convinced, if we truly grasped the biblical truth that Jesus, because of the incarnation, can relate to how we feel and what we face?

_____

_____

_____

3. How would embracing this concept change your prayer life? your hunger to read the Word?

_____

_____

_____

GETTING STARTED

VIDEO—In video segment number 9, Max tells about an experience he had at the Texas Open Golf Tournament. (The script is reprinted on page 230.)

4. At what sports do you excel? Which ones do you consider the biggest waste of time? Why?

_____

_____

_____

5. When were you the worst player on a sports team? What was that experience like? What happened?

_____

_____

_____

DIGGING IN

6. Max compares his experience of playing in a golf tournament on a team with more skilled golfers to what Christ has done for us. He says: "I get credit for the good work of someone else simply by virtue of being on his team. Hasn't Christ done the same for you?" What my team did for me on Monday, your Lord does for you every day of the week. Because of his performance you close your round with a perfect score." What does it mean to you to be on the Lord's "team"?

_____

_____

_____

7. Max also wrote about seeing minor, gradual improvements in his golf game during the eighteen-hole tournament. The reason? He received ongoing help from the golf pro who was on his team. In what areas of your life would you like to see some improvemnt this week? month? year?

_____

_____

_____

8. _Max writes:_ "Marriage is both a done deal and a daily development; something you did and something you do. The same is true of our walk with God. Can you be more saved than you were on the first day of your salvation? No. But can a person grow in salvation? Absolutely. It, like marriage, is a done deal and a daily development." In what ways is your walk with God like a marriage? How is it different?

_____

_____

_____

9. In what way is marriage a "done deal"? In what way is it a "daily development"?

_____

_____

_____

GOING DEEPER

John 19:31–37

31Therefore, because it was the Preparation Day, that the bodies should not remain on the cross on the Sabbath (for that Sabbath was a high day), the Jews asked Pilate that their legs might be broken, and that they might be taken away.
32Then the soldiers came and broke the legs of the first and of the other who was crucified with Him.
33But when they came to Jesus and saw that He was already dead, they did not break His legs.
34But one of the soldiers pierced His side with a spear, and immediately blood and water came out.
35And he who has seen has testified, and his testimony is true; and he knows that he is telling the truth, so that you may believe.
36For these things were done that the Scripture should be fulfilled, "Not [one] of His bones shall be broken."
37And again another Scripture says, "They shall look on Him whom they pierced." (NKJV)

10. Why were the legs of the two criminals broken? Why were Jesus' legs not broken?

_____

_____

_____

And Can It Be?

And can it be that I should gain
An int'rest in the Savior's blood?
Died He for me, who caused His pain?
For me, who Him to death pursued?
Amazing love! how can it be
That Thou, my God shouldst die for me?

He left His Father's throne above,
So free, so infinite His grace!
Emptied Himself of all but love,
And bled for Adam's helpless race!
'Tis mercy all, immense and free,
For, O my God, it found out me.

Long my imprisoned spirit lay
Fast bound in sin and nature's night.
Thine eye diffused a quick'ning ray:
I woke—the dungeon flamed with light!
My chains fell off, my heart was free,
I rose, went forth, and followed Thee.

No condemnation now I dread:
Jesus, and all in Him, is mine!
Alive in Him, my living Head,
And clothed in righteousness divine,
Bold I approach th'eternal throne,
And claim the crown, through Christ my own.

Chorus
Amazing love! how can it be
That Thou, my God, shouldst die for me!

(Charles Wesley, 1738)

11. Why did the soldier pierce Jesus' side? What happened when he did so?

_____

_____

_____

12. In verse 35 John tells his readers that he related the information about Jesus' pierced side so that "you may believe." What does he mean?

_____

_____

_____

_____

Jesus had already died so his legs were not broken. Instead, just to make sure, a soldier pierced Jesus' side with a spear. The result was a sudden flow of blood and water. This flow has been interpreted in various ways. Some have seen this as evidence that Jesus died of a broken heart so that his pericardium was full of blood and serum. Others see a symbolic or sacramental significance of the stream that heals people. More likely, it indicates that Jesus was a real human who died a real death. Possibly the spear struck the stomach and the heart, which accounted for the flow. The one who saw this (v. 35) saw saving significance in the sign. At the time of the writing of this Gospel, Gnosticism and Docetism were current problems. These ideologies denied the reality of Jesus' incarnation and death. But the blood and water are firm answers against those heresies. . . . John explained that soldiers not administering the *crurifragium* to Jesus but simply piercing his side fulfilled two specific prophecies or types. Jesus, as the true Passover Lamb, did not have any of his bones . . . broken (Exod. 12:46; Num. 9:12; Ps. 34:20) and people in the future will look on the pierced One (Zech. 12:10; see Rev. 1:7).

(© 1985 Cook Communications Ministries. *Bible Knowledge Commentary New Testament* by Walvoord and Zuck. Reprinted with permission. May not be further reproduced. All rights reserved.)

Hebrews 9:11–12, 22

11So Christ has now become the High Priest over all the good things that have come. He has entered that great, perfect sanctuary in heaven, not made by human hands and not part of this created world.
12Once for all time he took blood into that Most Holy Place, but not the blood of goats and calves. He took his own blood and with it he secured our salvation forever.
22In fact, we can say that according to the law of Moses, nearly everything was purified by sprinkling with blood. Without the shedding of blood, there is no forgiveness of sins. (NLT)

13. What do these verses teach about forgiveness?

14. Why was Christ able to enter the heavenly Most Holy Place?

15. What do these verses suggest about the flow of blood recorded by John?

We are in Christ, and Christ is in us. The first truth points upward, the second points downward. We must first be in Him with all our being—with our sin and weakness, and even with death. We know that in God's eyes we are freed, redeemed, and saved from these through Christ.
Then, we must swing above and beyond ourselves to Christ. Yes, we must be totally one with Christ and his people—those who are baptized in him and receive the Lord's supper.
Martin Luther

John 7:37–39

37On the last and most important day of the feast Jesus stood up and said in a loud voice, "Let anyone who is thirsty come to me and drink.
38If anyone believes in me, rivers of living water will flow out from that person's heart, as the Scripture says."
39Jesus was talking about the Holy Spirit. The Spirit had not yet been given, because Jesus had not yet been raised to glory. But later, those who believed in Jesus would receive the Spirit. (NCV)

16. What promise does Jesus give in this passage?

17. Is this an offer of a singular drink of water? How do you know?

18. In what way is the Spirit like a stream of living water?

_____

_____

_____

19. What must a person do to avail himself or herself of this water?

_____

_____

_____

20. *Max writes:* "Even a casual student of Scripture notes the connection between blood and mercy. As far back as Adam, worshipers knew ' . . . without the shedding of blood there is no forgiveness' (Hebrews 9:22, NIV). But . . . after Christ's sacrifice there would be no more need to shed blood.

    "If his work for us is seen in the blood, what might the water represent? You got it. His work in us. . . . He's not working to save us, mind you, that work is done. He's working to change us.

    "Some accept the blood, but forget the water. They want to be saved but don't want to be changed. Others accept the water, but forget the blood. They are busy for Christ, but never at peace in Christ. What about you? Do you tend to lean one way or the other?"

    How would you answer Max's question?

_____

_____

_____

21. How can someone who is saved mature in the faith so that he or she wants to be changed?

_____

_____

_____

22. How can someone who is frantically busy for Christ also find peace in Christ?

_____

_____

_____

MAKING IT REAL

23. *Max writes:* "Positional sanctification comes because of Christ's work *for* us. Progressive sanctification comes because of Christ's work *in* us. Both are gifts from God.

    "Positional and progressive sanctification: God's work for us and God's work in us. Neglect the first and you grow lazy. Neglect the second and you grow fearful. Both are essential, and both are seen in the moistened dirt at the base of the cross of Christ."

    In your own words, describe what "positional sanctification" means.

_____

_____

_____

24. In your own words, describe what "progressive sanctification" means.

_____

_____

_____

SANCTIFICATION—the process of God's grace by which the believer is separated from sin and becomes dedicated to God's righteousness. Accomplished by the Word of God (John 17:7) and the Holy Spirit (Rom. 8:3–4), sanctification results in holiness, or purification from the guilt and power of sin.

Sanctification as separation from the world and setting apart for God's service is a concept found throughout the Bible. Spoken of as "holy" or "set apart" in the Old Testament were the land of Canaan, the city of Jerusalem, the tabernacle, the Temple, the Sabbath, the feasts, the prophets, the priests, and the garments of the priests. God is sanctified by the witness of believers (1 Pet. 3:15) and by his judgments upon sin (Ezek. 38:16). Jesus also was "sanctified and sent into the world" (John 10:36, NKJV).

Sanctification in the Atonement
As the process by which God purifies the believer, sanctification is based on the sacrificial death of Christ. In his letters to the churches, the apostle Paul noted that God has "chosen" and "reconciled" us to himself in Christ for the purpose of sanctification (Eph. 1:4; 5:25–27; Titus 2:14).

Old Testament sacrifices did not take away sin, but they were able to sanctify "for the purifying of the flesh" (Heb. 9:13, NKJV). The blood of the new covenant (Heb. 10:29), however, goes far beyond this ritual purification of the body. The offering of Christ's body (Heb. 10:10) and blood (Heb. 13:12) serves to purge our conscience from "dead works to serve the living God" (Heb. 9:14). Because our cleansing from sin is made possible only by Christ's death and resurrection, we are "sanctified in Christ Jesus" (1 Cor. 1:2; Acts 20:32; 1 Cor. 1:30; 6:11).

Sanctification: God's Work
We are sanctified by God the Father (Jude 1), God the Son (Heb. 2:11), and God the Holy Spirit (2 Thess. 2:13; 1 Pet. 1:2). Perfect holiness is God's command (1 Thess. 4:7) and purpose. As Paul prayed, "Now may the God of peace Himself sanctify you completely" (1 Thess. 5:23, NKJV). Sanctification is a process that continues during our lives as believers (Heb. 10:14). Only after death are the saints referred to as "perfect" (Heb. 12:23).

Sanctification: The Believer's Work
Numerous commands in the Bible imply that believers also have a responsibility in the process of sanctification. We are commanded to "be holy" (Lev. 11:44; 1 Pet. 1:15–16); to "be perfect" (Matt. 5:48); and to "present your members as slaves of righteousness for holiness" (Rom. 6:19). Writing to the church of the Thessalonians, the apostle Paul made a strong plea for purity: "This is the will of God, your sanctification: that you should abstain from sexual immorality; that each of you should know how to possess his own vessel in sanctification and honor, not in passion of lust, like the Gentiles who do not know God" (1 Thess. 4:3–5, NKJV).

These commands imply effort on our part. We must believe in Jesus, since we are "sanctified by faith in Him" (Acts 26:18, NKJV). Through the Holy Spirit we must also "put to death the evil deeds of the body" (Rom. 8:13, NKJV). Paul itemized the many "works of the flesh" from which we must separate ourselves (Gal. 5:19–21). Finally, we must walk in the Spirit in order to display the fruit of the Spirit (Gal. 5:22–24).

(adapted from Ronald F. Youngblood, Ed., *Nelson's New Illustrated Bible Dictionary,* [Nashville, TN: Thomas Nelson Publishers, 1997], CD-ROM)

25. *Max writes:* "Do you feel so saved that you never serve? Are you so happy with the score of your team that you aren't getting out of the golf cart? If that is you, let me ask you a question. Why does God have you on the course? Why didn't he beam you up the moment he saved you? The fact is, you and I are here for a reason, and that reason is to glorify God in our service.

"Or is your tendency the opposite? Perhaps you always serve for fear of not being saved. Perhaps you don't trust your team. You're worried that a secret scorecard exists on which your score is being written. Is that you? If so, know this: The blood of Jesus is enough to save you."

What new insights have you gained from this study about what God has done for you?

_____

_____

_____

26. What new insights have you discovered about your own responsibility to grow in holiness?

_____

_____

_____

27. On what one or two specific things would you like to focus this week?

_____

_____

_____

THINKING IT THROUGH

Spend some time thinking back over the truths you've just studied. Thank God for the grace demonstrated in the blood. Ask God for the grace promised by the water. Then listen to "When I Remember" by Kim Hill on the CD.

PERSONAL NOTES

TAKING IT HOME

Memory Verses
Philippians 2:12, 13

So then, my beloved, just as you have always obeyed, not as in my presence only, but now much more in my absence, work out your salvation with fear and trembling;
13for it is God who is at work in you, both to will and to work for [His] good pleasure. (NKJV)

Therefore, my dear friends, as you have always obeyed—not only in my presence, but now much more in my absence—continue to work out your salvation with fear and trembling,
13for it is God who works in you to will and to act according to his good purpose. (NIV)

Dearest friends, you were always so careful to follow my instructions when I was with you. And now that I am away you must be even more careful to put into action God's saving work in your lives, obeying God with deep reverence and fear.
13For God is working in you giving you the desire to obey him and the power to do what pleases him. (NLT)

During the next week, study the following passages.

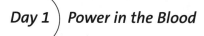

Day 1) *Power in the Blood*

Read
Exodus 12:1–24

Now the LORD spoke to Moses and Aaron in the land of Egypt, saying,
2This month shall be your beginning of months; it shall be the first month of the year to you.
3Speak to all the congregation of Israel, saying: 'On the tenth day of this month every man shall take for himself a lamb, according to the house of his father, a lamb for a household.
4And if the household is too small for the lamb, let him and his neighbor next to his house take it according to the number of the persons; according to each man's need you shall make your count for the lamb.
5Your lamb shall be without blemish, a male of the first year. You may take it from the sheep or from the goats.
6Now you shall keep it until the fourteenth day of the same month. Then the whole assembly of the congregation of Israel shall kill it at twilight.
7And they shall take some of the blood and put it on the two doorposts and on the lintel of the houses where they eat it.
8'Then they shall eat the flesh on that night; roasted in fire, with unleavened bread and with bitter herbs they shall eat it.
9Do not eat it raw, nor boiled at all with water, but roasted in fire—its head with its legs and its entrails.
10You shall let none of it remain until morning, and what remains of it until morning you shall burn with fire.
11And thus you shall eat it: with a belt on your waist, your sandals on your feet, and your staff in your hand. So you shall eat it in haste. It is the LORD's Passover.
12For I will pass through the land of Egypt on that night, and will strike all the firstborn in the land of Egypt, both man and beast; and against all the gods of Egypt I will execute judgment: I am the LORD.
13Now the blood shall be a sign for you on the houses where you are. And when I see the blood, I will pass over you; and the plague shall not be on you to destroy you when I strike the land of Egypt.
14So this day shall be to you a memorial; and you shall keep it as a feast to the LORD throughout your generations. You shall keep it as a feast by an everlasting ordinance.
15Seven days you shall eat unleavened bread. On the first day you shall remove leaven from your houses. For whoever eats leavened bread from the first day until the seventh day, that person shall be cut off from Israel.
16On the first day there shall be a holy convocation, and on the seventh day there shall be a

holy convocation for you. No manner of work shall be done on them; but that which everyone must eat—that only may be prepared by you.

17So you shall observe the Feast of Unleavened Bread, for on this same day I will have brought your armies out of the land of Egypt. Therefore you shall observe this day throughout your generations as an everlasting ordinance.

18In the first month, on the fourteenth day of the month at evening, you shall eat unleavened bread, until the twenty-first day of the month at evening.

19For seven days no leaven shall be found in your houses, since whoever eats what is leavened, that same person shall be cut off from the congregation of Israel, whether he is a stranger or a native of the land.

20You shall eat nothing leavened; in all your dwellings you shall eat unleavened bread.'"

21Then Moses called for all the elders of Israel and said to them, "Pick out and take lambs for yourselves according to your families, and kill the Passover lamb.

22And you shall take a bunch of hyssop, dip it in the blood that is in the basin, and strike the lintel and the two doorposts with the blood that is in the basin. And none of you shall go out of the door of his house until morning.

23For the LORD will pass through to strike the Egyptians; and when He sees the blood on the lintel and on the two doorposts, the LORD will pass over the door and not allow the destroyer to come into your houses to strike you.

24And you shall observe this thing as an ordinance for you and your sons forever." (NKJV)

Hebrews 10:3, 4, 9, 10

3But these sacrifices remind them of their sins every year,

4because it is impossible for the blood of bulls and goats to take away sins.

9Then he said, "Look, I have come to do what you want." God ends the first system of sacrifices so he can set up the new system.

10And because of this, we are made holy through the sacrifice Christ made in his body once and for all time. (NCV)

Realize

1. In God's instructions for the Passover, what kind of animal was required for sacrifice?

_____

_____

_____

2. What were the families to do with the blood of the slain animal?

_____

_____

_____

3. What did God promise to do when he saw the blood?

_____

_____

_____

_____

4. What does Hebrews say about animal sacrifices?

_____

_____

_____

_____

5. What did God do to end the need for animal sacrifices?

_____

_____

_____

Hebrews 9:14 The blood of Christ is clearly the price involved in the atonement. The atonement of Christ is one of the themes of the book of Hebrews and the pivotal doctrine of the entire Bible. The sacrifices of the Old Testament were forerunners of this work of Christ. The incarnation of Jesus was for the purpose of his suffering death in behalf of humankind. Atonement is a multifaceted concept which includes reconciliation—the restoration of human beings to fellowship with God (Rom. 5:10; 2 Cor. 5:19); propitiation—the satisfying of the just demands of God's holiness for the punishment of sin (Rom. 3:25, note); and redemption—the purchasing of the enslaved sinner to make him or her free (Col. 1:13–14). The atonement of Christ made it possible for God to justify men and women and to be just in so doing (Rom. 3:26). No passage could be any more lucid than Leviticus 17:11, which declares, "the life of the flesh is in the blood" (NKJV). This life poured out in substitutionary sacrifice makes atonement for the soul. Nor is there any other possible approach to God. "Without shedding of blood there is no remission" (9:22, NKJV). Christ's death on Golgotha was substitutionary (in our place). It is the act of Christ that makes possible forgiveness in that it satisfies the just and holy wrath of God.

10:18 The blood of sacrificial animals effected a temporary atonement, but the sacrificial system in itself could not take away sin and its consequent debt (which required forgiveness), slavery (which called for redemption), or alienation (which demanded reconciliation). Christ through his death made the perfect atonement (see 9:14) with everlasting efficacy. The key contrast is between "remission" . . . and "offering." . . . The Old Testament sacrifices were merely an "offering," a divinely appointed temporary means to bring people to God; Christ's redemptive work, "remission," was the perfect completion of atonement.

(adapted from W.A. Criswell, Ed., *The Believer's Study Bible, electronic ed.* [Nashville: Thomas Nelson Publishers, *Logos Library System*, 1997, c1991 by the Criswell Center for Biblical Studies])

Theological Insight

The Gospel of John gives us a picture of Christ's death as being a fountain of water and a fountain of blood—both being symbols of life given to others at the cost of Jesus' death.

The first depiction of Christ's death providing a fountain of water is found in John 7, where it tells about Jesus going to Jerusalem to attend the Festival of Tabernacles. During this festival, the Jewish people commemorated God's provision (of water and food) for his people in the wilderness and presence among them (in the pillar of fire) by pouring out water on a rock and by lighting lamps. Every day during this festival (except the last one) a priest, standing in front of the temple, would take a golden pitcher of water and pour it on a rock, in commemoration of the water flowing out of the smitten rock (see Exod. 17:6). While the water flowed out, the people standing by would chant, "With joy you will draw water from the wells of salvation" (Isa. 12:3, NRSV).

Jesus here presents himself as the true fulfillment of the smitten rock, providing spiritual nourishment. This comes in conjunction with the portion of John's narrative in which there is emphasis on Jesus' sufferings encountered during his ministry. From the end of John 6 through John 7 and following, we see a suffering Jesus—one constantly pierced with the jabs of unbelief and even hostile slander. It is in the midst of this suffering that one figure emerges—the smitten Rock. The more the Rock was smitten, the more he gave life-giving water. It was no accident that on the last day, the great day of the Festival of Tabernacles, Jesus stood and cried, "If anyone thirst, let him come to me and drink." Ultimately, Jesus would fulfill this promise when he died on the cross, for his wounds became the founts of life—as John said, "pierced his side with a spear, and at once blood and water came out" (19:34, NRSV).

This statement reveals the other element poured out at Christ's death: his blood, which symbolizes the loss of life to give others life. As the source of life, blood takes on a special significance in the whole matter of Christ's sacrifice. In order to fully appreciate this, we need to look back to the Day of Atonement (Lev. 16), when the blood of a bull and of a goat was sprinkled upon the altar as an atonement for the people's sin. Life was poured out in death. Animal life was given up on behalf of the life of the people. Judgment and atonement were carried out through a transfer of the sin of the people to the animal sacrifice (see Lev. 16:20–22). In the first Passover (Exod. 12:1–13), the "blood" had the same meaning. Blood put on each door was a sign that a death had already taken place, so the Angel of Death passed over.

In the New Testament, the primary reference is to the blood of Christ—with constant reference to the Old Testament sacrifices. In the first three Gospels, Jesus spoke of his blood at the Last Supper with reference to a new covenant (Matt. 26:28; Mark 14:24; Luke 22:20). Jesus was speaking of his sacrificial death and its redemptive significance. The Gospel of John expresses the same thought in a different context: "Unless you eat the flesh of the Son of Man and drink his blood, you cannot have eternal life in you" (6:53, NLT). Jesus' death is the means by which believers can have life.

Respond

6. Many people read the Old Testament accounts of animal sacrifice and are horrified. Why do you think God required such grave consequences for sin?

_____

_____

_____

7. How would it affect you if you had to slaughter a bull or goat regularly to pay for your sin?

_____

_____

_____

8. How are you motivated to live a holy life by the biblical requirement of "blood for sin"?

_____

_____

_____

9. What two things do you want to change about your life in light of what you're studying?

_____

_____

_____

Day 2) *The Living Water*

Read
John 4:4–14

4Now he had to go through Samaria.
5So he came to a town in Samaria called Sychar, near the plot of ground Jacob had given to his son Joseph.
6Jacob's well was there, and Jesus, tired as he was from the journey, sat down by the well. It was about the sixth hour.
7When a Samaritan woman came to draw water, Jesus said to her, "Will you give me a drink?"
8(His disciples had gone into the town to buy food.)
9The Samaritan woman said to him, "You are a Jew and I am a Samaritan woman. How can you ask me for a drink?" (For Jews do not associate with Samaritans.)
10Jesus answered her, "If you knew the gift of God and who it is that asks you for a drink, you would have asked him and he would have given you living water."
11"Sir," the woman said, "you have nothing to draw with and the well is deep. Where can you get this living water?
12Are you greater than our father Jacob, who gave us the well and drank from it himself, as did also his sons and his flocks and herds?"
13Jesus answered, "Everyone who drinks this water will be thirsty again,
14but whoever drinks the water I give him will never thirst. Indeed, the water I give him will become in him a spring of water welling up to eternal life." (NIV)

John 7:37–39
(Even though you read this as part of your lesson 9 study, it is such a critical passage that it bears further study.)
37On the last day, that great day of the feast, Jesus stood and cried out, saying, "If anyone thirsts, let him come to Me and drink.

38He who believes in Me, as the Scripture has said, out of his heart will flow rivers of living water."
39But this He spoke concerning the Spirit, whom those believing in Him would receive; for the Holy Spirit was not yet given, because Jesus was not yet glorified. (NASB)

Realize

1. To what kind of thirst was Jesus referring in his conversation with the Samaritan woman?

2. How did Jesus describe the kind of water he could provide?

3. Did the woman at the well understand Jesus? How do you know?

4. What did Jesus promise at the Feast of Tabernacles?

5. What were the conditions of the promise?

6. To what was Jesus referring?

The Feast of Tabernacles was celebrated with certain festival rituals. One was a solemn procession each day from the temple to the Gihon Spring. A priest filled a gold pitcher with water while the choir sang Isaiah 12:3. Then they returned to the altar and poured out the water. This ritual reminded them of the water from the rock during the wilderness wanderings (Num. 20:8–11; Ps. 78:15–16). It also spoke prophetically of the coming days of Messiah (see Zech. 14:8, 16–19). The Feast's seventh and last day was its greatest (see Lev. 23:36). Jesus stood, in contrast with the Rabbis' usual position of being seated while teaching. "Cried out" (John 1:15; 7:28; 12:44) refers to a way of introducing a solemn announcement. His statement, "Come to Me and drink," was an offer of salvation (4:14; 6:53–56).

Streams of living water will flow from within one who believes in Jesus. That is, that person will have a continual source of satisfaction that will provide life continually (4:14). When Jesus added, "as the Scripture has said," he did not identify the Old Testament passage(s) he had in mind. But he may have thought of Psalm 78:15, 16 and Zechariah 14:8 (see also Ezek. 47:1–11; Rev. 22:1, 2).

John explained that the "living water" (v. 38) was the coming gift of the Holy Spirit. The Spirit within a believer satisfies the believer's need of God, and provides him or her with regeneration, guidance, and empowerment. In the earliest Greek manuscripts, the words, "for the Holy Spirit was not yet [given]," are simply, "for there was not yet Spirit." This cannot be taken in an absolute sense since the Spirit had actively worked among people in the Old Testament era. Jesus referred to the special baptizing, sealing, and indwelling work of the Spirit in the Church Age, which would start on the day of Pentecost

(Acts 1:5, 8). Jesus said he would "send the Spirit" to His followers (John 15:26; 16:7). The Spirit had not yet been given to indwell believers permanently (see Ps. 51:11). That happened after Jesus was glorified, that is after his death, resurrection, and ascension. "Glorified," "glory," and "glorify" are used frequently in John's Gospel (John 7:39; 11:4; 12:16, 23, 28; 13:31–32; 14:13; 15:8; 16:14; 17:1, 4-5, 10)

(adapted from W.A. Criswell, Ed., *The Believer's Study Bible, electronic ed.* [Nashville: Thomas Nelson Publishers, *Logos Library System* 1997, c1991 by the Criswell Center for Biblical Studies])

Respond

7. What are some uses of water?

_____

_____

_____

8. Why do you think Jesus compared the Spirit's presence and work to "rivers of living water"?

_____

_____

_____

_____

9. What are some of the powerful ways the Spirit has worked in your life?

_____

_____

_____

_____

10. In what areas of your life does the Spirit need to flood and flow?

_____

_____

_____

_____

11. What can you do to facilitate this process?

_____

_____

_____

_____

Mark 15:24

The order of events culminating in the death of Christ may be outlined as follows: (1) the Passover meal is eaten with the disciples (Luke 22:14–16, 24–30); (2) Jesus washes the feet of the disciples (John 13:1–20); (3) Judas leaves the Upper Room (John 13:21–30); (4) Jesus institutes the memorial Supper (Luke 22:17–20); (5) the disciples accompany Jesus to Gethsemane (14:26, 32–42); (6) Judas betrays the Lord (John 18:2–12); (7) Annas, the former high priest, examines Jesus (John 18:12–14, 19–23); (8) Caiaphas and the Sanhedrin condemn Jesus (14:53, 55–65); (9) Peter denies the Lord three times (John 18:15–18, 25–27); (10) Jesus is formally condemned by the Sanhedrin (Luke 22:66–71); (11) Jesus appears before Pilate (John 18:28–38); (12) Jesus appears briefly before Herod Antipas (Luke 23:6–12); (13) Pilate sentences Jesus (Luke 23:13–25); (14) soldiers scourge and mock Jesus (John 19:1–14); (15) Jesus is placed on the cross after refusing to drink of the wine and myrrh (15:23–32); (16) the veil of the temple is torn (Matt. 27:51–56); and (17) the side of Jesus is pierced (John 19:31–37).

(adapted from W.A. Criswell, Ed., *The Believers Study Bible,* electronic ed. [Nashville, TN: Thomas Nelson Publishers, *Logos Library System* 1997, c1991 by the Criswell Center for Biblical Studies])

Read
Philippians 2:12, 13
12So then, my beloved, just as you have always obeyed, not as in my presence only, but now much more in my absence, work out your salvation with fear and trembling;
13for it is God who is at work in you, both to will and to work for [His] good pleasure. (NASB)

Hebrews 10:14
With one sacrifice he made perfect forever those who are being made holy. (NCV)

Realize
1. What did Paul urge the Philippians to do?

_____

_____

_____

2. What did Paul say God was doing in the lives of the Philippian saints?

_____

_____

_____

3. Are these two verses (Philippians 12 and 13) complementary or contradictory? Why?

_____

_____

_____

The saints at Philippi . . . were told to "work out," to put into practice in their daily living, what God had worked in them by his Spirit. They were not told to work for their salvation but to work out the salvation God had already given them. In view of the apparent problems of disunity and pride among those believers, this interpretation seems correct. Some were not doing their work selflessly and with the interests of others ahead of their own (see 2:3–4).

Some writers understand Paul's challenge to refer to the corporate life of the whole assembly in Philippi. Those who hold this view find support in the immediate context where Paul argued against their looking exclusively to their own needs (v. 4). In this view "salvation" refers to the whole assembly's deliverance from disunity, pride, and selfishness.

Perhaps it is best to see both the outworking of personal salvation and the corporate salvation or deliverance of the whole assembly from whatever held them back from experiencing God's best. This outworking was to be done "with fear and trembling," with a complete trust in God and not in themselves.

The only way this could be realized was through God who would enable them to do it (v. 13). Paul told the Philippian saints that God worked in them so that they could do his good pleasure and accomplish his good purpose. Both divine enablement and human responsibility are involved in getting God's work done. Believers are partners with God, laboring together with him. The verb works (v. 13) means "energizes" or "provides enablement." God makes his own both willing and desirous to do his work

(© 1985 Cook Communications Ministries. *Bible Knowledge Commentary New Testament* by Walvoord and Zuck. Reprinted with permission. May not be further reproduced. All rights reserved.)

4. What verb tenses does the writer of Hebrews use in 10:14?

_____

_____

5. How do these phrases illustrate both positional and progressive sanctification?

_____

_____

_____

_____

"Sanctify" means to "make holy," to set apart from sin for God (see 1 Thess. 4:3). When Christ fulfilled the will of God, he provided for the believer a continuing, permanent condition of holiness (Eph. 4:24; 1 Thess. 3:13). This is the believer's positional sanctification as opposed to the progressive sanctification that results from daily walking by the will of God.

(adapted from *The MacArthur Study Bible* [Nashville, TN: Word Bibles, 1997], 1913)

Respond

6. How much "fear and trembling" is part of your daily walk? Is your level of reverence and soberness appropriate or not? Why do you think?

_____

_____

_____

7. How would you answer a new Christian who confided in you: "I'm confused. I know God is living in me and wants to change me. But I also read the Bible and see all the commands that I'm supposed to carry out. So what gives? Who does what? How much should I be doing and how much should I let him do?"

_____

_____

_____

_____

8. To borrow the expression of Philippians 2:12–13, what areas of your salvation need an extra workout today?

_____

_____

_____

Day 4) *Transformed!*

Read
Romans 8:29
For those God foreknew he also predestined to be conformed to the likeness of his Son, that he might be the firstborn among many brothers. (NIV)

Romans 12:2
And do not be conformed to this world, but be transformed by the renewing of your mind, that you may prove what [is] that good and acceptable and perfect will of God. (NKJV)

2 Corinthians 3:18
Our faces, then, are not covered. We all show the Lord's glory, and we are being changed to be like him. This change in us brings ever greater glory, which comes from the Lord, who is the Spirit. (NCV)

Philippians 1:6
There has never been the slightest doubt in my mind that the God who started this great work in you would keep at it and bring it to a flourishing finish on the very day Christ Jesus appears.
(The Message)

Philippians 3:12–14
¹²I do not claim that I have already succeeded or have already become perfect. I keep striving to win the prize for which Christ Jesus has already won me to himself.
¹³Of course, my brothers, I really do not think that I have already won it; the one thing I do, however is to forget what is behind me and do my best to reach what is ahead.
¹⁴So I run straight toward the goal in order to win the prize, which is God's call through Christ Jesus to the life above. (TEV)

1 John 3:2
Dear friends, now we are children of God, and what we will be has not yet been made known. But we know that when he appears, we shall be like him, for we shall see him as he is. (NIV)

Realize

1. What does Paul say that believers have been predestined to?

_____

_____

_____

2. Romans 12 and 2 Corinthians 3 speak of being "transformed" and "changed." What does this mean? What does it look like practically in the life of a Christian?

_____

_____

_____

_____

WordFocus

TRANSFORM (Gk. *metamorphoo*) (Rom. 12:2; Matt. 17:2; 2 Cor. 3:18)
The Greek word means "to change form," as does the English derivative "metamorphosis." In the New Testament, this word is used to describe an inward renewal of our mind through which our inner spirit is changed into the likeness of Christ. Paul told the Roman believers: "Be transformed by the renewing of your minds" (12:2, NKJV). As our Christian life progresses, we should gradually notice that our thought life is being changed from Christlessness to Christlikeness. Transformation does not happen overnight. Our regeneration is instantaneous, but our transformation is continuous. We are conformed to Christ's image gradually as we spend time in intimate fellowship with Him (see 2 Cor. 3:18).

(adapted from *The Nelson Study Bible* [Nashville, TN: Thomas Nelson Publishers, 1997], 1903)

3. What is the great promise of Philippians 1:6?

_____

_____

_____

_____

4. How did Paul describe to the Philippians the process of sanctification in his own life? What imagery did he use? Did he view himself as a finished product or a work in progress? Why?

_____

_____

_____

_____

5. When, according to 1 John 3, will our progressive sanctification catch up with our positional sanctification?

_____

_____

_____

Respond

6. How different is your life (attitudes, behaviors, etc.) since meeting Christ from what it was before your conversion?

_____

_____

_____

Yet though the work of Christ is finished for the sinner, it is not yet finished in the sinner.
Donald Bloesch[1]

7. Who in your sphere of influence doesn't know you are a Christian and would be shocked to learn this fact? Why? What needs to change?

_____

_____

_____

8. The key to transformation (according to Romans 12:1–2) is a renewed mind. What does this mean? What does it look like?

_____

_____

_____

9. What specifically needs to stop happening or start happening in order for your mind to be filled with the things of God?

_____

_____

_____

Day 5 ⟩ *Walking in the Spirit*

Read
Galatians 5:13–26

13For you, brethren, have been called to liberty; only do not use liberty as an opportunity for the flesh, but through love serve one another.

14For all the law is fulfilled in one word, even in this: "You shall love your neighbor as yourself."

15But if you bite and devour one another, beware lest you be consumed by one another!

16I say then: Walk in the Spirit, and you shall not fulfill the lust of the flesh.

17For the flesh lusts against the Spirit, and the Spirit against the flesh; and these are contrary to one another, so that you do not do the things that you wish.

18But if you are led by the Spirit, you are not under the law.

19Now the works of the flesh are evident, which are: adultery, fornication, uncleanness, lewdness,

20idolatry, sorcery, hatred, contentions, jealousies, outbursts of wrath, selfish ambitions, dissensions, heresies,

21envy, murders, drunkenness, revelries, and the like; of which I tell you beforehand, just as I also told you in time past, that those who practice such things will not inherit the kingdom of God.

22But the fruit of the Spirit is love, joy, peace, longsuffering, kindness, goodness, faithfulness,

23gentleness, self-control. Against such there is no law.

24And those who are Christ's have crucified the flesh with its passions and desires.

²If we live in the Spirit, let us also walk in the Spirit.
²⁶Let us not become conceited, provoking one another, envying one another. (NKJV)

Realize

1. What two options for living does Paul describe?

_____

_____

_____

2. What is the relationship between the "flesh" and the "Spirit"?

_____

_____

_____

3. What are the consequences of a fleshly life?

_____

_____

_____

WordFocus

FLESH (Gk. *sarx*) (Gal. 5:19, 24; 6:8, 12, 13; Rom. 7:18; 8:3, 13)
In Greek literature, the word sarx usually meant nothing more than the human body. It was also used this way in the New Testament (see John 1:14; Rev. 17:16; 19:18, 21). Paul, however, often used the word to denote the entire fallen human being—not just the sinful body but the entire being, including the soul and mind, as affected by sin. Thus Paul often pitted the "flesh" against the "Spirit" as being two diametrically opposed forces. The unbeliever can live only in the flesh, but believers can live in the flesh or in the Spirit. Paul repeatedly encourages the believers to overcome the deeds of the flesh by living in the Spirit.

(adapted from *The Nelson Study Bible* [Nashville, TN: Thomas Nelson Publishers, 1997], 1978).

4. What qualities are the product of a Spirit-led life?

_____

_____

_____

5. Why, according to verse 24, is fleshly behavior incompatible with Christian identity?

_____

_____

_____

Respond

6. In what areas of your life are you most keenly aware of the war between the flesh and the Spirit?

_____

_____

_____

_____

7. What are the most evident qualities in your life over the last week? Why?

_____

_____

_____

8. How would you advise a new believer to "walk in the Spirit"? What is involved in that process?

_____

_____

_____

When I Survey the Wondrous Cross

When I survey the wondrous cross,
On which the Prince of glory died,
My richest gain I count but loss,
And pour contempt on all my pride.

Forbid it Lord that I should boast,
Save in the death of Christ my God;
All the vain things that charm me most,
I sacrifice them to His blood.

See, from His head, His hands, His feet,
Sorrow and love flow mingled down;
Did e'er such love and sorrow meet,
Or thorns compose so rich a crown?

Were the whole realm of nature mine
That were a present far too small;
Love so amazing, so divine,
Demands my soul, my life, my all.

(Isaac Watts, 1707)

Jesus Christ is not looking for people who want to add him to their sin as an insurance against hell. He is not looking for people who want to apply his high moral principles to their unregenerate lives. He is not looking for those who want only to be outwardly reformed by having their old nature improved.

Jesus Christ calls to himself those who are willing to be inwardly transformed by him, who desire an entirely new nature that is created in his own holy likeness. He calls to himself those who are willing to die with him in order to be raised with him, who are willing to relinquish slavery to their sin for slavery to his righteousness. And when men come to him on his terms, he changes their destiny from eternal death to eternal life.
—*John MacArthur*[2]

LESSON 10

"I Will Love You Forever"

God's Promise in the Cross

LOOKING BACK

The last lesson focused on the doctrine of sanctification—the positional holiness that is ours because of the shed blood of Christ and the progressive transformation that takes place in our lives as we walk in the power of the Holy Spirit, allowing him to change us. See if you can say our memory verses from that lesson—Philippians 2:12, 13.

1. The hope of Christianity is that Jesus pledges to make us into new creatures and that, with his power, we can move beyond old, destructive thought and habit patterns. What are the major evidences of sanctification in your life?

   _____
   _____
   _____

2. *Max writes:* "Jesus allows your mistakes to be lost in his perfection. When you and I stand in heaven to receive our prize, only one will know of all our sins, but he won't embarrass you—he has already forgiven them." How does the prospect of full and unconditional forgiveness motivate you to live a holy life?

   _____
   _____
   _____

3. *Max writes:* "Your life can improve the longer and closer you walk with Jesus. The work for us is complete; but the progressive work in us is ongoing." Where do you sense God working in you most at this stage of your life?

   _____
   _____
   _____
   _____

4. During the daily studies of the last lesson, what truths, insights, or principles had the greatest impact on you?

   _____
   _____
   _____

GETTING STARTED

VIDEO—In video segment number 10, Max talks about how to pronounce his name. (The script has been reprinted on page 230.)

5. What's the funniest name you've ever heard?

   _____
   _____

6. Do you like your name? Why or why not?

_____

_____

_____

_____

7. If you were to change your name, to what would you change it?

_____

_____

_____

8. Did you ever and do you now have a nickname? What is it?

_____

_____

_____

DIGGING IN

Max's encounter with the woman who repeatedly mispronounced his name illustrates the tension between what is right and what is loving. Bringing this dilemma over into the theological realm, he questions: "How can [God] be both just and kind? How can he dispense truth and mercy? How can he redeem the sinner without endorsing sin?

"Can a holy God overlook our mistakes? Can a kind God punish our mistakes? From our perspective there are only two equally unappealing solutions. But from his perspective there is a third. It's called 'The Cross of Christ.'"

9. In what ways was Max's plight similar to the situation God faced with his creatures?

_____

_____

_____

10. *Max writes:* "The cross is the universal symbol of Christianity. An odd choice, don't you think? Strange that a tool of torture would come to embody a movement of hope. The symbols of other faiths are more upbeat: the six-pointed star of Jerusalem, the crescent moon of Islam, a lotus blossom for Buddhism. Yet a cross for Christianity? An instrument of execution?

    "Would you wear a tiny electric chair on your neck? Suspend a gold-plated hangman's noose on the wall? Would you print a picture of a firing squad on a business card? Yet we do so with the cross."

    How do you feel about the cross as a symbol for Christianity?

_____

_____

_____

11. Do you wear a cross or display one in your home, office, or car? If so, how often do you think about what it actually represents?

_____

_____

_____

Do not let your hearts be troubled. Trust in God; trust also in me. In my Father's house are many rooms; if it were not so, I would have told you. I am going there to prepare a place for you. And if I go and prepare a place for you, I will come back and take you to be with me that you also may be where I am.

John 14:1-3

Soon Jesus would die on the cross, rise from the dead, and ascend into heaven, leaving his disciples on earth. To help prepare them for life without him, Jesus explained that he would be going to his Father in heaven and would be preparing a place for them there. He also promised to return.

The disciples were confused, not really believing that Jesus would have to die, not realizing that he would come back to life, and thus not understanding at all what he meant by going to the Father and "preparing a place" for them.

But we have the perspective of history. We know that Jesus died on the cross. And we know that he rose from the grave and later ascended into heaven. Thus, we can be confident that he is there now preparing for us.

What a great promise! If you have trusted in Christ as your Savior, your future is secure—he has a place for you in the "Father's house." No one can stop you; nothing can deter you; no one can steal your hope...because Jesus has promised.

And he's coming back to take you there.

(from David R. Veerman, *On Eagle's Wings*, [Wheaton, IL: Tyndale House Publishers, 1995] 54)

12. What are the pros and cons of making prominent displays of our faith (for example, jewelry, bumper stickers, Christian T-shirts, etc.)?

_____

_____

_____

_____

13. Have we (as Christians, as a culture, etc.) become unhealthily familiar with the cross? What can be done to recover the wonder of its symbolism?

_____

_____

_____

_____

GOING DEEPER

John 19:16–19, 25–31

16So he delivered Him to them to be crucified. So they took Jesus and led Him away.

17And He, bearing His cross, went out to a place called the Place of a Skull, which is called in Hebrew, Golgotha,

18where they crucified Him, and two others with Him, one on either side, and Jesus in the center.

19Now Pilate wrote a title and put it on the cross. And the writing was: JESUS OF NAZARETH, THE KING OF THE JEWS.

25Now there stood by the cross of Jesus His mother, and His mother's sister, Mary the wife of Clopas, and Mary Magdalene.

26When Jesus therefore saw His mother, and the disciple whom He loved standing by, He said to His mother, "Woman, behold your son!"

27Then He said to the disciple, "Behold your mother!" And from that hour that disciple took her to his own home.

28After this, Jesus, knowing that all things were now accomplished, that the Scripture might be fulfilled, said, "I thirst!"

29Now a vessel full of sour wine was sitting there; and they filled a sponge with sour wine, put it on hyssop, and put it to His mouth.

30So when Jesus had received the sour wine, He said, "It is finished!" And bowing His head, He gave up His spirit.

31Therefore, because it was the Preparation Day, that the bodies should not remain on the cross on the Sabbath (for that Sabbath was a high day), the Jews asked Pilate that their legs might be broken, and that they might be taken away. (NKJV)

_____

_____

_____

_____

CROSS—an upright wooden stake or post on which condemned people were executed. Before the manner of Jesus' death caused the cross to symbolize the very heart of the Christian faith, the Greek word for cross referred primarily to a pointed stake used in rows to form the walls of a defensive stockade.

It was common in the biblical period for the decapitated bodies of executed persons to be publicly displayed by impaling them on stakes to discourage civil disobedience and to mock defeated military foes (Gen. 40:19; 1 Sam. 31:8–13). This gruesome practice may explain how the stake eventually came to be used as an instrument of civil and military punishment. Such stakes came to be eventually fitted with crossbeams as instruments of humiliation, torture, and execution for persons convicted as enemies of the state (foreign soldiers, rebels, and spies, for example) or of civil criminals (such as robbers). . . .

From the early days of the Roman Republic, death on the cross was used for rebellious slaves and bandits although Roman citizens were rarely subjected to this method of execution. The practice continued well beyond the New Testament period as one of the supreme punishments for military and political crimes such as desertion, spying, revealing secrets, rebellion, and sedition. Following the conversion of the emperor Constantine to Christianity, the cross became a sacred symbol, and its use by Romans as a means of torture and death was abolished.

Death on a Cross
Those sentenced to death on a cross in the Roman period were usually beaten with leather lashes—a procedure that often resulted in severe loss of blood. Victims were then generally forced to carry the upper crossbeam to the execution site, where the central stake was already set up.

After being fastened to the crossbeam on the ground with ropes—or, in rare cases, nails through the wrist—the naked victim was then hoisted with the crossbeam against the standing vertical stake. A block or peg was sometimes fastened to the stake as a crude seat. The feet were then tied or nailed to the stake.

The recent discovery near Jerusalem of the bones of a crucifixion victim suggests that the knees were bent up side by side, parallel to the crossbeam, and the nail was then driven through the sides of the ankles. Death by suffocation or exhaustion normally followed only after a long period of agonizing pain.

The Shape of the Cross
In time the simple pointed stake first used for execution was modified. The four most important of the resulting crosses are: (1) the Latin cross (shaped like a lower case "t"), on which it seems likely that Jesus died for our sins, because of the notice placed above his head (Matt. 27:37); (2) the St. Anthony's cross, which has the crossbeam at the top (shaped like a capital "T"); (3) the St. Andrew's cross, which is shaped like a capital "X"; (4) the so-called Greek cross, which has the crossbeam in the center (shaped like a plus sign).

Significance of the Cross
The authors of the Gospels tell us that the Lord Jesus spoke of the cross before his death (Matt. 10:38; Mark 10:21; Luke 14:27) as a symbol of the necessity of full commitment (even unto death) for those who would be his disciples. But the major significance of the cross after Jesus' death and resurrection is its use as a symbol of Jesus' willingness to suffer for our sins (Phil. 2:8; Heb. 12:2) so that we might be reconciled (2 Cor. 5:19; Col. 1:20) to God and know his peace (Eph. 2:16).

Thus the cross symbolizes the glory of the Christian gospel (1 Cor. 1:17): the fact that through this

offensive means of death (1 Cor. 1:23; Gal. 5:11), the debt of sin against us was "nailed to the cross" (Col. 2:14, NKJV), and we, having "been crucified with Christ" (Gal. 2:20, NKJV), have been freed from sin and death and made alive to God (Rom. 6:6–11).

The cross, then, is the symbol of Jesus' love, God's power to save, and the thankful believer's unreserved commitment to Christian discipleship. To those who know the salvation that Christ gained for us through his death, it is a wondrous cross indeed.

(adapted from Ronald F. Youngblood, Ed., *Nelson's New Illustrated Bible Dictionary* [Nashville, TN: Thomas Nelson Publishers, 1997, c1995], CD-ROM)

15. What is remarkable about verses 26 and 27?

_____

_____

_____

_____

16. What did Jesus mean when he cried, "It is finished!"?

_____

_____

_____

_____

I thank God for that word "whosoever." If God had said there was mercy for Richard Baxter, I am so vile a sinner, that I would have thought he meant some other Richard Baxter; but, when he says "whosoever," I know that includes me, the worst of all Richard Baxters.
—Richard Baxter[1]

John 3:16
For God so loved the world that He gave His only begotten Son, that whosoever believes in Him should not perish but have everlasting life.(KJV).

17. According to this very familiar verse, what prompted the giving of Christ to the world?

_____

_____

_____

_____

18. From God's perspective, why was this a great sacrifice?

_____

_____

_____

_____

The Love of God

Could we with ink the ocean fill,
    and were the skies of parchment made.
And every stalk on earth a quill,
    and every man a scribe by trade.
To write the love of God above
    would drain the ocean dry.
Nor would the scroll contain the whole,
    though stretched from sky to sky.

(F. M. Lehman, 1917)

19. What are the conditions for everlasting life?

_____

_____

_____

_____

20. What is the consequence of unbelief?

_____

_____

_____

Romans 5:8–11

⁸But God shows his great love for us in this way: Christ died for us while we were still sinners.
⁹So through Christ we will surely be saved from God's anger, because we have been made right with God by the blood of Christ's death.
¹⁰While we were God's enemies, he made friends with us through the death of his Son. Surely, now that we are his friends, he will save us through his Son's life.
¹¹And not only that, but now we are also very happy in God through our Lord Jesus Christ. Through him we are now God's friends again. (NCV)

21. What did Christ's death demonstrate?

_____

_____

_____

22. What was our condition when God chose to rescue us? Why is this significant?

_____

_____

_____

23. From what are believers spared by the death of Christ?

_____

_____

_____

Christianity does not ask us to live in the shadow of the cross, but in the fire of its creative action.
Teilhard De Chardin

24. What did the death of the Lord Jesus make possible for believers?

_____

_____

_____

1 John 4:10

This is love: not that we loved God, but that he loved us and sent his Son as an atoning sacrifice for our sins. (NIV)

25. According to the Bible, who took the initiative in salvation?

_____

_____

_____

26. Is divine love primarily an emotion, an action, or both? How do you know?

_____

_____

_____

What motivated John to write five of the books of the New Testament? What sustained him through those turbulent first years of the church when persecution was rampant—when eleven of his fellow apostles died violent deaths? What enabled him to cope with his own lonely exile on the isle of Patmos?

Perhaps the answer is found in an idea that John mentioned repeatedly in his writings. That recurring theme is love. The words "love," "loves," and "loved" are used more than fifty times in John's Gospel, and there are at least that many references to love in John's epistles. John was so amazed by God's unconditional love and acceptance that he even began referring to himself as "the disciple whom Jesus loved"!

It feels wonderful to be loved by another human, but when we catch a glimpse of the depths of the love of God, we are awestruck. His love comes with no conditions, no strings attached. And once embraced, it has transforming power, taking ordinary sinners like John and changing them into extraordinary servants of God.

Have you ever pondered God's infinite love for you? More than that, have you accepted the priceless gift of forgiveness and salvation that he offers? God's love not only liberates us, it gives us a reason for living.

(adapted from Michael Kendrick & Daryl Lucas, Eds., *365 Life Lessons from Bible People* [Wheaton, IL: Tyndale House Publishers, 1996], 255)

27. *Max writes:* "Why is the cross the symbol of our faith? To find the answer look no further than the cross itself. Its design couldn't be simpler. One beam horizonta—the other vertical. One reaches out—like God's love. The other reaches up—as does God's holiness. The cross is the intersection. The cross is where God forgave his children without lowering his standard. How could he do this? In a sentence: God put our sin on his Son and punished it there." Describe what the cross means to you personally.

_____

_____

_____

28. What is your response to God's gift of absolute pardon and eternal life?

_____

_____

_____

MAKING IT REAL

29. *Max writes:* "Envision the moment. God on his throne. You on the earth. And between you and God, suspended between you and heaven, is Christ on his cross. Your sins have been placed on Jesus. God, who punishes sin, releases his rightful wrath on your mistakes. Jesus receives the blow. Since Christ is between you and God, you don't. The sin is punished, but you are safe, safe in the shadow of the cross." Take a few moments, close your eyes, and do what Max suggests. How does it feel to be "safe in the shadow of the cross"?

_____

_____

_____

Theological Insight

God created man with the intention of having many sons and daughters with whom he could fellowship. Out of all the universe, no other creature was suited for this purpose. Adam and Eve were unique and special, for they alone were created in the image of God (Gen. 1:26), and they alone enjoyed daily fellowship with God (implicit in Gen. 3:8). According to the details in Genesis 2 and 3, Adam and Eve could have partaken of the tree of life (see Gen. 2:7; 3:22), thereby obtaining immortality and the everlasting bliss of having unbroken, untainted fellowship with God. But we all know the tragic story. Adam and Eve, deceived by the serpent, disobeyed God; they partook of the fruit of the tree of the knowledge of good and evil. Through this disobedience, sin entered the human race, and death through sin (Rom. 5:12). They lost the chance to live forever; even worse, they became consciously separate from God. How grievous it is to read how Adam and Eve hid themselves from the God whose fellowship they had enjoyed. But not all was lost. God promised that the woman's seed would crush the enemy. That seed, as we know, would be the Savior, Jesus Christ (see Gal. 3:16). In addition, God provided animal skins to cover Adam and Eve's shameful nakedness. This prefigured the death of Christ and the garment of righteousness provided for all believers. A long time had to pass, however, before the Son of God would actually come to accomplish redemption. The believers in the Old Testament anticipated that day (see John 8:56; Heb. 11), a day when the Savior's blood would pay the price for their redemption. The blood of bulls and goats served as an earnest until the actual payment was made (Rom. 3:25).

The Bible says that Christ, as the Lamb of God, was foreordained to crucifixion (1 Pet. 1:19–20). His death on the cross was not an afterthought or merely a remedy; it was the fulfillment of the determined counsel and foreknowledge of God (Acts 2:23). Thus, the Scripture can speak of "the Lamb slain from the foundation of the world" (Rev. 13:8). Redemption could not have been accomplished if God had not partaken of flesh and blood—that is, mortality. God cannot die because he is immortal; he had to partake of actual humanity in order to participate in mortality. The Son of God, out of love for his Father, willingly relinquished his equality with the Father to become subservient to him for the purpose of accomplishing redemption. He was sent by the Father to experience incarnation, human living, and crucifixion. This involved an "emptying-out" (in Greek called *kenosis*—"the process of emptying") of his divine prerogatives and equalities with the Father (see Phil. 2:5–11). The Son did it because he loved the Father.

But God's great act of sending his Son to die on the cross was done not only for the sake of accomplishing a legal redemption; it was done for the purpose of demonstrating God's ultimate love for humanity (see Rom. 5:8). God went all the way—to the extent that he sacrificed his own Son—to show how much he loved the world. Mysteriously, the cross of Christ became an attracting force, drawing people's hearts to God like a great magnet. Christ knew that when he was lifted up on the cross, he would draw all people to him. He declared this prior to his crucifixion (see John 12:32).

Millions of people have been drawn to God by the constraining power manifested in Christ's cross. Paul, as if speaking for all who have known that love, exclaimed, "For the love of Christ constrains me. Because we thus judge, if one died for all, then all died. And he died for all, that those who live might no longer live for themselves but for him who for their sake died and was raised" (2 Cor. 5:14–15). This is the invitation extended to the whole world: believe in Jesus Christ's death for your sins and be forgiven by God eternally.

THINKING IT THROUGH

Max writes: "Consider what he did. He gave his son. His only son. Would you do that? Would you offer the life of your child for someone else? I wouldn't. There are those for whom I would give my life. But ask me to make a list of those for whom I would kill my daughter? The sheet will be blank. I don't need a pencil. The list has no names."

Ponder this truth: Jesus came for you. Jesus went to the cross for you. Spend some time in heartfelt praise for God's amazing gift as you listen to "The Lamb That Was Slain" by Jeff Nelson and The Oak Hills Choir on the CD.

Memory Verse
Romans 5:8

But God demonstrates his own love for us in this: While we were still sinners, Christ died for us. (NIV)

But God demonstrates His own love toward us, in that while we were still sinners, Christ died for us. (NKJV)

But God showed his great love for us by sending Christ to die for us while we were still sinners. (NLT)

During the next week, study the following passages.

Day 1) *God's Justice*

Read
1 Samuel 2:10
The adversaries of the LORD shall be broken in pieces; From heaven He will thunder against them. The LORD will judge the ends of the earth. (NKJV)

Psalm 7:8–9, 11
8Lord, judge the people.
Lord, defend me because I am right,
because I have done no wrong, God Most High.
9God, you do what is right.
You know our thoughts and feelings.
Stop those wicked actions done by evil people,
and help those who do what is right.
God judges by what is right,
and God is always ready to punish the wicked.
11God judges by what is right, and God is always ready to punish the wicked. (NCV)

Psalm 89:32
I will punish their sin with the rod, their iniquity with flogging. (NIV)

Proverbs 11:21
Evil people will certainly be punished,
but those who do right will be set free. (NCV)

Ezekiel 7:8
Soon I will pour out my fury to complete your punishment for all your disgusting behavior. (NLT)

Romans 1:18
God's anger is shown from heaven against all the evil and wrong things people do. By their own evil lives they hide the truth. (NCV)

Romans 2:12
For as many as have sinned without law will also perish without law, and as many as have sinned in the law will be judged by the law. (NKJV)

Realize
1. What do these verses say about the destiny of those who oppose God?

_____

_____

_____   168

2. Can anyone at anytime accuse God of being an unfair judge? Why?

_____

_____

_____

3. Why does God punish sin? Why can't he just look the other way?

_____

_____

_____

4. Are there any sins that will escape God's notice? How do you know?

_____

_____

_____

5. Why is "ignorance of the law" not an acceptable excuse in God's sight?

_____

_____

_____

Respond

6. Do most people not know God's promise to judge every sin, or do they simply not believe it?

_____

_____

_____

7. Does God's wrath due to sin seem like a reasonable response to you? Or does it seem a little harsh? What does your answer reveal about your understanding of holiness?

_____

_____

_____

_____

WRATH—the personal manifestation of God's holy, moral character in judgment against sin. Wrath is neither an impersonal process nor irrational and fitful like anger. It is in no way vindictive or malicious. It is holy indignation—God's anger directed against sin.

God's wrath is an expression of his holy love. If God is not a God of wrath, his love is no more than frail, worthless sentimentality; the concept of mercy is meaningless; and the Cross was a cruel and unnecessary experience for his Son.

The Bible declares that all people are "by nature children of wrath" (Eph. 2:3, NKJV) and that "the wrath of God is revealed from heaven against all ungodliness and unrighteousness of men, who suppress the truth in unrighteousness" (Rom. 1:18, NKJV). Because Christians have been "justified by His blood, we shall be saved from wrath through Him" (Rom. 5:9, NKJV). The magnitude of God's love is manifested in the Cross, where God's only Son experienced wrath on our behalf.

"The day of the Lord's wrath" (Zeph. 1:18, NKJV) is identical with "the great day of the Lord" (Zeph. 1:14, NKJV). These terms refer to "the wrath of the Lamb" (Rev. 6:16, NKJV), Jesus Christ, that will fall on the ungodly at his Second Coming.

(adapted from Ronald F. Youngblood, Ed., *Nelson's New Illustrated Bible Dictionary* [Nashville, TN: Thomas Nelson Publishers, 1997, c1995], CD-ROM)

8. How does it make you feel to know that Christ willingly endured God's wrath for the sins of the world? for your sins?

_____

_____

_____

Day 2) God's Love

Read

1 John 4:7–21

⁷Beloved, let us love one another, for love is of God; and everyone who loves is born of God and knows God.

⁸He who does not love does not know God, for God is love.

⁹In this the love of God was manifested toward us, that God has sent His only begotten Son into the world, that we might live through Him.

¹⁰In this is love, not that we loved God, but that He loved us and sent His Son to be the propitiation for our sins.

¹¹Beloved, if God so loved us, we also ought to love one another.

¹²No one has seen God at any time. If we love one another, God abides in us, and His love has been perfected in us.

¹³By this we know that we abide in Him, and He in us, because He has given us of His Spirit.

¹⁴And we have seen and testify that the Father has sent the Son as Savior of the world.

¹⁵Whoever confesses that Jesus is the Son of God, God abides in him, and he in God.

¹⁶And we have known and believed the love that God has for us. God is love, and he who abides in love abides in God, and God in him.

¹⁷Love has been perfected among us in this: that we may have boldness in the day of judgment; because as He is, so are we in this world.

¹⁸There is no fear in love; but perfect love casts out fear, because fear involves torment. But he who fears has not been made perfect in love.

¹⁹We love Him because He first loved us.

²⁰If someone says, "I love God," and hates his brother, he is a liar; for he who does not love his brother whom he has seen, how can he love God whom he has not seen?

²¹And this commandment we have from Him: that he who loves God must love his brother also. (NKJV)

Realize

1. Who or what is the source of all love?

_____

_____

2. How did God demonstrate his love?

_____

_____

_____

3. How should God's love for us change the way we relate to others?

_____

_____

_____

4. Why is hate incompatible with someone who claims the name of Christ?

_____

_____

5. What, according to verse 18, happens when we really understand and embrace God's love?

_____

_____

_____

_____

Clearly, John's readers were struggling with the topic of love—where to find it and how to rightly share it with others. (How else can we explain the lengthy sections of this epistle that address the issue?) As the ultimate example of love, John pointed to the cross, where Jesus laid down his life for us. Then he added that we should do the same for one another.

What does it mean to lay down your life for a brother or a sister? It means giving up your rights. It means seeking his best, even it when it hurts or costs you deeply. It means putting her needs and interests above your own desires. Real love is an action, not a feeling. It produces selfless, sacrificial giving. The greatest act of love is giving oneself for others, serving others with no thought of receiving anything in return. Sometimes it is easier to say that we'll die for others than to truly live for them—that involves putting others' desires first. Jesus taught this same principle of love in John 15:13. In what specific way could you "lay down your life" for a family member or friend today?

John dismissed the idea that God's love is a mere theoretical concept. He rejected the notion that sentimental words are an adequate expression of love to others. On the contrary, he argued, love must take action! Biblical love is a verb! It begins with feelings of concern and compassion for those in need and always results in tangible, substantial sacrifice. So easily we rationalize away biblical demands. In most of the world, our Christian brothers and sisters lack proper food, clothing, and jobs to live decent lives. John 3:16 provides the best example of this truth, "God so loved the world that he gave . . ." (KJV). Consider the people God has placed in your life and ask yourself, "What does an active love require me to do for him or her today?" Consider people around the world and ask what you can do to help.

(adapted from _Life Application Bible Commentary: 1, 2 & 3 John_ [Wheaton, IL: Tyndale House Publishers, 1998], 75, 77)

Respond

6. Can someone who rejects God really love others? Why or why not?

_____

_____

_____

_____

7. If you had to rate yourself in the area of love from 1 to 10, (one being awful and 10 being awesome), what mark would you earn?

_____

_____

_____

8. How does knowing you are loved and accepted unconditionally and eternally free you to care for others?

_____

_____

_____

9. Who in your world needs an expression of love and the reminder that God is perfect in love?

_____

_____

_____

Read
Isaiah 55:1
Come, all you who are thirsty, come to the waters; and you who have no money, come, buy and eat! Come, buy wine and milk without money and without cost. (NIV)

John 4:14
(Jesus is speaking) "Whoever drinks the water I give will never be thirsty. The water I give will become a spring of water gushing up inside that person, giving eternal life." (NCV)

Acts 10:43
He is the one all the prophets testified about, saying that everyone who believes in him will have their sins forgiven through his name. (NLT)

1 John 5:1
Whoever believes that Jesus is the Messiah is a child of God. (TEV)

Revelation 22:17
The Spirit and the bride say, "Come." Let each one who hears them say, "Come." Let the thirsty ones come—anyone who wants to. Let them come and drink the water of life without charge. (NLT)

Realize
1. What do these verses suggest about God's invitation to salvation?

_____

_____

_____

2. Which of these verses limit salvation to a certain group? Are any automatically disqualified from responding to God's offer?

_____

_____

_____

> *Jesus did not die in order to spare the indignities of the wounded creation. He died that we might see those wounds as our own.*
> Peter J. Gomes

3. What is the significance of the word "come"? What does it say about God?

_____

_____

_____

4. Why are there so many references to thirst and drinking? Why is this such a common biblical metaphor for faith and salvation?

_____

_____

_____

5. What does it mean, really, to believe in Jesus? How can a person know if his or her faith is real?

_____

_____

_____

6. What, according to Revelation, does salvation cost?

_____

_____

Respond

7. Some people speak of the "wooing of the Spirit," referring to God's convicting people of their sin and calling them to respond. Did you ever have such a time in your life when it seemed as though God were knocking on your heart or summoning you to himself?

_____

_____

_____

8. How have the deep thirsts of your soul been quenched by Christ? Do you ever still feel thirsty? Why do you think?

_____

_____

_____

9. In your circle of friends and neighbors who do not yet know Christ, who seems to be most open to a spiritual conversation? How can you broach the subject of Christ in a natural way?

_____

_____

_____

In one school where I have taught, the student aid was handled in this way. People make gifts to the student aid fund. Needy students apply for help from that fund. A committee decides who will receive aid and how much. But when the actual money is distributed, it is done by issuing a check to the student, who then is expected to endorse it back to the school, which will then place the credit on his account. The money was not moved directly from the aid fund to the individual student's account. The student had to receive it personally and place it on his account. Let us suppose you gave a gift to cover one student's tuition for one year. You could properly say that his tuition was fully paid. But until the selection is made by the committee, and until the student receives the gift and places it on his account, his tuition is not paid. If he fails to endorse the check, it will never be paid, even though it has been paid! The death of Christ pays for all the sins of all people. But not one individual has his own account settled until he believes. If he never believes, then even though the price has been fully paid, his sins will not be forgiven. The death of Christ is like some benefactor paying the tuitions of all students in all schools everywhere. If that could be true, what should we be telling students? The good news that their tuitions are paid. Christ died for all. What should we be telling the world?

(© 1986 Cook Communications Ministries. _Bible Knowledge Commentary_ by Walvoord and Zuck. Reprinted with permission. May not be further reproduced. All rights reserved.)

Day 4) Crucified with Christ

Read
Romans 6:1–14
1What shall we say then? Shall we continue in sin that grace may abound?
2Certainly not! How shall we who died to sin live any longer in it?
3Or do you not know that as many of us as were baptized into Christ Jesus were baptized into His death?
4Therefore we were buried with Him through baptism into death, that just as Christ was raised from the dead by the glory of the Father, even so we also should walk in newness of life.
5For if we have been united together in the likeness of His death, certainly we also shall be in the likeness of His resurrection,
6knowing this, that our old man was crucified with Him, that the body of sin might be done away with, that we should no longer be slaves of sin.
7For he who has died has been freed from sin.

8Now if we died with Christ, we believe that we shall also live with Him,

9knowing that Christ, having been raised from the dead, dies no more. Death no longer has dominion over Him.

10For the death that He died, He died to sin once for all; but the life that He lives, He lives to God.

11Likewise you also, reckon yourselves to be dead indeed to sin, but alive to God in Christ Jesus our Lord.

12Therefore do not let sin reign in your mortal body, that you should obey it in its lusts.

13And do not present your members as instruments of unrighteousness to sin, but present yourselves to God as being alive from the dead, and your members as instruments of righteousness to God.

14For sin shall not have dominion over you, for you are not under law but under grace. (NKJV)

Galatians 2:19–20

19I have been put to death with Christ on the cross,

20so that it is no longer I who live, but it is Christ who lives in me. This life that I live now, I live by faith in the Son of God, who loved me and gave his life for me. (TEV)

Realize

1. What is the believer's relationship to sin?

_____

_____

_____

2. How can this be?

_____

_____

_____

3. What are the implications of being crucified with Christ?

_____

_____

_____

> *The author of Hebrews writes, "Consider him who endured such opposition from sinful men, so that you will not grow weary and lose heart" (12:2-3 NIV). Yes, consider Him. In our suffering and tribulations Jesus Himself must be our chief consideration. We must fix our eyes upon Him. He who suffered for us shows us how we are to bear our sufferings.*
> *Billy Graham[2]*

4. What is the believer's relationship to God and righteousness?

_____

_____

_____

5. If what Paul says here is true, why do Christians still sin?

_____

_____

_____

6. How does Paul summarize the Christian life in Galatians 2:19, 20?

_____

_____

_____

Respond

7. To what degree is sin reigning in your life? What's behind this, do you think?

_____

_____

_____

8. What does it look like, practically speaking, to present yourself "to God as being alive from the dead, and your members as instruments of righteousness to God" (verse 13)?

How does someone do this?

In every Christian's heart there is a cross and a throne, and the Christian is on the throne till he puts himself on the cross; if he refuses the cross he remains on the throne. Perhaps this is at the bottom of the backsliding and worldliness among gospel believers today. We want to be saved but we insist that Christ do all the dying. No cross for us, no dethronement, no dying. We remain king within the little kingdom of Mansoul and wear our tinsel crown with all the pride of a Caesar; but we doom ourselves to shadows and weakness and spiritual sterility.

A.W. Tozer [3]

9. Is this a once-for-all thing? A daily requirement? What?

10. What needs to happen in your life immediately so that it becomes obvious to all that "Christ lives in you" (Galatians 2:20)?

Day 5) *Taking Up Our Cross*

Read
Luke 9:18–26
[18]*And it happened, as He was alone praying, that His disciples joined Him, and He asked them, saying, "Who do the crowds say that I am?"*
[19]*So they answered and said, "John the Baptist, but some say Elijah; and others say that one of the old prophets has risen again."*
[20]*He said to them, "But who do you say that I am?" Peter answered and said, "The Christ of God."*
[21]*And He strictly warned and commanded them to tell this to no one,*
[22]*saying, "The Son of Man must suffer many things, and be rejected by the elders and chief priests and scribes, and be killed, and be raised the third day."*
[23]*Then He said to them all, "If anyone desires to come after Me, let him deny himself, and take up his cross daily, and follow Me.*
[24]*"For whoever desires to save his life will lose it, but whoever loses his life for My sake will save it.*
[25]*"For what profit is it to a man if he gains the whole world, and is himself destroyed or lost?*
[26]*"For whoever is ashamed of Me and My words, of him the Son of Man will be ashamed when He comes in His own glory, and in His Father's, and of the holy angels. (NKJV)*

Luke 14:25–35
[25]*Large crowds were traveling with Jesus, and turning to them he said:*
[26]*"If anyone comes to me and does not hate his father and mother, his wife and children, his brothers and sisters—yes, even his own life—he cannot be my disciple.*
[27]*"And anyone who does not carry his cross and follow me cannot be my disciple.*
[28]*"Suppose one of you wants to build a tower. Will he not first sit down and estimate the cost to see if he has enough money to complete it?*
[29]*"For if he lays the foundation and is not able to finish it, everyone who sees it will ridicule him,*
[30]*saying, 'This fellow began to build and was not able to finish.'*
[31]*"Or suppose a king is about to go to war against another king. Will he not first sit down and consider whether he is able with ten thousand men to oppose the one coming against him with twenty thousand?*
[32]*"If he is not able, he will send a delegation while the other is still a long way off and will ask for terms of peace.*
[33]*"In the same way, any of you who does not give up everything he has cannot be my disciple.*

[34]*"Salt is good, but if it loses its saltiness, how can it be made salty again?*

35*"It is fit neither for the soil nor for the manure pile; it is thrown out. He who has ears to hear, let him hear." (NIV)* LESSON 10 NOTES

Realize

1. Would you categorize Jesus' remarks to his followers as upbeat and user-friendly? Why or why not?

_____

_____

_____

2. By speaking such hard and demanding words, what risk was Jesus taking?

_____

_____

_____

3. What does it mean to "deny" oneself?

_____

_____

_____

4. What did Jesus intend by the command to take up one's cross daily and follow him?

_____

_____

_____

The cross effects its ends by destroying one established pattern, the victim's, and creating another pattern, its own. Thus it always has its way. It wins by defeating its opponent and imposing its will upon him. It always dominates. It never compromises, never dickers nor confers, never surrenders a point for the sake of peace. It cares not for peace; it cares only to end its opposition as fast as possible.

With perfect knowledge of all this Christ said, "If any man will come after me, let him deny himself, and take up his cross, and follow me." So the cross not only brings Christ's life to an end, it ends also the first life, the old life, of every one of his true followers. It destroys the old pattern, the Adam pattern, in the believer's life, and brings it to an end. Then the God who raised Christ from the dead raises the believer and a new life begins.

This, and nothing less, is true Christianity.

We must do something about the cross, and one of two things only we can do—flee it or die upon it. If we are wise we will do what Jesus did: endure the cross and despise its shame for the joy that is set before us. The cross will cut into our lives where it hurts worst, sparing neither us nor our carefully cultivated reputations. It will defeat us and bring our selfish lives to an end. Only then can we rise in fullness of life to establish a pattern of living wholly new and free and full of good works

(adapted from A.W. Tozer, *The Root of the Righteous* [Harrisburg, PA: Christian Publications, Inc., 1955], 62–64).

5. What is the point of the parable about counting the cost?

_____

_____

_____

6. How do you understand Luke 14:33? What does that look like in a believer's life?

_____

_____

_____

Respond

7. What are you willing to do or to endure for Christ?

_____

_____

_____

8. In what ways or situations are you reluctant to boldly and unreservedly follow Christ?

_____

_____

_____

9. Some researchers have noted that more Christians were martyred for their faith in the twentieth century than in the previous nineteen centuries combined. If called upon, do you think you could die for Christ? How can believers be changed so that they are willing, if necessary, to die for the Faith?

_____

_____

_____

ETERNAL LIFE—a person's new and redeemed existence in Jesus Christ that is granted by God as a gift to all believers

Eternal life refers to the quality or character of our new existence in Christ as well as the unending character of that life. The phrase, "everlasting life," is found in the Old Testament only once (Dan. 12:2). But the idea of eternal life is implied by the prophets in their pictures of the glorious future promised to God's people.

The majority of references to eternal life in the New Testament are oriented to the future. The emphasis, however, is upon the blessed character of the life that will be enjoyed endlessly in the future. Jesus made it clear that eternal life comes only to those who make a total commitment to him (Matt. 19:16–21; Luke 18:18–22). Paul's letters refer to eternal life relatively seldom, and again primarily with a future rather than a present orientation (Rom. 5:21; 6:22; Gal. 6:8).

The phrase, "eternal life," appears most often in the Gospel of John and the epistle of 1 John. John emphasizes eternal life as the present reality and possession of the Christian (John 3:36; 5:24; 1 John 5:13). John declares that the believer has already begun to experience the blessings of the future even before their fullest expression: "And this is eternal life, that they may know You, the only true God, and Jesus Christ whom You have sent" (John 17:3, NKJV).

(adapted from Ronald F Youngblood, Ed., _Nelson's New Illustrated Bible Dictionary_ [Nashville, TN: Thomas Nelson Publishers, 1997, c1995], CD-ROM)

LESSON

11

"I Can Turn Your Tragedy into Triumph"

God's Promise in the Burial Clothing

LOOKING BACK

Lesson 10 offered us the chance to explore in depth the perfect justice and immeasurable love of God demonstrated on the cross. How odd that an instrument of execution became an invitation extended to the whole human race to find life—new life, rich life, eternal life. Our memory verse for lesson 10 was Romans 5:8. Can you say it without any prompting?

1. How was the death of Christ just? Why was it the greatest act of love ever?

_____

_____

_____

_____

2. *Max writes:* "It's nice to be included. You aren't always. Universities exclude you if you aren't smart enough. Businesses exclude you if you aren't qualified enough, and, sadly, some churches exclude you if you aren't good enough. But though they may exclude you, Christ includes you. When asked to describe the width of his love, he stretched one hand to the right and the other to the left and had them nailed in that position so you would know he died loving you." When you see artistic renditions of the crucifixion, how are you affected? Why?

_____

_____

_____

3. What movie version of the life, death, and resurrection of Jesus do you consider the most powerful? Why?

_____

_____

_____

4. As you think back over the daily studies from lesson 10, what details made the biggest impression on you? Why?

_____

_____

_____

GETTING STARTED

VIDEO—In video segment number 11, Max talks about John at the cross and God turning tragedy into triumph. (The script is reprinted on page 231.)

5. You've probably been to enough funerals to know what you want (and don't want!) at your own. What have you decided and why?

6. What have been the three greatest tragedies of human history? of American history? of your own life?

7. Everyone claims to hate bad news and depressing stories, but the truth is we switch on our TVs and radios almost daily to catch all the bad news. Why? Could a newspaper or TV station be successful by concentrating strictly on positive and uplifting stories? Would you watch or listen?

8. What truths, people, or things have been your greatest help in times of tragedy?

DIGGING IN

9. Max begins this lesson talking about symbols of tragedy. Specifically he makes the point that God can take a token of tragedy and turn it into a symbol of triumph. *He writes:* "We all face tragedy. What's more, we've all received the symbols of tragedy. Yours might be a telegram from the war department, an ID bracelet from the hospital, a scar, or a court subpoena. We don't like these symbols, nor do we want these symbols. Like wrecked cars in a junkyard, they clutter up our hearts with memories of bad days. Could God use such things for something good?" What symbols of tragedy have you collected over the years?

10. *Max writes:* "On the first Easter Sunday, God took clothing of death and made it a symbol of life. Could he do the same for you?"

How would you answer Max's question? Explain.

Sometimes what looks like a defeat will be seen later to have been a positive victory. When the soldiers of Pilate flung Christ to the ground and began to drive in the nails, everything looked as if our Lord had ended a failure. Surely this ignominious death would not come to a man of God. There must be some mistake. The man Jesus had been an idealist, a visionary, but now his hopes and the hopes of his followers were collapsing under the brutal attacks of tough, practical men. So reasoned the onlookers. But our Lord could die with the same calm in which he had lived. He had known all along how things would turn out. He had looked beyond the cross to the triumphant resurrection. He knew that his apparent defeat would eventuate in universal glory for the human race.

(adapted from A.W. Tozer, *The Root of the Righteous* [Harrisburg, PA: Christian Publications, Inc., 1955], 138, 140)

GOING DEEPER

John 19:38–20:10

³⁸*After this, Joseph of Arimathea, being a disciple of Jesus, but secretly, for fear of the Jews, asked Pilate that he might take away the body of Jesus; and Pilate gave [him] permission. So he came and took the body of Jesus.*

³⁹*And Nicodemus, who at first came to Jesus by night, also came, bringing a mixture of myrrh and aloes, about a hundred pounds.*

40 *Then they took the body of Jesus, and bound it in strips of linen with the spices, as the custom of the Jews is to bury.*

⁴¹*Now in the place where He was crucified there was a garden, and in the garden a new tomb in which no one had yet been laid.*

⁴²*So there they laid Jesus, because of the Jews' Preparation Day, for the tomb was nearby.*

²⁰:¹*Now on the first day of the week Mary Magdalene went to the tomb early, while it was still dark, and saw that the stone had been taken away from the tomb.*

²*Then she ran and came to Simon Peter, and to the other disciple, whom Jesus loved, and said to them, "They have taken away the Lord out of the tomb, and we do not know where they have laid Him."*

³*Peter therefore went out, and the other disciple, and were going to the tomb.*

⁴*So they both ran together, and the other disciple outran Peter and came to the tomb first.*

⁵*And he, stooping down and looking in, saw the linen cloths lying there; yet he did not go in.*

⁶*Then Simon Peter came, following him, and went into the tomb; and he saw the linen cloths lying there,*

⁷*and the handkerchief that had been around His head, not lying with the linen cloths, but folded together in a place by itself.*

⁸*Then the other disciple, who came to the tomb first, went in also; and he saw and believed.*

⁹*For as yet they did not know the Scripture, that He must rise again from the dead.*

¹⁰*Then the disciples went away again to their own homes. (NKJV)*

Love Divine, All Loves Excelling

Love divine, all loves excelling,
Joy of heav'n to earth come down;
Fix in us Thy humble dwelling;
All thy faithful mercies crown.
Jesus, Thou art all compassion,
Pure, unbounded love Thou art;
Visit us with Thy salvation;
Enter ev'ry trembling heart.

Breathe, O breathe Thy loving Spirit,
Into ev'ry troubled breast!
Let us all in Thee inherit,
Let us find the promised rest;
Take away our bent to sinning;
Alpha and Omega be;
End of faith, as its beginning,
Set our hearts at liberty.

Come, Almighty to deliver,
Let us all Thy grace receive;
Suddenly return, and never,
Nevermore Thy temples leave.
Thee we would be always blessing,
Serve Thee as Thy host above,
Pray, and praise Thee without ceasing,
Glory in Thy perfect love.
Finish, then, Thy new creation;

Pure and spotless let us be;
Let us see Thy great salvation
Perfectly restored in Thee:
Changed from glory into glory,
Till in heav'n we take our place,
Till we cast our crowns before Thee,
Lost in wonder, love, and praise.

(Charles Wesley, 1747)

11. What evidence from this passage proves that Jesus was certifiably dead?

_____

_____

_____

12. What did Nicodemus bring with him when he came to retrieve the body of Jesus? Why?

_____

_____

_____

13. What was Mary's interpretation of the events of that first Easter morning?

_____

_____

_____

We don't need to wipe away our own sins, or try to conquer death and the devil. Everything has already been done for us. We're not fighting the real battle. We're only suffering now in order to share in Christ's victory. All of our suffering combined, even all the suffering of the martyrs and saints, wouldn't give us the victory. It's not accomplished by what we do. Some people claim that we ought to be able to conquer sin, death, and hell on our own. By saying this they insult Christ. But our struggles and fighting come way too late. The battle must be won beforehand if we are to have any comfort and peace. Christ says, "I have already won. Accept my victory. Sing about it and glorify it. Take comfort in it."
Martin Luther

14. What did Simon Peter and John do when they arrived at the tomb? What did they see?

_____

_____

_____

15. How did the situation affect them?

_____

_____

_____

Myrrh was a very fragrant gummy resin, which the Jews turned into a powdered form and mixed with aloes, a powder from the aromatic sandalwood. The Jews did not embalm but did this procedure to stifle the smell of putrefaction. The spices most likely were laid on the entire length of the strips of linen that were then wound around Jesus' body. More spices were laid under the body and perhaps packed around it. The sticky resin would help the cloth adhere.

(adapted from *The MacArthur Study Bible* [Nashville, TN: Word Bibles, 1997], 1625)

Romans 8:28
We know that in everything God works for the good of those who love him. They are the people he called, because that was his plan. (NCV)

16. What is significant about the phrase "in everything"?

_____

_____

_____ 182

17. Does this verse teach that bad things are, in actuality, good? Explain.

_____

_____

_____

18. What are the conditions for seeing God work everything (including bad things) for good?

_____

_____

_____

19. How can this verse give us hope in difficult times?

_____

_____

_____

Romans 8:28 God works in "everything"—not just isolated incidents—for our good. This does not mean that all that happens to us is good. Evil is prevalent in our fallen world, but God is able to turn every circumstance around for our long-range good. Note that God is not working to make us happy, but to fulfill his purpose. Note also that this promise is not for everybody. It can be claimed only by those who love God and are called according to his purpose. Those who are "called" are those the Holy Spirit convinces and enables to receive Christ. Such people have a new perspective, a new mind-set on life. They trust in God, not life's treasures; they look for their security in heaven, not on earth; they learn to accept, not resent, pain and persecution because God is with them.

(adapted from the _Life Application Bible/NLT_ [Wheaton, IL: Tyndale House Publishers, 1996], 1782)

Great hearts can only be made by great troubles. The spade of trouble digs the reservoir of comfort deeper, and makes more room for consolation. God comes into our heart—he finds it full—he begins to break our comforts and to make it empty; then there is more room for grace. The humbler a man lies, the more comfort he will always have, because he will be more fitted to receive it. Another reason why we are often most happy in our troubles, is this—_then we have the closest dealings with God._ When the barn is full, man can live without God: when the purse is bursting with gold, we try to do without so much prayer. But once take our _gourds_ away, and we want our _God;_ once cleanse the idols out of the house, then we are compelled to honor Jehovah. "Out of the depths have I cried unto thee, O Lord." There is no cry so good as that which comes from the bottom of the mountains; no prayer half so hearty as that which comes up from the depths of the soul, through deep trials and afflictions. Hence they bring us to God, and we are happier; for nearness to God is happiness. Come, troubled believer, fret not over your heavy troubles, for they are the heralds of weighty mercies.

(Charles H. Spurgeon, _Morning and Evening_, [30 Hunt Valley Circle, New Kensington, PA: Whitaker House © 1997. Used by permission of the publisher.] 86.)

Isaiah 64:8
_Yet, O L_ORD_, you are our Father. We are the clay, you are the potter; we are all the work of your hand. (NIV)_

20. What do you know about pottery making, potters, and clay?

_____

_____

_____

21. What does this verse teach about God?

_____

_____

_____

22. What does this verse teach about human beings?

_____

_____

_____

23. Why is this an important truth to keep in mind?

_____

_____

_____

1 Peter 5:10
And the God of all grace, who called you to his eternal glory in Christ, after you have suffered a little while, will himself restore you and make you strong, firm and steadfast. (NIV)

24. How is God described in this verse?

_____

_____

_____

25. What does this verse teach that God does _to_ us and _for_ us? What does he allow in us?

_____

_____

_____

26. Would this verse be encouraging to a suffering saint? Why or why not?

_____

_____

_____

27. Max writes: "When it's Saturday in your life, how do you react? When you are somewhere between yesterday's tragedy and tomorrow's triumph, what do you do? Do you leave God—or do you linger near him?" What does Max mean by "Saturday in your life"?

_____

_____

_____

> _So call it what you wish: An act of grace. A plan of redemption. A martyr's sacrifice. But whatever you call it, don't call it an accident. It was anything but that._
> Max Lucado[1]

28. After tragedy strikes, do you leave God or do you linger near him?

_____

_____

_____

Making It Real

John's experience with the grave clothes of Christ is a good reminder of our sovereign God's ability to take the bleakest and worst of situations and turn them into occasions for joyful worship.

Luke 1:37
(an angel is speaking) _"God can do anything!" (NCV)_

29. Why is it so difficult to believe that God controls everything?

_____

_____

_____

30. Why is it important to believe that God has control?

_____

_____

_____

THINKING IT THROUGH

The truth of God's sovereignty, as revealed in this lesson, is critically important for everyday life. Reflect on all that you've read and studied. Listen to "He Reigns" by Glenn Wagner, Bernie Herms, and Bryan Lenox on the CD and let it move your heart to sincere praise.

PERSONAL NOTES

Memory Verse
Romans 8:28

And we know that in all things God works for the good of those who love him, who have been called according to his purpose. (NIV)

And we know that all things work together for good to those who love God, to those who are the called according to His purpose. (NKJV)

And we know that God causes everything to work together for the good of those who love God and are called according to his purpose for them. (NLT)

During the next week, study the following passages.

Day 1) *The Sovereignty of God*

Read
Isaiah 45:9–19

⁹*How terrible it will be for those who argue with the God who made them. They are like a piece of broken pottery among many pieces. The clay does not ask the potter, 'What are you doing?' The thing that is made doesn't say to its maker, 'You have no hands.'*
¹⁰*How terrible it will be for the child who says to his father, 'Why are you giving me life?' How terrible it will be for the child who says to his mother, 'Why are you giving birth to me?'"*
¹¹*This is what the LORD, the Holy One of Israel, and its Maker, says: "You ask me about what will happen. You question me about my children. You give me orders about what I have made.*
¹²*I made the earth and all the people living on it. With my own hands I stretched out the skies, and I commanded all the armies in the sky.*
¹³*I will bring Cyrus to do good things, and I will make his work easy. He will rebuild my city and set my people free without any payment or reward. The LORD All-Powerful says this."*
¹⁴*The LORD says, "The goods made in Egypt and Cush, and the tall people of Seba will come to you and will become yours. The Sabeans will walk behind you, coming along in chains. They will bow down before you and pray to you, saying, 'God is with you, and there is no other God.'"*
¹⁵*God and Savior of Israel, you are a God that people cannot see.*
¹⁶*All the people who make idols will be put to great shame; they will go off together in disgrace.*
¹⁷*But Israel will be saved by the LORD, and that salvation will continue forever. Never again will Israel be put to shame.*
¹⁸*The LORD created the heavens. He is the God who formed the earth and made it. He did not want it to be empty, but he wanted life on the earth. This is what the LORD says: "I am the LORD. There is no other God.*
¹⁹*I did not speak in secret or hide my words in some dark place. I did not tell the family of Jacob to look for me in empty places. I am the LORD, and I speak the truth; I say what is right." (NCV)*

Realize
1. Isaiah 45 is a detailed prophecy given some 150 years in advance about how God would raise up and use a Persian monarch named Cyrus to orchestrate his divine plan for his people.

   What different names or titles are ascribed to God in this passage?

_____
_____
_____
_____

186

2. Why do you think God emphasized his role as Creator here?

_____

_____

_____

3. How would this passage have been a comfort to the people of God?

_____

_____

4. What does this chapter reveal about God's direct control of human affairs and world events?

_____

_____

_____

SOVEREIGNTY OF GOD—a theological term that refers to the unlimited power of God, who has sovereign control over the affairs of nature and history (Isa. 45:9–19; Rom. 8:18–39)

The Bible declares that God is working out his sovereign plan of redemption for the world and that the conclusion is certain. Immediately after the Fall he spoke of the curse of human sin and specified the cure for it. To the serpent he said, "I will put enmity between you and the woman, and between your seed and her seed; He shall bruise your head, and you shall bruise His heel" (Gen. 3:15, NKJV). The whole redemptive story of the Bible is the fulfillment of this prophecy by the sovereign God, as Paul clearly teaches in Romans 8—11.

The story of redemption from Genesis to Revelation is possible only because the sovereign God loves the created world, fallen though it is, and is able to do something about it. Without the sovereign love of the Father ministered to us through the Son and the Holy Spirit, there would be no real human freedom and no hope of everlasting life.

(adapted from Ronald F. Youngblood, Ed., *Nelson's New Illustrated Bible Dictionary* [Nashville, TN: Thomas Nelson Publishers, 1997, c1995], CD-ROM).

Respond

5. How would you answer the person who said: "If God is in control of all things, then God must, obviously, be in control of natural disasters and wars. Sorry, but I have a hard time trusting a God like that!"

_____

_____

_____

6. In what specific situation of your life is it most difficult to believe that God is in control?

_____

_____

7. How does a person strengthen his or her faith?

_____

_____

_____

Theological Insight

As we read the Gospel accounts of Jesus' crucifixion, it becomes clear that God was in control of all the events. This is made especially clear in the Gospel of John (cited throughout). While this Gospel depicts Jesus' crucifixion at the hands of sinful people, we must keep in mind that ultimately God is in control here, not human beings. The crucifixion was his plan, not theirs. All happened as it was supposed to happen. No one but Jesus, however, was aware of this. Since he knew his destiny (see John 18:37), he walked into death boldly and calmly—carrying his own cross to Calvary (19:17). The Jews and the Romans were not taking his life from him; he was laying it down of his own accord. When he had accomplished salvation—when it was all "finished," Jesus of his own volition gave up his spirit (19:30). As he had foretold, no one took his life from him; he had authority to give it up and then retake it in resurrection (10:18). From the cross, Jesus was exalted as if it were his throne. On the cross was nailed the royal proclamation for all the world to read (it was written in the three major languages): "Jesus, King of the Jews!" A king went to the cross to conquer death. He did so, then he rose to enjoy a glorious victory!

Everything that happened in connection with Jesus' betrayal and crucifixion transpired according to the prearranged, divine plan. The hour was predetermined; it could not happen before or after the Passover. The betrayer, Judas Iscariot, was picked by Jesus. He knew from the beginning that Judas was a devil and would be his betrayer (see 6:64, 70). The method of death—crucifixion—was prearranged, so Jesus knew that he would be lifted up on the cross (see 12:32–33). Thus, it was clear that his executors would be the Romans (for they were the unique administrators of this kind of capital punishment) and not the Jews, who executed by stoning (18:32). The Jews attempted to stone Jesus many times, but they never succeeded because it was not in accord with the divine plan.

Many of the events that occurred during Jesus' arrest and crucifixion were destined to happen because they had been prophesied. Only Jesus was arrested, not one of his disciples, in fulfillment of the Scripture, "that I should lose nothing of all that he has given to me" (18:9, from John 6:39, NRSV). When Jesus was on the cross, the soldiers cast lots for his tunic without realizing that they were carrying out a part of predictive prophecy (19:24, from Ps. 22:18). But Jesus knew that what was transpiring was in accord with God's predetermined will. Near the end of his crucifixion Jesus, "knowing that all things had now been accomplished," said, "I thirst." This fulfilled the Scriptures (19:28, from Ps. 69:21). After Jesus died, the soldiers refrained from breaking his legs. This also fulfilled Scripture: "not a bone of him shall be broken" (19:36, from Ps. 34:20; see also Exod. 12:46; Num. 9:12). Instead of breaking his bones, one of the soldiers pierced his side, from which blood and water then issued. This also fulfilled prophecy: "They will look on the one whom they have pierced" (19:37, from Zech. 12:10, NRSV).

All happened as it was supposed to happen. No one but Jesus, however, was aware of this. Since he knew his destiny (see 18:37), he walked into death boldly and courageously. He walked into death as the Son of God. John's narrative does not describe the agony in the Garden of Gethsemane and Jesus crying out, "My God, My God, why have you forsaken me!" on the cross. The other Gospels show us his human side. They describe the sufferings of the man who would become our sympathetic high priest. John shows us the God-man. He is the man in whom Pilate could find no fault. He is the man who, while dying on the cross, showed his concern for the well-being of his mother. He is the man who laid down his life of his own accord. When it was all finished, Jesus, of his own volition, gave up his spirit. As was foretold, no one took his life from him. He had authority to give it up and then retake it. He, the king of life, was the king over death.

Day 2) *Tragedy and Triumph in Joseph's Life*

Read
Genesis 37:18–28

¹⁸*Now when they saw him afar off, even before he came near them, they conspired against him to kill him.*
¹⁹*Then they said to one another, "Look, this dreamer is coming!*
²⁰"Come therefore, let us now kill him and cast him into some pit; and we shall say, 'Some wild beast has devoured him.' We shall see what will become of his dreams!"*
²¹*But Reuben heard it, and he delivered him out of their hands, and said, "Let us not kill him."*
²²*And Reuben said to them, "Shed no blood, but cast him into this pit which is in the wilderness, and do not lay a hand on him"—that he might deliver him out of their hands, and bring him back to his father.*
²³*So it came to pass, when Joseph had come to his brothers, that they stripped Joseph of his tunic, the tunic of many colors that was on him.*
²⁴*Then they took him and cast him into a pit. And the pit was empty; there was no water in it.*

25And they sat down to eat a meal. Then they lifted their eyes and looked, and there was a company of Ishmaelites, coming from Gilead with their camels, bearing spices, balm, and myrrh, on their way to carry them down to Egypt.

26So Judah said to his brothers, "What profit is there if we kill our brother and conceal his blood?

27Come and let us sell him to the Ishmaelites, and let not our hand be upon him, for he is our brother and our flesh." And his brothers listened.

28Then Midianite traders passed by; so the brothers pulled Joseph up and lifted him out of the pit, and sold him to the Ishmaelites for twenty shekels of silver. And they took Joseph to Egypt. (NKJV)

Genesis 45:1–15

1Then Joseph could no longer control himself before all his attendants, and he cried out, "Have everyone leave my presence!" So there was no one with Joseph when he made himself known to his brothers.

2And he wept so loudly that the Egyptians heard him, and Pharaoh's household heard about it.

3Joseph said to his brothers, "I am Joseph! Is my father still living?" But his brothers were not able to answer him, because they were terrified at his presence.

4Then Joseph said to his brothers, "Come close to me." When they had done so, he said, "I am your brother Joseph, the one you sold into Egypt!

5And now, do not be distressed and do not be angry with yourselves for selling me here, because it was to save lives that God sent me ahead of you.

6For two years now there has been famine in the land, and for the next five years there will not be plowing and reaping.

7But God sent me ahead of you to preserve for you a remnant on earth and to save your lives by a great deliverance.

8So then, it was not you who sent me here, but God. He made me father to Pharaoh, lord of his entire household and ruler of all Egypt.

9Now hurry back to my father and say to him, 'This is what your son Joseph says: God has made me lord of all Egypt. Come down to me; don't delay.

10You shall live in the region of Goshen and be near me—you, your children and grandchildren, your flocks and herds, and all you have.

11I will provide for you there, because five years of famine are still to come. Otherwise you and your household and all who belong to you will become destitute.'

12You can see for yourselves, and so can my brother Benjamin, that it is really I who am speaking to you.

13Tell my father about all the honor accorded me in Egypt and about everything you have seen. And bring my father down here quickly."

14Then he threw his arms around his brother Benjamin and wept, and Benjamin embraced him, weeping.

15And he kissed all his brothers and wept over them. Afterward his brothers talked with him. (NIV)

Realize

1. What did Joseph's brothers do first to try to make sure his dreams of greatness (see Genesis 37:1–11) did not come true?

_____

_____

_____

2. Why did they change their minds?

_____

_____

3. Where did Joseph end up?

_____

_____

4. **While in Egypt (for more than twenty years), Joseph was a slave, then a falsely accused prisoner, before rising to the rank of prime minister. What happened when Joseph revealed himself to his brothers?**

_____

_____

_____

5. Why were Joseph's brothers afraid?

_____

_____

_____

6. What reason did Joseph give his brothers for not being afraid?

_____

_____

_____

Respond

7. What emotions and thoughts do you suppose would have filled your heart and mind had you been in Joseph's shoes?

_____

_____

_____

8. What experiences in your life appeared (on the surface) to be meant for evil but which God transformed into good?

_____

_____

_____

9. How can a deep, abiding belief in God's sovereignty make a difference in your daily life?

_____

_____

_____

When Joseph finally revealed himself to his brothers, they were terrified . . . and rightly so. After all, they had nearly killed him before finally deciding to sell him into slavery. Somehow, however, much to their amazement, Joseph had become the second most powerful man in Egypt. The brothers recognized that their lives were in Joseph's hands. They cowered before him, trembling and waiting for him to pronounce judgment.

Instead they heard their long-lost brother speak words of consolation. Joseph told them not to be angry with themselves, for God had sent him to Egypt so that he could preserve his family from the famine that had engulfed the land. Joseph encouraged his brothers to make the reunion complete by bringing their father, Jacob, to Egypt.

Rather than being vengeful, Joseph was thrilled. "Isn't it amazing?" he seemed to be saying. "God orchestrated this whole episode!" By standing back and looking at the big picture, Joseph saw the sovereign hand of God. He realized that God can master terrible situations to benefit his children.

What a marvelous, comforting truth! God is in control of your life today. Trusting in that fact can be the difference between joy and despair.

Few truths can change our lives like the knowledge that God is in control.

(from Michael Kendrick & Daryl Lucas, Eds., _365 Life Lessons from Bible People_ [Wheaton, IL: Tyndale House Publishers, 1996], 41)

190

Read

Psalm 30

¹*I will extol You, O LORD, for You have lifted me up, and have not let my foes rejoice over me.*

²*O LORD my God, I cried out to You, and You healed me.*

³*O LORD, You brought my soul up from the grave; You have kept me alive, that I should not go down to the pit.*

⁴*Sing praise to the LORD, you saints of His, and give thanks at the remembrance of His holy name.*

⁵*For His anger is but for a moment, His favor is for life; weeping may endure for a night, but joy comes in the morning.*

⁶*Now in my prosperity I said, "I shall never be moved."*

⁷*LORD, by Your favor You have made my mountain stand strong; You hid Your face, and I was troubled.*

⁸*I cried out to You, O LORD; and to the LORD I made supplication:*

⁹*What profit is there in my blood, When I go down to the pit? Will the dust praise You? Will it declare Your truth?*

¹⁰*Hear, O LORD, and have mercy on me; LORD, be my helper!"*

¹¹*You have turned for me my mourning into dancing; You have put off my sackcloth and clothed me with gladness,*

¹²*To the end that my glory may sing praise to You and not be silent. O LORD my God, I will give thanks to You forever. (NKJV)*

Realize

1. What reason did David give for praising the Lord? (30:1–3)

_____

_____

2. What images did David use to describe how the Lord delivered him?

_____

_____

_____

> *It was not human beings who accomplished anything here [on the cross]; no, God alone did it. He came to human beings in infinite love. He judged what is human. And he granted grace beyond merit.*
> *Dietrich Bonhoeffer*

3. Why did David experience divine discipline? What sinful attitude was he guilty of?

_____

_____

_____

4. What do verses 5 and 12 teach about how God can turn dark and distressing situations around?

_____

_____

_____

5. Why did David want God to save him?

_____

_____

Respond

6. Which is a better description of your life right now—weeping at night or joy in the morning? Why?

_____

_____

_____

7. How has God delivered you in the past?

_____

_____

_____

_____

8. How can you become more trusting—even during hard or uncertain times?

_____

_____

_____

_____

9. How do you plan to follow the example of this psalm?

_____

_____

_____

_____

Troubles and Complaints in the Psalms

We can relate to the psalms because they express our feelings. We all face troubles, as did the psalm writers hundreds of years ago, and we often respond as they did. In Psalm 3, David told God how he felt about the odds against him. But within three verses, the king realized that God's presence and care made the odds meaningless. This experience is repeated in many of the psalms. Usually, the hope and confidence in God outweigh the fear and suffering; sometimes they do not. Still, the psalm writers consistently poured out their thoughts and emotions to God. When they felt abandoned by God, they told him so. When they were impatient with how slowly God seemed to be answering their prayers, they also told him so. Because they recognized the difference between themselves and God, they were free to be human and to be honest with their Creator. That is why so many of the dark psalms end in the light. The psalm writers started by expressing their feelings and ended up remembering to whom they were speaking!

Although we have much in common with the psalm writers, we may differ in two ways: we might not tell God what we are really thinking and feeling; therefore, we also might not recognize, even faintly, who is listening to our prayers!

Notice this pattern as you read Psalms, and put the psalm writers' insight to the test. You may well find that your awareness and appreciation of God will grow as you are honest with him. (See Psalms 3; 6; 13; 31; 37; 64; 77; 102; 121; 142.)

(adapted from the *Life Application Bible/NLT* [Wheaton, IL: Tyndale House Publishers, 1996], 833)

Day 4) *When All Seems Lost!*

Read
John 11:1–44

¹*A man named Lazarus was sick. He lived in the town of Bethany, where Mary and her sister Martha lived.*

²*Mary was the woman who later put perfume on the Lord and wiped his feet with her hair. Mary's brother was Lazarus, the man who was now sick.*

³*So Mary and Martha sent someone to tell Jesus, "Lord, the one you love is sick."*

⁴*When Jesus heard this, he said, "This sickness will not end in death. It is for the glory of God, to bring glory to the Son of God."*

⁵*Jesus loved Martha and her sister and Lazarus.*

⁶*But when he heard that Lazarus was sick, he stayed where he was for two more days.*

⁷Then Jesus said to his followers, "Let's go back to Judea."

⁸The followers said, "But Teacher, the Jews there tried to stone you to death only a short time ago. Now you want to go back there?"

⁹Jesus answered, "Are there not twelve hours in the day? If anyone walks in the daylight, he will not stumble, because he can see by this world's light.

¹⁰But if anyone walks at night, he stumbles because there is no light to help him see."

¹¹After Jesus said this, he added, "Our friend Lazarus has fallen asleep, but I am going there to wake him."

¹²The followers said, "But Lord, if he is only asleep, he will be all right."

¹³Jesus meant that Lazarus was dead, but his followers thought he meant Lazarus was really sleeping.

¹⁴So then Jesus said plainly, "Lazarus is dead.

¹⁵And I am glad for your sakes I was not there so that you may believe. But let's go to him now."

¹⁶Then Thomas (the one called Didymus) said to the other followers, "Let us also go so that we can die with him."

¹⁷When Jesus arrived, he learned that Lazarus had already been dead and in the tomb for four days.

¹⁸Bethany was about two miles from Jerusalem.

¹⁹Many of the Jews had come there to comfort Martha and Mary about their brother.

²⁰When Martha heard that Jesus was coming, she went out to meet him, but Mary stayed home.

²¹Martha said to Jesus, "Lord, if you had been here, my brother would not have died.

²²But I know that even now God will give you anything you ask."

²³Jesus said, "Your brother will rise and live again."

²⁴Martha answered, "I know that he will rise and live again in the resurrection on the last day."

²⁵Jesus said to her, "I am the resurrection and the life. Those who believe in me will have life even if they die.

²⁶And everyone who lives and believes in me will never die. Martha, do you believe this?"

²⁷Martha answered, "Yes, Lord. I believe that you are the Christ, the Son of God, the One coming to the world."

²⁸After Martha said this, she went back and talked to her sister Mary alone. Martha said, "The Teacher is here and he is asking for you."

²⁹When Mary heard this, she got up quickly and went to Jesus.

³⁰Jesus had not yet come into the town but was still at the place where Martha had met him.

³¹The Jews were with Mary in the house, comforting her. When they saw her stand and leave quickly, they followed her, thinking she was going to the tomb to cry there.

³²But Mary went to the place where Jesus was. When she saw him, she fell at his feet and said, "Lord, if you had been here, my brother would not have died."

³³When Jesus saw Mary crying and the Jews who came with her also crying, he was upset and was deeply troubled.

³⁴He asked, "Where did you bury him?"

"Come and see, Lord," they said.

³⁵Jesus cried.

³⁶So the Jews said, "See how much he loved him."

³⁷But some of them said, "If Jesus opened the eyes of the blind man, why couldn't he keep Lazarus from dying?"

³⁸Again feeling very upset, Jesus came to the tomb. It was a cave with a large stone covering the entrance.

³⁹Jesus said, "Move the stone away."

Martha, the sister of the dead man, said, "But, Lord, it has been four days since he died. There will be a bad smell."

⁴⁰Then Jesus said to her, "Didn't I tell you that if you believed you would see the glory of God?"

⁴¹So they moved the stone away from the entrance. Then Jesus looked up and said, "Father, I thank you that you heard me.

⁴²I know that you always hear me, but I said these things because of the people here around me. I want them to believe that you sent me."

⁴³After Jesus said this, he cried out in a loud voice, "Lazarus, come out!"

⁴⁴The dead man came out, his hands and feet wrapped with pieces of cloth, and a cloth around his face. Jesus said to them, "Take the cloth off of him and let him go." (NCV)

Realize

1. What in this chapter tells you that Jesus had an especially close relationship with Lazarus and his sisters?

_____

_____

_____

2. Why do you think Jesus delayed going to the bedside of Lazarus? Does verse 6 seem cruel to you? Why or why not?

_____

_____

_____

_____

3. Try to describe what those days of waiting must have felt like to Mary and Martha.

_____

_____

_____

4. When Jesus did finally arrive, do you think Mary and Martha's identical comment to him was a statement of gentle rebuke or a simple exclamation of faith?

_____

_____

_____

5. How did these events affect Jesus emotionally? Why?

_____

_____

_____

_____

_____

We are not necessarily doubting that God will do the best for us; we are wondering how painful the best will turn out to be.
C.S. Lewis²

6. What, according to Jesus, was the ultimate reason for the resurrection of Lazarus?

_____

_____

_____

_____

Respond

7. How do you handle tough situations when you have to wait and it seems like no help is forthcoming from God?

_____

_____

_____

8. What is the most helpless and hopeless you've ever been?

_____

_____

_____

9. Who in your immediate world is in the midst of a dark time? What specifically can you do to encourage that person?

_____

_____

_____

Timing Is Everything

Sometimes we offer a passionate prayer of need, and God answers quickly. We are thankful and excited, and our faith is often strengthened. At other times, it seems that God will never answer our prayers. We can't understand, because we know that we prayed for God's will. What should we do? We should wait in faith, knowing that God has our best interests in mind. We may never see our prayer answered in our lifetime; we may wait many years only to see God answer the prayer in another way altogether; we may find that God's final answer is no. Whatever the case, God's decision is best, and his timing is right.

(adapted from *Life Application Bible Commentary: John* [Wheaton, IL: Tyndale House Publishers, Inc., 1993], 227).

Day 5) When Storms Come

Read
Mark 4:35–41

35As evening came, Jesus said to his disciples, "Let's cross to the other side of the lake."
36He was already in the boat, so they started out, leaving the crowds behind (although other boats followed).
37But soon a fierce storm arose. High waves began to break into the boat until it was nearly full of water.
38Jesus was sleeping at the back of the boat with his head on a cushion. Frantically they woke him up, shouting, "Teacher, don't you even care that we are going to drown?"
39When he woke up, he rebuked the wind and said to the water, "Quiet down!" Suddenly the wind stopped, and there was a great calm.
40And he asked them, "Why are you so afraid? Do you still not have faith in me?"
41And they were filled with awe and said among themselves, "Who is this man, that even the wind and waves obey him?" (NLT)

Mark 4:37 It is not unusual even today for a sudden fierce storm to appear on the Sea of Galilee during the evening hours. The warm tropical air from the lake's surface rises and meets the colder air from the nearby hills. The resulting turbulence stirs up great waves that make boating extremely treacherous.

4:38 The mention of Jesus "sleeping . . . on a cushion" shows his true humanity. He was fully human and needed food and rest just as all people do.

4:39 Jesus' command over the wind and the sea demonstrates his full and complete deity. Only God the Creator can calm wind and sea.

(adapted from *The Nelson Study Bible* [Nashville, TN: Thomas Nelson Publishers, 1997], 1648)

"Quiet down!" Storms normally subside gradually, but when the Creator gave the order, the natural elements of this storm ceased immediately.

"they were filled with awe" This was not fear of being harmed by the storm, but a reverence for the supernatural power Jesus had just displayed. The only thing more terrifying than having a storm outside the boat was having God in the boat!

(adapted from *The MacArthur Study Bible* [Nashville, TN: Word Publishing, 1997], 1467)

Matthew 14:22–33
22 Immediately Jesus made the disciples get into the boat and go on ahead of him to the other side, while he dismissed the crowd.

²³*After he had dismissed them, he went up on a mountainside by himself to pray. When evening came, he was there alone,*
²⁴*but the boat was already a considerable distance from land, buffeted by the waves because the wind was against it.*
²⁵*During the fourth watch of the night Jesus went out to them, walking on the lake.*
²⁶*When the disciples saw him walking on the lake, they were terrified. "It's a ghost," they said, and cried out in fear.*
²⁷*But Jesus immediately said to them: "Take courage! It is I. Don't be afraid."*
²⁸*"Lord, if it's you," Peter replied, "tell me to come to you on the water."*
²⁹*"Come," he said. Then Peter got down out of the boat, walked on the water and came toward Jesus.*
³⁰*But when he saw the wind, he was afraid and, beginning to sink, cried out, "Lord, save me!"*
³¹*Immediately Jesus reached out his hand and caught him. "You of little faith," he said, "why did you doubt?"*
³²*And when they climbed into the boat, the wind died down.*
³³*Then those who were in the boat worshiped him, saying, "Truly you are the Son of God." (NIV)*

Realize

1. Some of the disciples were professional fishermen who practically lived on the water. What does their reaction in Mark 4 suggest about the severity of this sudden storm?

_____

_____

_____

2. What was Jesus doing? What does this suggest?

_____

_____

_____

3. What false assumption or accusation did the disciples hurl at Jesus?

_____

_____

_____

4. What did Jesus do?

_____

_____

_____

5. List some adjectives that describe the emotions of the disciples during the storm. How about before the calming of the storm? after this incident?

_____

_____

_____

_____

6. In the other incident, when Peter tried to walk on the water out to Jesus, what happened?

_____

_____

_____

7. When did he begin to sink?

_____

_____

_____

8. What does this suggest about where our focus needs to be in uncertain or scary times?

_____

_____

_____

Respond

9. Why do you think Peter was eager to walk on water (when, apparently, no one else was)?

_____

_____

_____

10. How bold are you? On a scale of 1—10 (with 1 being "terrible" and 10 being "terrific"), how would you rate the health of your trust in God?

_____

_____

_____

11. How quick are you to become despairing when all seems lost? Why?

_____

_____

_____

12. What "storm" in your life needs the Master's touch today?

_____

_____

_____

_____

L E S S O N

12

What Will You Leave at the Cross?

LOOKING BACK

In Lesson 11 we pondered the truth of God's sovereignty (that is, the truth that he controls all things). Practically, we were reminded that God can turn our tragedies in triumphs. Go ahead and say our memory verse, Romans 8:28, from that lesson.

1. Why is God's sovereignty one of the most important concepts a believer can ever grasp?

_____

_____

_____

2. *Max writes:* "The Bible says that 'in everything God works for the good of those who love him' (Rom. 8:28, NCV). Remove the word *everything* and replace it with the symbol of your tragedy. For the Apostle John, the verse would read: 'In burial clothing God works for the good of those who love him.'

   "How would Romans 8:28 read in your life?

   "*In hospital stays* God works for the good.

   "*In divorce papers* God works for the good.

   "*In a prison term* God works for the good.

   "If God can change John's life through a tragedy, could it be he will use a tragedy to change yours?

   "As hard as it may be to believe, you could be only a Saturday away from a resurrection. You could be only hours from that precious prayer of a changed heart, 'God, did you do this for me?'"

   What kind of "resurrection" do you need right now?

_____

_____

_____

3. What Bible passage, principle, or insight from your daily studies of the previous lesson was the most powerful and meaningful to you? Why?

_____

_____

_____

GETTING STARTED

VIDEO—In video segment number 12, Max tells of playing football in fields of burrs. (The script has been reprinted on page 233.)

4. Max mentioned playing football as a kid. What sports or hobbies did you engage in as a youngster? What were the upsides of this experience? What were the downsides?

_____

_____

5. Max tells of his experiences with grass burrs. When you get a thorn, sticker, or splinter, do you try to remove it yourself, do you seek the help of another, or do you ignore it as long as possible? Why?

_____

_____

_____

6. Why are so many people (especially men) reluctant to seek help when hurt or injured?

_____

_____

_____

7. Most Christians follow a fairly predictable routine when they realize they've sinned. What's yours?

_____

_____

_____

_____

Digging In

8. In summarizing the scene of the cross, *Max writes:* "Absurdities and ironies. The hill of Calvary is nothing if not both. We would have scripted the moment differently. Ask us how a God should redeem his world, and we will show you! White horses, flashing swords. Evil on his back. God on his throne. But God on a cross?

"A split-lipped, puffy-eyed, blood-masked God on a cross?"

What absurdities surround the hill of Calvary?

_____

_____

_____

_____

9. What ironies surround the hill of Calvary?

_____

_____

_____

_____

The cross is more than an example. It is more than a system of ethics. It is the mighty act of God's justice and love. God is saying to the whole world, "I love you. I am willing to forgive your sins." God is saying to all of those who are filled with guilt today, "Your sins are forgiven because of the cross." God is saying to all those who are lonely today, "Behold, I am with you until the end of the age" (cf. Matthew 28:20). Every person reading these words is guilty of sin, and there is no way to remove the stain of guilt except by the sacrifice of Christ.
Billy Graham[1]

10. What intrigues you the most, the absurdities or the ironies? Why?

_____

_____

_____

11. *Max writes:* "We wouldn't have written the drama of redemption this way. But, then again, we weren't asked to. These players and props were heaven picked and God ordained. We were not asked to design the hour. But we have been asked to respond to it. In order for the cross of Christ to be the cross of your life, you and I need to bring something to the hill."

How would you have written the drama of redemption, had you been asked to dream up a plan for the redemption of the world?

_____

_____

_____

Going Deeper

Mark 15:22–41

22And they brought Him to the place Golgotha, which is translated, Place of a Skull.

23Then they gave Him wine mingled with myrrh to drink, but He did not take it.

24And when they crucified Him, they divided His garments, casting lots for them to determine what every man should take.

25Now it was the third hour, and they crucified Him.

26And the inscription of His accusation was written above: THE KING OF THE JEWS.

27With Him they also crucified two robbers, one on His right and the other on His left.

28So the Scripture was fulfilled which says, "And He was numbered with the transgressors."

29And those who passed by blasphemed Him, wagging their heads and saying, "Aha! You who destroy the temple and build it in three days,

30save Yourself, and come down from the cross!"

31Likewise the chief priests also, mocking among themselves with the scribes, said, "He saved others; Himself He cannot save.

32Let the Christ, the King of Israel, descend now from the cross, that we may see and believe." Even those who were crucified with Him reviled Him.

33Now when the sixth hour had come, there was darkness over the whole land until the ninth hour.

34And at the ninth hour Jesus cried out with a loud voice, saying, "Eloi, Eloi, lama sabachthani?" which is translated, "My God, My God, why have You forsaken Me?"

35Some of those who stood by, when they heard that, said, "Look, He is calling for Elijah!"

36Then someone ran and filled a sponge full of sour wine, put it on a reed, and offered it to Him to drink, saying, "Let Him alone; let us see if Elijah will come to take Him down."

37And Jesus cried out with a loud voice, and breathed His last.

38Then the veil of the temple was torn in two from top to bottom.

39So when the centurion, who stood opposite Him, saw that He cried out like this and breathed His last, he said, "Truly this Man was the Son of God!"

40There were also women looking on from afar, among whom were Mary Magdalene, Mary the mother of James the Less and of Joses, and Salome,

41who also followed Him and ministered to Him when He was in Galilee, and many other women who came up with Him to Jerusalem. (NKJV)

12. You've been studying in detail the individual components of the crucifixion. How are you affected as you read the entire scene one final time from Mark's concise Gospel?

_____

_____

_____

13. What individuals are recorded by Mark as having been there at the scene of the cross when Jesus breathed his last?

_____

_____

_____

14. Comment on the centurion. What does his comment mean? Do you think he had been involved in the arrest and beating of Jesus? Why or why not?

_____

_____

_____

15. What women were there? What does their presence indicate? Where were the male followers of Jesus?

_____

_____

_____

Mark 15:39

centurion The Roman officer in charge of the crucifixion. Centurions, considered the backbone of the Roman army, commanded 100 soldiers.

saw that he cried out like this The centurion had seen many crucified victims die, but none like Jesus. The strength he possessed at his death, as evidenced by his loud cry (v. 37), was unheard of for a victim of crucifixion. That, coupled with the earthquake that coincided with Christ's death (Matt. 27:51–54) convinced the centurion that Jesus "truly was the Son of God." According to tradition, this man actually became a believer.

(adapted from *The MacArthur Study Bible* [Nashville, TN: Word Publishing, 1997], 1501)

Mark 15:40, 41

The women mentioned in these verses were true disciples of Christ. They had ministered to Jesus' needs and would be the first witnesses of his resurrection. Mark does not name Jesus' mother here but includes other prominent women. Three Marys were present along with many other women, and Salome, whom only Mark mentions by name (see also 16:1). Salome was the wife of Zebedee and the mother of the disciples James and John (Matt. 27:56). She may have been the unnamed sister of Jesus' mother (John 19:25). If so, James and John were Jesus' first cousins.

(adapted from *The Nelson Study Bible* [Nashville, TN: Thomas Nelson Publishers, 1997], 1679)

Seven Words From the Cross—the seven utterances of Jesus from the cross:

1. "Father, forgive them, for they do not know what they do" (Luke 23:34, NKJV). Jesus taught that we should forgive those who sin against us. How appropriate that his first words from the cross should be words of forgiveness.
2. "Assuredly, I say to you, today you will be with Me in Paradise" (Luke 23:43, NKJV). As he hung on the cross, Jesus certainly did not appear to be a king. Yet, what faith the repentant thief displayed when he asked, "Lord, remember me when You come into Your kingdom" (Luke 23:42, NKJV). Jesus' reply was good news indeed to this dying sinner.
3. "Woman, behold your son! . . . Behold your mother!" (John 19:26–27). Despite his grief and pain, Jesus continued to think of others. His earthly father, Joseph, probably had died by this time. Jesus asked his beloved disciple, John, to take care of his mother, Mary.
4. *"Eloi, Eloi, lama sabachthani?"* My God, My God, why have You forsaken Me?" (Matt. 27:46, NKJV; Mark 15:34). These words came from Jesus' lips about 3:00 P.M., after he had hung on the cross for nine hours. Death was near, and Jesus was feeling the pain and loneliness that sin causes. But the sin in this case was our sin and not his. To express his anguish and grief, Jesus quoted the opening words of Psalm 22, using the same words that King David had used a thousand years earlier (Ps. 22:1).
5. "I thirst!" (John 19:28, NKJV). The Old Testament had prophesied that Jesus would suffer for the sins of the world. In his death, that prophecy was being fulfilled. Jesus suffered spiritual torment as well as physical agony as he hung on the cross. His spirit thirsted to win the spiritual battle against evil while his body thirsted for water.
6. "It is finished!" (John 19:30, NKJV). The word translated "finished" shows clearly that Jesus' victory has been achieved. It carries the idea of perfection or fulfillment. God's plan of salvation had been accomplished through Jesus' sacrifice on the cross.
7. "Father, into Your hands I commend My spirit" (Luke 23:46, NKJV; also see Ps. 31:5; Matt. 27:50; Mark 15:37). Jesus did not die a failure. He died a victorious Savior. He finished his work triumphantly and entrusted his spirit to God his Father.

(adapted from Ronald F. Youngblood, Ed., *Nelson's New Illustrated Bible Dictionary* [Nashville, TN: Thomas Nelson Publishers, 1997, c1995], CD-ROM)

---

1 Peter 5:7

Give all your worries to him, because he cares about you. (NCV)

16. What does this verse instruct us to do?

_____

_____

_____

17. How is this to be done, practically speaking?

_____
_____
_____

18. What promise does this verse give us?

_____
_____
_____

19. What do we have to leave at the cross in order to benefit from the promise of this verse?

_____
_____
_____

"Thou shalt not be afraid for the terror by night" (Psalm 91:5, KJV).

What is this terror? It may be the cry of fire, or the noise of thieves, or fancied appearances, or the shriek of sudden sickness or death. We live in the world of death and sorrow, we may therefore look for ills as well in the night-watches as beneath the glare of the broiling sun. Nor should this alarm us, for be the terror what it may, the promise is that the believer shall not be afraid. Why should he? Let us put it more closely, why should we? God our Father is here, and will be here all through the lonely hours; he is an almighty Watcher, a sleepless Guardian, a faithful Friend. Nothing can happen without his direction, for even hell itself is under his control. Darkness is not dark to him. He has promised to be a wall of fire around his people—and who can break through such a barrier? Worldlings may well be afraid, for they have an angry God above them, a guilty conscience within them, and a yawning hell beneath them; but we who rest in Jesus are saved from all these through rich mercy. If we give way to foolish fear we shall dishonor our profession, and lead others to doubt the reality of godliness. We ought to be afraid of being afraid, lest we should vex the Holy Spirit by foolish distrust. Down, then, ye dismal forebodings and groundless apprehensions, God has not forgotten to be gracious, nor shut up his tender mercies; it may be night in the soul, but there need be no terror, for the God of love changes not. Children of light may walk in darkness, but they are not therefore cast away, nay, they are now enabled to prove their adoption by trusting in their heavenly Father as hypocrites cannot do.

"Though the night be dark and dreary,
Darkness cannot hide from thee;
Thou art he, who, never weary,
Watchest where thy people be."

(Charles H. Spurgeon, _Morning and Evening_ [30 Hunt Valley Circle, New Kensington, PA: Whitaker House, © 1997. Used by permission of the publisher.], 229).

---

1 John 1:9
But if we confess our sins to him, he is faithful and just to forgive us and to cleanse us from every wrong. (NLT)

20. What promise is given in this verse?

_____
_____
_____
_____

21. What confession do you need to leave at Calvary?

_____
_____
_____

Amazing Grace

Amazing grace! how sweet the sound,
That saved a wretch like me!
I once was lost, but now am found,
Was blind, but now I see.

'Twas grace that taught my heart to fear,
And grace my fears relieved;
How precious did that grace appear
The hour I first believed!

Thru many dangers, toils, and snares,
I have already come;
'Tis grace hath bro't me safe this far,
And grace will lead me home.

The Lord has promised good to me,
His Word my hope secures;
He will my shield and portion be
As long as life endures.

When we've been there ten thousand years,
Bright shining as the sun,
We've no less days to sing God's praise
Than when we'd first begun.

(John Newton, 1779)

Proverbs 3:5–6

⁵*Trust in the LORD with all your heart, and lean not on your own understanding;*
⁶*In all your ways acknowledge Him, and He shall direct your paths.* (NKJV)

22. What instruction is given in this verse? Or, to use the metaphor Max presents in the chapter, what does this command require us to leave at the cross?

_____

_____

_____

23. What promise is given in this verse?

_____

_____

24. Can you think of a time in your life when you obeyed this verse and experienced its promise? Describe it.

_____

_____

_____

The Christian way is different: harder, and easier. Christ says, "Give me all. I don't want so much of your time and so much of your money and so much of your work: I want you. I have not come to torment your natural self, but to kill it. No half-measures are any good. I don't want to cut off a branch here and a branch there, I want to have the whole tree down. I don't want to drill the tooth, or crown it, or stop it, but to have it out. Hand over the whole natural self, all the desires which you think innocent as well as the ones you think wicked—the whole outfit. I will give you a new self instead. In fact, I will give you myself: my own will shall become yours."

Both harder and easier than what we are all trying to do. You have noticed, I expect, that Christ himself sometimes describes the Christian way as very hard, sometimes as very easy. He says, "Take up your cross"—in other words, it is like going to be beaten to death in a concentration camp. Next minute he says, "My yoke is easy and my burden light." He means both. And one can just see why both are true.
C.S. Lewis²

25. *Max writes:* "We have seen what Jesus brought. With scarred hands he offered forgiveness. Through torn skin he promised acceptance. He took the path to take us home. He wore our garments to give us his own. We have seen the gifts he brought. Now we ask, what will we bring?

"We aren't asked to paint the sign or carry the nails. We aren't asked to wear the spit or bear the crown. But we are asked to walk the path and leave something at the cross. You can observe the cross and analyze the cross. You can read about it, even pray to it. But until you leave something there, you haven't embraced the cross."

How have you responded to Calvary? What have you brought to the hill at Golgotha?

_____

_____

_____

MAKING IT REAL

VIDEO—In video segment number 13, Max tells about the special letter from his father. The script is on page 233.

26. *Max writes:* "Spend a few moments looking again at the pieces of passion. Run your thumb over the tip of the spear. Balance a spike in the palm of your hand. Read the wooden sign written in your own language. And as you do, touch the velvet dirt, moist with the blood of God.

"Blood he bled for you. The spear he took for you. The nails he felt for you. The sign he left for you. He did all of this for you. Knowing this, knowing all he did for you there, don't you think he'll look out for you here?"

How would you answer Max's question?

_____

_____

_____

Romans 8:32
Since God did not spare even his own Son but gave him up for us all, won't God, who gave us Christ, also give us everything else? (NLT)

27. What gifts have you received from God? Describe them.

_____

_____

_____

_____

28. List several "gifts of the cross" and describe how each reveals God's love.

_____

_____

_____

_____

29. What gifts of the cross speak most profoundly to your heart? Why?

_____

_____

_____

_____

THINKING IT THROUGH

Take some time for silent reflection. Consider all that you've read and pondered during these twelve lessons. Thank God for the ultimate act of love that was Calvary. Listen to "These Hands" by Jeff Deyo on the CD, and let it move you first to praise and then to a deeper commitment to trust and obey the Lord.

In video segment Number 14, Max concludes this series. (The script is on page 234.)

TAKING IT HOME

Memory Verse
Romans 8:32
He who did not spare his own Son, but gave him up for us all—how will he not also, along with him, graciously give us all things? (NIV)

He who did not spare His own Son, but delivered Him up for us all, how shall He not with Him also freely give us all things? (NKJV)

Since God did not spare even his own Son but gave him up for us all, won't God, who gave us Christ, also give us everything else? (NLT)

During the next week, study the following passages.

Day 1) *Leaving Your Old Life*

Read
Acts 9:1–31
¹*In Jerusalem Saul was still threatening the followers of the Lord by saying he would kill them. So he went to the high priest*
²*and asked him to write letters to the synagogues in the city of Damascus. Then if Saul found any followers of Christ's Way, men or women, he would arrest them and bring them back to Jerusalem.*
³*So Saul headed toward Damascus. As he came near the city, a bright light from heaven suddenly flashed around him.*
⁴*Saul fell to the ground and heard a voice saying to him, "Saul, Saul! Why are you persecuting me?"*
⁵*Saul said, "Who are you, Lord?"*
The voice answered, "I am Jesus, whom you are persecuting.
⁶*"Get up now and go into the city. Someone there will tell you what you must do."*
⁷*The people traveling with Saul stood there but said nothing. They heard the voice, but they saw no one.*
⁸*Saul got up from the ground and opened his eyes, but he could not see. So those with Saul took his hand and led him into Damascus.*
⁹*For three days Saul could not see and did not eat or drink.*
¹⁰*There was a follower of Jesus in Damascus named Ananias. The Lord spoke to Ananias in a vision, "Ananias!"*
Ananias answered, "Here I am, Lord."
¹¹*The Lord said to him, "Get up and go to Straight Street. Find the house of Judas, and ask for a man named Saul from the city of Tarsus. He is there now, praying.*
¹²*"Saul has seen a vision in which a man named Ananias comes to him and lays his hands on him. Then he is able to see again."*
¹³*But Ananias answered, "Lord, many people have told me about this man and the terrible things he did to your holy people in Jerusalem.*
¹⁴*"Now he has come here to Damascus, and the leading priests have given him the power to arrest everyone who worships you."*
¹⁵*But the Lord said to Ananias, "Go! I have chosen Saul for an important work. He must tell about me to those who are not Jews, to kings, and to the people of Israel.*
¹⁶*"I will show him how much he must suffer for my name."*
¹⁷*So Ananias went to the house of Judas. He laid his hands on Saul and said, "Brother Saul, the Lord Jesus sent me. He is the one you saw on the road on your way here. He sent me so that you can see again and be filled with the Holy Spirit."*
¹⁸*Immediately, something that looked like fish scales fell from Saul's eyes, and he was able to see again! Then Saul got up and was baptized.*
¹⁹*After he ate some food, his strength returned.*

Saul stayed with the followers of Jesus in Damascus for a few days.
²⁰*Soon he began to preach about Jesus in the synagogues, saying, "Jesus is the Son of God."*
²¹*All the people who heard him were amazed. They said, "This is the man who was in Jerusalem trying to destroy those who trust in this name! He came here to arrest the followers of Jesus and take them back to the leading priests."*
²²*But Saul grew more powerful. His proofs that Jesus is the Christ were so strong that the Jewish people in Damascus could not argue with him.*
²³*After many days, some Jewish people made plans to kill Saul.*
²⁴*They were watching the city gates day and night, but Saul learned about their plan.*
²⁵*One night some followers of Saul helped him leave the city by lowering him in a basket through an opening in the city wall.*
²⁶*When Saul went to Jerusalem, he tried to join the group of followers, but they were all afraid of him. They did not believe he was really a follower.*
²⁷*But Barnabas accepted Saul and took him to the apostles. Barnabas explained to them that Saul had seen the Lord on the road and the Lord had spoken to Saul. Then he told them how boldly Saul had preached in the name of Jesus in Damascus.*
²⁸*And so Saul stayed with the followers, going everywhere in Jerusalem, preaching boldly in the name of the Lord.*
²⁹*He would often talk and argue with the Jewish people who spoke Greek, but they were trying to kill him.*
³⁰*When the followers learned about this, they took Saul to Caesarea and from there sent him to Tarsus.*
³¹*The church everywhere in Judea, Galilee, and Samaria had a time of peace and became stronger. Respecting the Lord by the way they lived, and being encouraged by the Holy Spirit, the group of believers continued to grow. (NCV)*

Realize

1. What do verses 1 and 2 suggest about Saul's (that is, Paul's) values, passions, motives, and goals?

_____

_____

_____

2. Who did Saul meet unexpectedly on the road to Damascus?

_____

_____

_____

3. What happened to Saul over the next three days?

_____

_____

_____

4. What role did Ananias play in Saul's spiritual journey?

_____

_____

_____

5. Why did the church respond to Saul the way they did?

_____

_____

_____

6. How did this experience change Saul's life?

_____

_____

_____

7. What did Saul leave on the Damascus road?

_____

_____

Respond

8. When did you meet Christ?

_____

_____

9. In what ways has your life changed since then?

_____

_____

_____

10. What from this passage prompts you to live differently today?

_____

_____

_____

Day 2) *Genuine Faith*

Read

1 Thessalonians 1:1–10

¹Paul, Silvanus, and Timothy, to the church of the Thessalonians in God the Father and the Lord Jesus Christ: Grace to you and peace from God our Father and the Lord Jesus Christ.
²We give thanks to God always for you all, making mention of you in our prayers,
³remembering without ceasing your work of faith, labor of love, and patience of hope in our Lord Jesus Christ in the sight of our God and Father,
⁴knowing, beloved brethren, your election by God.
⁵For our gospel did not come to you in word only, but also in power, and in the Holy Spirit and in much assurance, as you know what kind of men we were among you for your sake.
⁶And you became followers of us and of the Lord, having received the word in much affliction, with joy of the Holy Spirit,
⁷so that you became examples to all in Macedonia and Achaia who believe.
⁸For from you the word of the Lord has sounded forth, not only in Macedonia and Achaia, but also in every place. Your faith toward God has gone out, so that we do not need to say anything.
⁹For they themselves declare concerning us what manner of entry we had to you, and how you turned to God from idols to serve the living and true God,
¹⁰and to wait for His Son from heaven, whom He raised from the dead, even Jesus who delivers us from the wrath to come. (NKJV)

Realize

1. What did Paul remember about his experience with the believers in Thessalonica?

_____

_____

_____

2. What evidence does Paul provide to indicate the genuine nature of the Thessalonian believers' faith?

_____

_____

3. What is significant about Paul's use of words like "work" of faith and "labor" of love (verse 3)?

_____

_____

_____

4. Describe the Thessalonians' lifestyle before turning to Christ.

_____

_____

_____

5. Were the Thessalonians vocal about their faith? How do you know?

_____

_____

_____

6. What makes you think the Thessalonians' allegiance to Christ cost them dearly?

_____

_____

_____

Respond

7. A person in your church earnestly claims to have "done business with Jesus at the cross." But for literally years you see no evidence of change, either in attitudes or actions. What can you conclude?

_____

_____

_____

8. If Paul were to write an epistle to you, what we he say about your growth in faith?

_____

_____

_____

9. How could accountability help stimulate you to a deeper, more consistent walk with God?

_____

_____

_____

_____

To many Christians Christ is little more than an idea, or at best an ideal; he is not a fact. Millions of professed believers talk as if he were real and act as if he were not. And always our actual position is to be discovered by the way we act, not by the way we talk.

We can prove our faith by our committal to it, and in no other way. Any belief that does not command the one who holds it is not real belief; it is a pseudo belief only. And it might shock some of us profoundly if we were brought suddenly face to face with our beliefs and forced to test them in the fires of practical living.

Many of us Christians have become extremely skillful in arranging our lives so as to admit the truth of Christianity without being embarrassed by its implications. We arrange things so that we can get on well enough without divine aid, while at the same time ostensibly seeking it. We boast in the Lord but watch carefully that we never get caught depending on him.

It would be a tragedy indeed to come to the place where we have no other but God and find that we had not really been trusting God during the days of our earthly sojourn. It would be better to invite God now to remove every false trust, to disengage our hearts from all secret hiding places and to bring us out into the open where we can discover for ourselves whether or not we actually trust him. That is a harsh cure for our troubles, but it is a sure one. Gentler cures may be too weak to do the work. And time is running out on us.
A.W. Tozer[3]

Day 3) *Living By Faith*

Read
Hebrews 11:1–40
¹Now faith is being sure of what we hope for and certain of what we do not see.
²This is what the ancients were commended for.
³By faith we understand that the universe was formed at God's command, so that what is seen was not made out of what was visible.
⁴By faith Abel offered God a better sacrifice than Cain did. By faith he was commended as a

210

righteous man, when God spoke well of his offerings. And by faith he still speaks, even though he is dead.

⁵By faith Enoch was taken from this life, so that he did not experience death; he could not be found, because God had taken him away. For before he was taken, he was commended as one who pleased God.

⁶And without faith it is impossible to please God, because anyone who comes to him must believe that he exists and that he rewards those who earnestly seek him.

⁷By faith Noah, when warned about things not yet seen, in holy fear built an ark to save his family. By his faith he condemned the world and became heir of the righteousness that comes by faith.

⁸By faith Abraham, when called to go to a place he would later receive as his inheritance, obeyed and went, even though he did not know where he was going.

⁹By faith he made his home in the promised land like a stranger in a foreign country; he lived in tents, as did Isaac and Jacob, who were heirs with him of the same promise.

¹⁰For he was looking forward to the city with foundations, whose architect and builder is God.

¹¹By faith Abraham, even though he was past age—and Sarah herself was barren—was enabled to become a father because he considered him faithful who had made the promise.

¹²And so from this one man, and he as good as dead, came descendants as numerous as the stars in the sky and as countless as the sand on the seashore.

¹³All these people were still living by faith when they died. They did not receive the things promised; they only saw them and welcomed them from a distance. And they admitted that they were aliens and strangers on earth.

¹⁴People who say such things show that they are looking for a country of their own.

¹⁵If they had been thinking of the country they had left, they would have had opportunity to return.

¹⁶Instead, they were longing for a better country—a heavenly one. Therefore God is not ashamed to be called their God, for he has prepared a city for them.

¹⁷By faith Abraham, when God tested him, offered Isaac as a sacrifice. He who had received the promises was about to sacrifice his one and only son,

¹⁸even though God had said to him, "It is through Isaac that your offspring will be reckoned."

¹⁹Abraham reasoned that God could raise the dead, and figuratively speaking, he did receive Isaac back from death.

²⁰By faith Isaac blessed Jacob and Esau in regard to their future.

²¹By faith Jacob, when he was dying, blessed each of Joseph's sons, and worshiped as he leaned on the top of his staff.

²²By faith Joseph, when his end was near, spoke about the exodus of the Israelites from Egypt and gave instructions about his bones.

²³By faith Moses' parents hid him for three months after he was born, because they saw he was no ordinary child, and they were not afraid of the king's edict.

²⁴By faith Moses, when he had grown up, refused to be known as the son of Pharaoh's daughter.

²⁵He chose to be mistreated along with the people of God rather than to enjoy the pleasures of sin for a short time.

²⁶He regarded disgrace for the sake of Christ as of greater value than the treasures of Egypt, because he was looking ahead to his reward.

²⁷By faith he left Egypt, not fearing the king's anger; he persevered because he saw him who is invisible.

²⁸By faith he kept the Passover and the sprinkling of blood, so that the destroyer of the firstborn would not touch the firstborn of Israel.

²⁹By faith the people passed through the Red Sea as on dry land; but when the Egyptians tried to do so, they were drowned.

³⁰By faith the walls of Jericho fell, after the people had marched around them for seven days.

³¹By faith the prostitute Rahab, because she welcomed the spies, was not killed with those who were disobedient.

³²And what more shall I say? I do not have time to tell about Gideon, Barak, Samson, Jephthah, David, Samuel and the prophets,

³³who through faith conquered kingdoms, administered justice, and gained what was promised; who shut the mouths of lions,

³⁴quenched the fury of the flames, and escaped the edge of the sword; whose weakness was

turned to strength; and who became powerful in battle and routed foreign armies.
35Women received back their dead, raised to life again. Others were tortured and refused to be released, so that they might gain a better resurrection.
36Some faced jeers and flogging, while still others were chained and put in prison.
37They were stoned; they were sawed in two; they were put to death by the sword. They went about in sheepskins and goatskins, destitute, persecuted and mistreated—
38the world was not worthy of them. They wandered in deserts and mountains, and in caves and holes in the ground.
39These were all commended for their faith, yet none of them received what had been prom-ised.
40God had planned something better for us so that only together with us would they be made perfect. (NIV)

FAITH

It's called God's Hall of Fame . . . or Hall of Faith. And it's certainly one of the more beloved passages in all the Bible. But what does Hebrews 11 really mean, and what is it saying to us?

The Jewish Christians to whom the epistle of Hebrews is addressed were a demoralized, discouraged bunch. Christianity had proven difficult. It was radical. It set aside centuries of tradition. It emphasized a vague, troubling kind of spiritual freedom. In short, it incurred the wrath of the religious establish-ment.

So many converts were ready to revert. To leave the uneasy, uncharted waters of faith for the com-fortable, familiar life of works and moral effort. That was the choice they faced: keeping the Law or fol-lowing Jesus, trying to please God or trusting in him, a complicated religious system or a simple rela-tionship with the living God through Christ.

After reminding these immature believers of the superiority of Jesus Christ, the writer, beginning in 10:19, begins demonstrating for them the superiority of faith. The word used is the Greek word *pistis*. It has the idea of belief, confidence, assurance, or trust. Faith means we can't see the outcome, we're not sure what lies ahead (11:1). But we are convinced of the reality of God (11:6). As the well-known phrase goes, "I don't know what the future holds, but I know who holds the future." Further faith also means clinging to the hope that God will eventually reward those who seek him (11:6). So we obey. We do his bidding, even when it seems crazy, even when submission is excruciating.

Interestingly, it seems to be that response—obedience—that qualifies the characters in chapter 11 as being people of great faith. They believed God; consequently they obeyed him, regardless of the con-sequences and with no thought to the cost. This kind of willing trust pleases God (11:6). Anything less will not do.

In short, the writer seems to be saying to the readers: "Those with no faith look only with their physi-cal eyes, only at their temporal circumstances. Consequently they can never know God or please him. Those, however, who open their spiritual eyes, and see all the realities beyond this world find the strength to endure and one day will receive great eternal reward."

When it comes to faith, the world scoffs. It seems like so much wishful thinking. It seems, at best, a great waste; at worst, suicidal. Do we really want to give up all that is tangible and tempting, for some-thing illusive and ethereal?

Faith is never easy. The expression "simple faith" is a contradiction in terms. But the more convinced we are of the reality of an all-good, all-powerful God, the more our trust will grow, and the less "driv-en and tossed" (James 1:6) we will be by doubts and temptations to go back.

(adapted from *The Prophecy Study Bible* [Nashville, TN: Thomas Nelson Publishers, 1997], CD-ROM)

Realize

1. How does the writer of Hebrews define and describe faith?

_____

_____

_____

2. According to this chapter, how necessary is faith?

_____

_____

_____

3. What are your overall impressions as you read this great litany of faith-full saints?

_____

_____

_____

4. Who is your favorite character from Hebrews 11? Why?

_____

_____

5. In 2 Corinthians 5:7, Paul writes: "We live by faith, not by sight" (NIV). What's the difference?

_____

_____

_____

We have to think of what a place we live in. The world is a howling wilderness to many of God's people. Some of us are greatly indulged in the providence of God, but others have a stern fight of it. We begin our day with prayer, and we very often hear the voice of holy song in our houses. But many good people have scarcely risen from their knees in the morning before they are saluted with blasphemy. They go out to work and all day long are vexed with filthy conversation like righteous Lot in Sodom. Can you even walk the open streets without your ears being afflicted with foul language? The world is no friend to grace. The best we can do with this world is to get through it with Jesus as close to us as possible. We live in an enemy's country. A robber lurks in every bush. Everywhere we need to travel with a "drawn sword" in our hand, or at least with that weapon which is called "all-prayer" at our side. We have to fight for every inch of our way. Make no mistake about this, or you will be rudely shaken out of your fond delusion. O God, help us and confirm us to the end, or where will we be?

True Christianity is supernatural at its beginning, supernatural in its continuance, and supernatural in its close. It is the work of God from first to last. There is great need that the hand of the Lord should be stretched out still. That need you are feeling now and I am glad that you should feel it. Now you will look for your own preservation to the Lord who alone is able to keep us from falling and glorify us with his Son.

(Charles H. Spurgeon, *All of Grace* [30 Hunt Valley Circle, New Kensington, PA: Whitaker House, © 1981. Used by permission of the publisher.], 119–120)

Respond

6. In what specific situations do you typically feel your faith waver? Why?

_____

_____

_____

7. How can the examples of the saints in Hebrews 11 spur you on to trust God more fully?

_____

_____

_____

8. A familiar New Testament verse says faith comes by hearing, and hearing by the Word of God (Romans 10:17). How can the Word of Christ build your faith this week?

_____

_____

FAITH—a belief in or confident attitude toward God, involving commitment to his will for one's life

According to Hebrews 11, faith was already present in the experience of many people in the Old Testament as a key element of their spiritual lives. In this chapter, the various heroes of the Old Testament (Abel, Enoch, Noah, Abraham, Sarah, Isaac, Jacob, Joseph, and Moses) are described as living by faith. In addition, the Old Testament itself makes the same point. Abraham "believed in the Lord" (Gen. 15:6, NKJV); the Israelites "believed" (Exod. 4:31, NKJV; 14:31); and the prophet Habakkuk taught that "the just shall live by his faith" (Hab. 2:4, NKJV).

In the New Testament, "faith" covers various levels of personal commitment. Mere intellectual agreement to a truth is illustrated in James 2:19, where even demons are said to believe that there is one God. Obviously, however, they are not saved by this type of belief. Genuine saving faith is a personal attachment to Christ, best thought of as a combination of two ideas—reliance on Christ and commitment to him. Saving faith involves personally depending on the finished work of Christ's sacrifice as the only basis for forgiveness of sin and entrance into heaven. But saving faith is also a personal commitment of one's life to following Christ in obedience to his commands: "I know whom I have believed and am persuaded that He is able to keep what I have committed to Him until that Day" (2 Tim. 1:12, NKJV).

Faith is part of the Christian life from beginning to end. As the instrument by which the gift of salvation is received (Eph. 2:8–9), faith is thus distinct from the basis of salvation, which is grace, and from the outworking of salvation, which is good works. The apostle Paul declared that salvation is through faith, not through keeping the law (Gal. 2:16).

Finally, in the New Testament, faith can refer to the teachings of the Bible, the faith that was once for all delivered to the saints (Jude 3). In modern times, faith has been weakened in meaning so that some people use it to mean self-confidence. But in the Bible, true faith is confidence in God or Christ, not in oneself.

(adapted from Ronald F. Youngblood, Ed.; *Nelson's New Illustrated Bible Dictionary,* [Nashville, TN: Thomas Nelson Publishers, 1997, c1995], CD-ROM)

Day 4) *A Certain Future*

Read
John 14:1–3
(Jesus is speaking) ¹*"Do not let your hearts be troubled. Trust in God; trust also in me.*
²*In my Father's house are many rooms; if it were not so, I would have told you. I am going there to prepare a place for you.*
³*And if I go and prepare a place for you, I will come back and take you to be with me that you also may be where I am. (NIV)*

Luke 10:20
(Jesus is speaking) "But you should not be happy because the spirits obey you but because your names are written in heaven." (NCV)

2 Corinthians 5:1
For we know that when this earthly tent we live in is taken down—when we die and leave these bodies—we will have a home in heaven, an eternal body made for us by God himself and not by human hands. (NLT)

Revelation 21:1–10, 22–27; 22:1–5
¹*And I saw a new heaven and a new earth; for the first heaven and the first earth passed away, and there is no longer any sea.*
²*And I saw the holy city, new Jerusalem, coming down out of heaven from God, made ready as a bride adorned for her husband.*
³*And I heard a loud voice from the throne, saying, "Behold, the tabernacle of God is among men, and He shall dwell among them, and they shall be His people, and God Himself shall be among them,*

⁴and He shall wipe away every tear from their eyes; and there shall no longer be any death; there shall no longer be any mourning, or crying, or pain; the first things have passed away."

⁵And He who sits on the throne said, "Behold, I am making all things new." "And He said, "Write, for these words are faithful and true."

⁶And He said to me, "It is done. I am the Alpha and the Omega, the beginning and the end. I will give to the one who thirsts from the spring of the water of life without cost.

⁷"He who overcomes shall inherit these things, and I will be his God and he will be My son.

⁸"But for the cowardly and unbelieving and abominable and murderers and immoral persons and sorcerers and idolaters and all liars, their part will be in the lake that burns with fire and brimstone, which is the second death."

⁹And one of the seven angels who had the seven bowls full of the seven last plagues, came and spoke with me, saying, "Come here, I shall show you the bride, the wife of the Lamb."

¹⁰And he carried me away in the Spirit to a great and high mountain, and showed me the holy city, Jerusalem, coming down out of heaven from God,

²²And I saw no temple in it, for the Lord God, the Almighty, and the Lamb, are its temple.

²³And the city has no need of the sun or of the moon to shine upon it, for the glory of God has illumined it, and its lamp is the Lamb.

²⁴And the nations shall walk by its light, and the kings of the earth shall bring their glory into it.

²⁵And in the daytime (for there shall be no night there) its gates shall never be closed;

²⁶and they shall bring the glory and the honor of the nations into it;

²⁷and nothing unclean and no one who practices abomination and lying, shall ever come into it, but only those whose names are written in the Lamb's book of life.

²²:¹And he showed me a river of the water of life, clear as crystal, coming from the throne of God and of the Lamb,

²in the middle of its street. And on either side of the river was the tree of life, bearing twelve kinds of fruit, yielding its fruit every month; and the leaves of the tree were for the healing of the nations.

³And there shall no longer be any curse; and the throne of God and of the Lamb shall be in it, and His bond-servants shall serve Him;

⁴and they shall see His face, and His name shall be on their foreheads.

⁵And there shall no longer be any night; and they shall not have need of the light of a lamp nor the light of the sun, because the Lord God shall illumine them; and they shall reign forever and ever. (NASB)

Realize

1. In John 14, what did Jesus promise his disciples?

_____

_____

_____

2. In Luke 10, what did Jesus say is the ultimate reason for rejoicing?

_____

_____

_____

3. According to Paul in his letter to the Corinthians, what will happen when we die?

_____

_____

_____

_____

4. What kind of place did John's vision of heaven in Revelation reveal?

_____

_____

5. List at least five ways heaven will be different from earth.

_____

_____

_____

Respond

6. Contrast the ugliness and obscenity of Calvary with the grandeur of heaven. What words come to mind?

_____

_____

_____

7. What promise of heaven is most encouraging to you?

_____

_____

_____

8. How can the promise of heaven one day make a difference in your life today?

_____

_____

_____

HEAVEN—a word that expresses several distinct concepts in the Bible

1. As used in a physical sense, heaven is the expanse over the earth (Gen. 1:8). The tower of Babel reached upward to heaven (Gen. 11:4). God is the possessor of heaven (Gen. 14:19). Heaven is the location of the stars (Gen. 1:14; 26:4) as well as the source of dew (Gen. 27:28).
2. Heaven is also the dwelling place of God (Gen. 28:17; Rev. 12:7–8). It is the source of the new Jerusalem (Rev. 21:2, 10). Because of the work of Christ on the cross, heaven is, in part, present with believers on earth as they obey God's commands (John 14:2, 23).
3. The word "heaven" is also used as a substitute for the name of God (Luke 15:18, 21; John 3:27). The kingdom of God and the kingdom of heaven are often spoken of interchangeably (Matt. 4:17; Mark 1:15).

(adapted from Ronald F. Youngblood, Ed., _Nelson's New Illustrated Bible Dictionary_ [Nashville, TN: Thomas Nelson Publishers, 1997, c1995], CD-ROM)

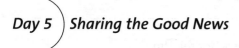

Day 5   _Sharing the Good News_

Read
Matthew 28:16–20
¹⁶Then the eleven disciples went away into Galilee, to the mountain which Jesus had appointed for them.
¹⁷When they saw Him, they worshiped Him; but some doubted.
¹⁸And Jesus came and spoke to them, saying, "All authority has been given to Me in heaven and on earth.
¹⁹Go therefore and make disciples of all the nations, baptizing them in the name of the Father and of the Son and of the Holy Spirit,
²⁰teaching them to observe all things that I have commanded you; and lo, I am with you always, even to the end of the age." Amen. (NKJV)

Acts 1:1–11
¹In my former book, Theophilus, I wrote about all that Jesus began to do and to teach

2until the day he was taken up to heaven, after giving instructions through the Holy Spirit to the apostles he had chosen.

3After his suffering, he showed himself to these men and gave many convincing proofs that he was alive. He appeared to them over a period of forty days and spoke about the kingdom of God.

4On one occasion, while he was eating with them, he gave them this command: "Do not leave Jerusalem, but wait for the gift my Father promised, which you have heard me speak about.

5For John baptized with water, but in a few days you will be baptized with the Holy Spirit."

6So when they met together, they asked him, "Lord, are you at this time going to restore the kingdom to Israel?"

7He said to them: "It is not for you to know the times or dates the Father has set by his own authority.

8But you will receive power when the Holy Spirit comes on you; and you will be my witnesses in Jerusalem, and in all Judea and Samaria, and to the ends of the earth."

9After he said this, he was taken up before their very eyes, and a cloud hid him from their sight.

10They were looking intently up into the sky as he was going, when suddenly two men dressed in white stood beside them.

11"Men of Galilee," they said, "why do you stand here looking into the sky? This same Jesus, who has been taken from you into heaven, will come back in the same way you have seen him go into heaven." (NIV)

Realize

1. What were the disciples thinking when they met the resurrected Christ on the designated mountain?

_____

_____

_____

_____

2. What was Jesus' command to his eleven followers (verses 19–20)?

_____

_____

_____

3. What assurances did Jesus give his disciples?

_____

_____

_____

4. According to Acts 1, what would the promised Holy Spirit give the disciples?

_____

_____

_____

_____

5. What was to be the extent of the disciples' witness?

_____

_____

_____

_____

6. Why did the angels essentially tell the gawking disciples to "get to work"?

_____

_____

_____

The Blessings and Responsibilities of Believers

Paul's letter to the Ephesian church divides neatly into two sections. The first describes the spiritual blessings all believers possess; the second outlines what God expects of believers, in light of all he has done for them.

The Blessings We Enjoy

Chosen by God 1:4
Adoption into God's family 1:5; 2:19
Acceptance before God 1:6
Redemption/forgiveness of sins 1:7
Insight into God's will 1:9
An eternal inheritance 1:11
The seal of the Holy Spirit 1:13; 2:18
Wisdom & knowledge 1:17
Divine power 1:19–20; 3:16, 20
Spiritual life 2:1, 5
God's mercy and love 2:4; 3:17–19
The promise of eternal kindness 2:7
The knowledge that God has a plan of
   "good works" for our lives 2:10
Unity and peace with all the saints of God
   from all ages 2:11–18; 3:6
Heavenly citizenship 2:19
Access to God through Christ 3:12
The opportunity to be "filled with
   all the fullness of God" 3:19
Participation with the church in bringing
   glory to God 3:21

The Responsibilities We Have

To keep the unity of the Spirit 4:3–6
To use our gifts and abilities and share in the
   ministry with other believers 4:7–13
To keep growing and maturing 4:14–15
To put away old, sinful ways of living and
   relating 4:17–24; 5:2–14
To speak honestly and purely 4:25, 29
   (signifying security and ownership)
To do the things the Spirit leads us to do 4:30
To imitate God 5:1
To walk in love 5:2
To find out what is acceptable to the Lord 5:10
To make the most of our time 5:16
To be filled with the Spirit 5:18
To submit to one another 5:21
To have God-honoring marriages 5:22–33
To honor God in our families 6:1–4
To demonstrate integrity and fairness in the
   workplace 6:5–9
To stand strong (in God's strength) against
   the forces of evil 6:10–18

(adapted from *The Nelson Study Bible* [Nashville, TN: Thomas Nelson Publishers, 1997], 1991)

Respond

7. Are you involved in making disciples? If not, why not?

_____

_____

_____

8. Which of your neighbors do not know Christ? What can you do to bring them to the cross?

_____

_____

_____

9. When did you experience the power of the Holy Spirit in witnessing to others? What happened?

_____

_____

_____

10. Most churches reach out to their "Jerusalem, Judea, and Samaria" (that is, locally, and perhaps even cross-culturally), but many stop short of taking the gospel to the ends of the earth. What about yours?

_____

_____

11. Rank the following 1–10 (1 being the most likely and 10 the least likely) in terms of which you would be most likely to do:
   ___ pray faithfully for an unreached people group

___ financially support a missionary
___ go on a short-term mission trip
___ serve on your church's missions committee
___ open your home to a missionary on furlough
___ read a missions biography
___ pray about going overseas long-term
___ help plan and pull off a missions conference
___ subscribe to (and read) a missions magazine
___ read the book of Acts in one sitting

Alas! And Did My Savior Bleed?

Alas and did my Savior bleed
And did my Sov'reign die?
Would he devote that sacred head
for sinners such as I?

Was it for crimes that I had done
He groaned upon the tree?
Amazing pity, grace unknown,
And love beyond degree!

Well might the sun in darkness hide,
And shut His glories in,
When Christ the mighty Maker died
For man, the creature's sin.

But drops of grief can ne'er repay
The debt of love I owe;
Here, Lord, I give myself away,
'Tis all that I can do.

(Isaac Watts, 1707)

VIDEO SCRIPTS

VIDEO SEGMENT NUMBER 1

He deserves our compassion. When you see him, do not laugh. Do not turn away or shake your head. Just gently lead him to the nearest bench and help him sit down.

Have pity on the man. He is so fearful, so wide-eyed. He's like a beached whale, wondering how he got here, and how he'll get out.

Who is this forlorn creature? Well, he's the man in the women's department. Looking for a gift.

The occasion may be her birthday or their anniversary or Christmas. Whatever the reason, he has left behind his familiar habitat of sporting goods stores, food courts and the big-screen television in the appliance department, to venture into the unknown world of women's wear. You'll spot him easily. He's the motionless one in the aisle.

He is a man in a woman's world, and he's never seen so much underwear. At the Wal-Mart where he buys his, it's all wrapped up and fits on one shelf. But here he is in a forest of lace.

He moves on, but he doesn't know where to go. You see, not every man has been prepared for this moment like I was. My father saw the challenge of shopping for women as a rite of passage, right in there with birds and bees and tying neckties. He taught my brother and me how to survive when we shopped. I can remember the day when he sat us down and taught us two words: the language of the ladies department.

"There will come a time," he said solemnly, "when a salesperson will offer to help you and At that moment, take a deep breath and say this phrase, Es-tee Lau-der." On gift-giving occasions for years after, my mom received three gifts from the three men in her life: Estee Lauder, Estee Lauder and Estee Lauder.

My fear of the women's department was gone. But then I met Denalyn. Denalyn doesn't like Estee Lauder. Though I told her it made her smell motherly, she didn't change her mind. I've been in a bind ever since.

This year I opted to buy her a purse. Thought it would be easy. What could be complicated about selecting a tool for holding cards and money? I've used the same money clip for eight years. What would be difficult about buying a purse?

Oh, naïve soul that I am. Tell an attendant in the men's department that you want a wallet, and your only decision is black or brown. Tell an attendant in the ladies department that you want a purse, and you are escorted to a room. A room of shelves. Shelves with purses. Purses with price tags. Small but potent price tags . . . prices so potent that they should remove the need for a purse, right?

I was pondering this thought when the salesperson asked me some questions. "What kind of purse would your wife like?" Well, my blank look told her I was clueless, so she began listing the options: "Handbag? Shoulderbag? Glove bag? Back pack? Shoulder pack? Change purse?"

Well, dizzied by the number of choices, I had to sit down and put my head between my knees lest I faint. Didn't stop her. Leaning over me, she continued, "Money bag? Pocketbook? Satchel?"

"Satchel?" I perked up at the sound of a familiar word. Satchel Paige pitched in the major leagues. This must be the answer. I straightened my shoulders and said proudly "Satchel."

Well apparently she didn't like my answer. She began to curse at me in a foreign language. Forgive me for relating her vulgarity, but she was very crude. I didn't understand all she said, but I do know she called me a "Dooney-Bird" and threatened to "brighten" me with a spade that belonged to someone named Kate. When she laid claim to "our-mawny," I put my hand over the wallet in my hip pocket and said, "No, it's my money." And that was enough. I got out of there as fast as I could. But as I left the room, I gave her a bit of her own medicine, "Estee Lauder!" I shouted and ran as fast as I could.

Oh, the things we do to give gifts to those we love.

But we don't mind, do we? We would do it all again. Fact is, we do it all again. Every Christmas, every birthday, every so often we find ourselves in foreign territory. Grown-ups are in toy stores. Dads are in teen stores. Wives are in the hunting department, and husbands are in the purse department.

We are at our best when we are giving. In fact, we are most like God when we are giving. If we give gifts to show our love, how much more does he? If we, speckled with foibles and greed, love to give gifts, how much more does God, pure and perfect God, enjoy giving gifts to us?

You see, every gift reveals God's love . . . but no gift reveals his love more than the gifts of the cross. They came, not wrapped in paper, but in passion. Not placed around a tree, but a cross, not covered with ribbons, but sprinkled with blood.

The gifts of the cross. Have you considered them, the many gifts of the cross? The gifts of the nails, the crown of thorns, the garment taken, the garments given. Have you taken time to open these gifts?

He didn't have to give them, you know. The only *required* act for our salvation was the shedding of blood; yet he did so much more.

He gave gifts. Divine gifts intended to stir that moment, that split second where your face will brighten, your eyes will widen, and God will hear you whisper: "You did this for me?"

The diadem of pain
Which sliced your gentle face,
Three spikes piercing flesh and wood
To hold you in your place.

The need for blood, I understand.
Your sacrifice, I embrace.
But the bitter sponge, the cutting spear
The spit upon your face?

Did it have to be a cross?
Did not a kinder death exist
Than six hours hanging between life and death,
All spurred by a betrayer's kiss.

"Oh, Father," you pose,
heart-stilled at what could be,
"I'm sorry to ask, but I long to know,
did you do this for me?"

Dare we pray such a prayer? Dare we think such thoughts? Could it be that the hill of the cross is rich with God's gifts? Let's examine them, shall we? Let's unwrap these gifts of grace as if—or perhaps, indeed—for the very first time. And as you touch them—as you feel the timber of the cross, and trace the braid of the crown and finger the point of the spike—pause and listen. Perchance you will hear him whisper:

"I did it just for you."

VIDEO SEGMENT NUMBER 2

Before the shadow of sin fell across the garden of Adam, before the shadow of sin fell across the heart of Adam, humanity was beautiful and the world a pleasant place. But since sin entered the garden, we've been different. Beastly. Ugly. Defiant. Angry. We do things we know we shouldn't do, and we wonder why we did them.

The ugly part of me sure showed his beastly face the other night. I was driving on a two-lane road that was about to become a single lane. A woman in a car beside me was in the lane that continued. I was in the one that stopped. I needed to be ahead of her. My schedule was, no doubt, more important than hers. After all, am I not a man of the cloth? Am I not a courier of compassion? An ambassador of peace?

So I floored it.

Guess what? So did she. When my lane ended, she was a fender ahead of me. I growled and slowed and let her go ahead. Over her shoulder she gave me a sweet little bye-bye wave. Grrrr.

I started to dim my lights, but then I paused. The sinister part of me said, "Wait a minute." So I did. Am

222

I not called to shed light on dark places? Illuminate the shadows?

So I put a little high beam in her rearview mirror.

She retaliated by slowing down. To a crawl. This woman was mean. She wouldn't go more than fifteen miles per hour. And I wasn't going to take my lights out of her rearview mirror. Like two stubborn donkeys, she kept it slow and I kept it bright. Well, after more unkind thoughts than I dare confess, I started to pass her when the road returned to two lanes. Wouldn't you know it? A red light left the two of us side by side at an intersection. What happened next contains both good news and bad. The good news is, she waved at me. The bad news is, the wave was not one you'd want to imitate.

Moments later, conviction surfaced. "Why did I do that?" I'm typically a calm guy, but for fifteen minutes I was a beast! Only two facts comforted me: one, I don't have a fish symbol on my car, and two, the apostle Paul had similar struggles. "I do not do the good things I want to do, but I do the bad things I do not want to do" (Romans 7:15). Each of us could echo Paul's words, couldn't we?

Ever done some things that you knew were wrong? Ever promised yourself you'd never repeat the same sinful actions? Ever failed to live up to your promise? Ever gossiped, slandered? Ever raised your hand in anger or rolled your eyes in arrogance? Ever made someone feel bad so you would feel good?

What makes us act like this? What gets into us? Well, the answer, in a word, is sin. There is, within each one of us, a tendency to do bad. That's the bad news. The good news is, God knows. He knew you'd try to do better. He knew you would fail. He knew about sin. And that's what his plan was all about. And what an incredible plan it was. For when Jesus went to the cross, he who was sinless took on the face of a sinner, so that we sinners could take on the face of a saint. Remember that the next time you're trying to beat someone to the fast lane.

VIDEO SEGMENT NUMBER 3

We just moved into a new house and we're real happy here. But like most new houses a few mistakes were made during the construction, and so I'm making a list of mistakes. The builder never should have asked me to do so. In fact, I kind of dread showing it to him. He's a skilled builder and a fine friend. And we really like the house. But, still, there are a few mistakes.

Until this week I didn't see them. But, then again, until this week I didn't live in the house. Once you take up residence in a place, you see every flaw.

So I did what the builder said: I started a list. A bedroom door won't lock. The storage room window is cracked. Someone forgot to install towel racks in the girls' bathroom. Someone else forgot the knobs to the den door, and, well, the list is growing.

The list of the builder's mistakes then caused me to think about God making a list of mine. After all, hasn't he taken up residence in my heart? And if I see flaws in my house, imagine what God sees in *me*. Oh, dare we think of the list he could compile—the list of our weaknesses. Would you like anyone to see yours? Would you like your mistakes to be made public? How would you feel if they were posted high so that everyone, including Christ himself, could see?

You know, there was a moment when they were. There was a moment when that list was very evident to the Savior. Picture the scene of Calvary and watch as the soldiers shove the Carpenter to the ground and stretch his arms against the beams. One presses a knee against a forearm and a spike against a hand. Jesus turns his face toward the nail just as the soldier lifts the hammer to strike it.

Couldn't Jesus have stopped him? With a flex of the biceps, with a clench of the fist, he could have resisted. Is this not the same hand that stilled the sea and cleansed the temple? Summoned the dead?

But the fist doesn't clench. . .and the moment isn't aborted.

The mallet rings and the skin rips and the blood begins to drip and then rush. And then the questions follow. Why? Why didn't Jesus resist?

"Well, because he loves us," we reply and that is true, wonderfully true, but—forgive me—only partially true. There is more to his reason. He saw something that made him stay. As the soldier pressed his arm, Jesus rolled his head to the side, and with cheek resting on the wood, he saw the list. A long list. A list of our mistakes: our lusts, our lies, our greedy moments, our prodigal years. A record of our sins. This is why he refused to close his fist. He saw the list! He knew the price of those sins was death.

He knew the source of those sins was you, and since he couldn't bear the thought of eternity without you, he chose the nails.

And because he chose the nails—we read these words.

"He canceled the record that contained the charges against us. He took it and destroyed it by nailing it to Christ's cross." (Col. 2:14)

The list of your sins cannot be read. Your failures are hidden—blotted out by the blood of God's Son. That's why Jesus didn't resist. The nails were God's idea.

The hand that swung the hammer was the hand of God.

And as the hands of Jesus opened for the nail, the doors of heaven opened for you.

VIDEO SEGMENT NUMBER 4

Wise is the man who learns the nonverbal language of his wife; who notes the nod and discerns the gestures. It's not just about what is said, but how. Not just about how, but when. Not just about when, but where. Good husbanding is good decoding. You've got to read the signs.

I thought I was doing a pretty good job that weekend in Miami. Just a few months into our marriage, we were hosting company in our apartment. I'd invited a Sunday guest speaker to stay with us on Saturday night. Risky move on my part since this man wasn't a college chum; he was an older distinguished professor, and not just any professor, but a specialist in family relations. Our new family was hosting a family specialist!

When Denalyn heard the news, she gave me a sign, a verbal sign. "We better clean the apartment." On Friday night she issued a second sign, a nonverbal sign. She got down on her knees and began scrubbing the kitchen floor. Now, much to my credit, I put the two signs together, and I got the message. I got off the couch.

What can I do to help? I thought. Never one to tackle the simple jobs, I passed on dusting and vacuuming and looked for a more challenging task. After a diligent search, I thought of the perfect one. I would fill a picture frame with pictures. One of our wedding gifts was a collage picture frame. We hadn't even unpacked it, much less filled it. But all that would change tonight.

So, I got to work. With Denalyn scrubbing floors behind me and an unmade bed in the room beside me, I dumped a shoe-box of photos in front of me and started to assemble the pictures. (I don't know what I was thinking. I guess I would have told the guest, "Hey, step over the laundry on the floor and look at our photo collection.")

I had missed the message. When Denalyn, with a chill in her voice that would have frozen perdition, asked me what I was doing, I still missed the message. "Just making a collage of pictures," I replied joyfully. For the next half-hour or so, she didn't speak. No problem. I had assumed she was praying, thanking God for such a thoughtful mate. I had imagined her thinking, *Maybe he'll work on our scrapbook next.*

But such were not her thoughts. My first clue that something was wrong was her final pronouncement of the evening. Having single-handedly cleaned the entire apartment, she announced, "I'm going to bed. I'm very upset. Tomorrow morning I will tell you why."

Duh.

Sometimes we miss the signs.

God knows that we sometimes miss the signs. The framer of our destiny is familiar with our denseness. Maybe that's why he has given us so many. The rainbow after the Flood signified God's covenant. Circumcision identified God's chosen, and the stars portray the size of his family. Even today, we see signs in the New Testament church. Communion is a sign of his death. Baptism is a sign of our spiritual birth. Each of these signs symbolizes greater spiritual truth.

The most poignant sign, however, was found on the cross. A tri-lingual, hand-painted, Roman commissioned sign that read: "Jesus of Nazareth, King of the Jews." And this sign reveals two truths about God's desire to reach the world. First, there is no person God will not use. Remember, the sign was ordered by Pilate himself. And second, there is no language God will not speak. Every passerby could read the sign. Since Jesus was a king for all people, the message was stated in the tongues of all people.

God will speak to you in your language, too. Perhaps it's the language of abundance or the language of need or the language of loneliness. But be listening. Your Father is speaking, and you don't want to miss the signs.

VIDEO SEGMENT NUMBER 5

Jesus once asked, if we humans who are sinful have such a love, how much more would God, the sinless and selfless Father, love us? But what happens when the love isn't returned? What happens to the heart of the Father when his child turns away?

I want to tell you a story that will remind you of the lengths God will go to retrieve your heart. It's a story of a dad named Joe and his daughter, Madeline. A story of the constancy of love, through the inconstancy of life.

Five-year-old Madeline climbed into her father's lap after another of Grandma's famous Christmas Eve dinners. "Time for bed," said the dad.

Madeline put her little hands on either side of his big face, begging him for a few more minutes. "Poppa, this is Christmas Eve. You said we could dance."

Joe feigned a poor memory, and Madeline pleaded once more. "We always dance on Christmas Eve. Just you and me. Remember?"

A smile burst from beneath his thick mustache. He stood and took her hand, and for a moment, just a moment, his wife was alive again and the two were walking into the den again to dance away another Christmas Eve. They would have danced away their lives, but then came the surprise pregnancy and the complications. Madeline survived, but the mother did not. And Joe, the thick-handed butcher from Minnesota was left to raise Madeline. "Come on, Poppa, " she urged. And Joe scooped up his daughter and began to dance with her until the relatives descended on them, filling the house with hugs and laughter.

Joe and Madeline spent many similar Christmases, as the years passed. But then the little girl became a teenager, and rebellion flew into Joe's world like a Minnesota blizzard. About the time she was old enough to drive, Madeline decided she was old enough to lead her life. And that life did not include her father.

Joe didn't know what to do. He didn't know how to handle the pierced nose and the tight skirts. He didn't understand the late nights and the poor grades. And, most of all, he didn't know when to speak and when to be silent.

She, on the other hand, had it all figured out. She knew when to speak to her father: never. She knew when to be quiet: always. The pattern was reversed, however, with the lanky, tattooed kid from down the street. He was no good, and Joe knew it. And there was no way he was going to allow his daughter to spend Christmas Eve with that kid. Joe insisted Madeline spend Christmas Eve with him and Grandma, just as always.

Christmas Eve came, and though they were at the same table, they might as well have been on different sides of town. Madeline played with her food and said nothing. Joe was angry, heart-broken. Soon the relatives arrived, bringing with them a welcome end to the awkward silence. As the room filled with noise and people, Joe stayed on one side, Madeline sat sullenly on the other.

One of his brothers started the music, and Joe walked toward his daughter. "Will you dance with your Poppa tonight?" he invited.

Well, the way she huffed and turned, you would've thought that he'd insulted her. In full view of the family, she turned and walked out the door, marched down the sidewalk, leaving her father alone. Very much alone.

Madeline came back later that night, and for the next few weeks, Joe tried hard to recapture the relationship they had once known. He made her favorite dinner; she didn't want to eat. He invited her to a movie; she just stayed in her room. And then there was that spring day he left work early to be at the house when she arrived home from school.

Wouldn't you know that was the day she never came home.

A friend saw her and her boyfriend in the vicinity of the bus station. The authorities confirmed the purchase of a ticket to Chicago; later, Joe learned that Madeline and the scrawny boyfriend were staying with one of her cousins in Houston. The cousin let the two runaways stay in his apartment at night, but they had to be out during the day. Which was fine with them. They had big plans. He was going to be a mechanic, and Madeline just knew she could get a job at a department store. Of course, he knew nothing about cars, and she knew even less about getting a job, but you don't think of things like that when you're intoxicated on freedom.

After a couple of weeks, the cousin changed his mind. And the day he changed his mind and announced his decision, the boyfriend announced his. Madeline found herself facing the night with no place to sleep or hand to hold.

It was just the first of many.

She found a homeless shelter nearby. For a couple of bucks she could get a bowl of soup and a cot. A couple of bucks was about all she had. The room was so rowdy, it was hard to sleep. Madeline turned her face to the wall and thought of the whiskered face of her father kissing her goodnight. But as her eyes began to water, she refused to cry. She pushed the memory deep inside and determined not to think about it anymore. She'd gone too far to go back home.

The next morning, the girl in the cot next to hers showed her a fistful of tips she'd made from dancing on tables. She told Madeline the manager was looking for another girl. She gave Madeline a matchbook. "Here's the address."

Madeline's stomach turned at the thought. She spent the rest of the week looking for work. At the end of the week when it was time to pay her bill at the shelter, she reached into her pocket and pulled out the matchbook. It was all she had left.

"I won't be staying tonight," she said, and walked out the door.

Hunger has a way of softening convictions.

If Madeline knew anything, she knew how to dance. Her father had taught her. But now men her father's age would be watching her. She didn't rationalize it; she didn't think about it. Madeline just did it. She simply did her work, and she took their dollars.

She might have never thought about it, except for the letters. The cousin brought them. Not one, or two, but a boxful. All addressed to her. All from her father. "These come two or three a week," he complained. "Give him your address." Oh, but she couldn't do that. He might find her.

Nor could she bear to open the envelopes. She knew what they said; he wanted her home. But if he knew what she was doing, he would not be writing. It seemed less painful not to read them. So she didn't. She just kept them in her dressing room at the club.

Most days Madeline was able to numb the emotions. Thoughts of home and thoughts of shame were shoved into the same part of her heart. Then a few days before Christmas Eve another letter arrived. Same shape. Same color. But this one had no postmark. She found it sitting on her dressing-room table.

One of the other dancers told her that a big man stopped by and asked her to give Madeline the letter.

"He was here?" she asked anxiously. Madeline swallowed hard and looked at the envelope. She opened it. "I know where you are," the card read. "I know what you do. This doesn't change the way I feel. What I've said in each letter is still true."

"But I don't know what you've said," Madeline declared to herself. She pulled a letter from the top of the stack and read it. Then a second and a third. Each letter had the same exact sentence. Each sentence asked the same question.

In a matter of moments the floor was littered with paper and her face was streaked with tears. Within an hour she was on a bus. "I just might make it in time."

She barely did.

The relatives were starting to leave. Joe was helping his mother in the kitchen when his brother called from the suddenly quiet den. "Joe, someone is here to see you."

Joe stepped out of the kitchen and stopped. In one hand she held a backpack. In the other she held a card. He saw the question in her eyes.

"If the invitation is still good, the answer is 'yes,'" she said to her father.

Joe could hardly speak. "Of course, the invitation is good."

And so the two danced again on Christmas Eve.

On the floor, near the door, rested a letter with Madeline's name and her father's request. "Will you come home and dance with your Poppa again?'

VIDEO SEGMENT NUMBER 6

Oh, the maitre d' wouldn't change his mind. He didn't care that this was our honeymoon. Didn't matter that the evening at the classy country club restaurant was a wedding gift. He could care less that Denalyn and I had gone without lunch to save room for dinner. All of this was immaterial in comparison to the looming problem.

I wasn't wearing a jacket.

Didn't know I needed one. I thought a sport shirt was sufficient. It was clean and tucked in. But Mr. Black-Tie with the French accent was unimpressed. He seated everyone else. Mr. and Mrs. Debonair were given a table. Mr. and Mrs. Classier-Than-You were seated. But Mr. and Mrs. Didn't-Wear-a-Jacket?

If I'd had another option, I wouldn't have begged. But I didn't. The hour was late. Other restaurants were booked, and we were hungry. "There's got to be something you can do," I pleaded. He looked and me, then at Denalyn, and then let out a long sigh that puffed his cheeks.

"All right, let me see."

He disappeared into the cloakroom and emerged with a jacket. "Put this on." I did. The sleeves were too short. The shoulders were too tight. And the color was lime green. But I didn't complain. I had a jacket and we were taken to a table. (Don't tell anyone, but I took it off when the food came.)

For all the inconveniences of the evening, we ended up with a great dinner, and an even greater parable.

I needed a jacket, but all I had was a prayer. The fellow was too kind to turn me away, but too loyal to lower the standard. So, the very one who required a jacket gave me a jacket, and we were given a table.

Isn't this what happened at the cross? Seats at God's table are not available to the sloppy. But who among us is anything but? Unkempt morality. Untidy with truth. Careless with people. Our moral clothing is in disarray. Yes, the standard for sitting at God's table is high, but the love of God for his children is higher. So he offers a gift.

Not a lime-colored jacket, but a robe. A seamless robe. Not a garment pulled out of a cloakroom, but a robe worn by his Son, Jesus.

When Christ was nailed to the cross, he took off his robe of seamless perfection and assumed a different wardrobe, the wardrobe of sin. The clothing of Christ on the cross was sin—your sin and mine. All the sins of humanity.

No, he was not guilty. No, he had not committed a sin. And, no, he did not deserve to be sentenced. But you and I were, we had, and we did. We were left in the same position I was with the maitre d': with nothing to offer but a prayer. Jesus, however, goes further than the maitre d'. Can you imagine the restaurant host removing his tuxedo coat and offering it to me?

Jesus does, and we're not talking about a misfit, leftover jacket. He offers a robe of seamless purity and dons my patchwork coat of pride, greed and self-service. He wore our sin, so we could wear his righteousness. Indeed, we are dressed in Christ himself. The Bible says we have all put on Christ as a garment.

It wasn't enough for him to prepare you a feast.

It wasn't enough for him to reserve you a seat.

It wasn't enough for him to cover the cost and provide the transportation to the banquet.

He did something more. He let you wear his own clothes, so that you would be properly dressed.

He did that . . . just for you.

VIDEO SEGMENT NUMBER 7

Imagine yourself standing in front of the White House.

That's you on the sidewalk, peering through the fence, over the lawn at the residence of the president. That's you, in fine form—hair in place and shoes shined. That's you turning toward the entrance. Your pace is brisk, your stride is sure. It should be. You have come to meet with the president.

You have a few matters you wish to discuss with him.

First, there is the matter of the fire hydrant in front of your house. Could they soften the red just a shade? It's too bright. Then there's the issue of world peace. You are for it—would he create it? And college tuition is too high. Could he call the admissions office and see if they could lighten up just a bit?

All worthy issues, correct? Won't take more than a few minutes. Besides, you brought him some cookies that he can share with the first lady and the first puppy. So with bag in hand and smile on your face, you step up to the gate and announce to the guard, "I'd like to see the president please."

He asks for your name. He looks at his list and says, "We have no record of your appointment."

Oh, you need an appointment? Hmmm. Then you find out you have to go through the office staff to get an appointment, and guess what? The number is restricted!

So, you wonder how you can get in, and the guard tells you that you'll have to wait until the president calls you.

Fat chance!

So you sigh and turn and begin your journey home. Your questions are unanswered and your needs are unmet.

And you were so close! But there were too many barriers. The guard, the fence, the Secret Service.

And what about the invisible barriers? Barriers of time. (The president is too busy). Barriers of status. (You have no clout). Barriers of protocol. (You have to go through the right channels.) You leave the White House with nothing more than a hard lesson learned. You do not have access to the president. You'll have to take your problems about peace and your question about the fire hydrant with you.

That is, unless he takes the initiative. Unless he, spotting you on the sidewalk, takes pity on your plight and tells his chief of staff to bring the person with the sack of cookies in. If he gives such a command, all the barriers will drop. The Oval Office will call the head of security. The head of security will call the guard, and the guard will call your name.

And then, you'd stop and turn and straighten your shoulders and enter the same door where, only moments before, you were denied access. The guard is the same. The gates are the same. The security personnel are the same. But the situation is not the same. You can now go where once you could not.

And, what's more, you are not the same. You feel special, chosen. Why? Because the man up there saw you down here, and made it possible for you to come in.

Yeah, you're right. It's a fanciful story. You and I both know when it comes to the President, don't hold your breath—no invitation will come. But when it comes to God, pick up your cookies and walk in. It already has.

He has spotted you. He has heard you, and he has invited you. "What once separated you has been removed The Bible says . . . now in Christ Jesus you who were far away from God are brought near" (Eph 2:13). Nothing remains between you and God but an open door.

228

But how could this be? If we can't get in to see the president, how could we be granted an audience with God? What happened? Well, in a word, someone opened the curtain. Someone tore down the veil. Something happened in the death of Christ that opened the door for you and me. And that "something" is described by the writer of Hebrews in this verse:

"So, brothers and sisters, we are completely free to enter the Most Holy Place without fear because of the blood of Jesus' death. We can enter through a new and living way which Jesus opened for us. It leads through the curtain—Christ's body" (Hebrews 10:19, 20).

You see, Jesus hasn't left us with an unapproachable God. Yes, God is holy. Yes, we are sinful. But, yes, yes, yes, Jesus is our mediator.

We are welcome to enter into God's presence—any day, any time. God has removed the barrier that separates us from him. When Jesus went to the cross, he ripped apart the barrier of sin, and nothing remains between us. We have immediate, everlasting access to the ruler of heaven.

VIDEO SEGMENT NUMBER 8

Have you ever tried to convince a mouse not to worry? Have you ever succeeded in pacifying the panic of a rodent? Well, if so, you are wiser than I because my attempt was not successful. My comforting words fell on tiny, deaf ears.

Not that the little fellow deserved any kindness, mind you. Because of him, Denalyn screamed. And because of the scream, I was yanked out of dreamland and off my Lazy-Boy and called to defend my wife and country. Of course I was proud to go. With shoulders high, I marched into the garage.

The mouse never had a chance. I know jujitsu and karate and tae kwan do and several other . . . uh, phrases. I've even watched self-defense infomercials. This time the tiny mouse had met his match.

Besides, he was trapped in an empty trash can. Now how he got there only he knows, and he ain't telling. I know, I asked him. His only reply was a mad race around the base of the can.

The poor guy was scared to the tip of his whiskers. And who wouldn't be? Imagine being caged in a plastic container and looking up only to see the large (be it handsome) face of a human. Would be enough to make you chuck up your cheese.

"What are you going to do with him?" Denalyn asked me, clutching my arm for courage.

"Oh, don't worry, little darlin'," I replied with a swagger that made her swoon and would have made John Wayne jealous, "I'll go easy on the little fellow."

So off we went, the mouse, the trash can, and me, marching down the cul-de-sac toward an empty lot. "Stick with me, little guy, I'll have you home in no time." He didn't listen. You'd have thought we were walking to death row. Had I not placed a lid on the can, the furry fellow would have jumped out. "I'm not going to hurt you," I explained. "I'm going to release you. You got yourself into a mess; I'm going to get you out."

He never calmed down. He never, well, he never trusted me. Even at the last moment, when I tilted the can on the ground and set him free, did he turn around and say thank you? Did he invite me to his mouse house for a meal? No. He just ran. (Was it my imagination, or did I hear him shouting, "Get back! Get back! Max, the mouse-hater is here!)

Honestly. What would I have to do to win his trust? Learn to speak Mouse-agese? Grow beady eyes and a long tail? Get down in the trash can with him? Thanks, but no thanks. I mean, the mouse was cute and all, but he wasn't worth that much.

Apparently you and I are.

You think it's absurd for a man to become a mouse? The journey from your house to a trash can is far shorter than the one from heaven to earth. But Jesus took it. Why?

Because he wants us to trust him.

Why did Jesus live on the earth as long as he did? Couldn't his life have been much shorter? Why not step into our world just long enough to die for our sins and then leave? Why not a sinless week? Why did he have to live a sinless life? To take on our sins is one thing, but to take on our sunburns and our sore throats? To experience death, yes, but to put up with life? Why did he do it?

Because he wants you to trust him.

He has been where you are and can relate to how you feel. And if his life on earth doesn't convince you, his death on the cross should. He understands what you are going through. Our Lord does not patronize or scoff at our needs. The Bible says he responds "generously to all without finding fault" (James 1:5, NIV).

And, oh, don't we need someone to trust in? Don't we need someone to trust in who is bigger than we are? Aren't we tired of trusting in the people of this earth for understanding? Aren't we weary of trusting in the things of this earth for strength? You know a drowning sailor doesn't call on another drowning sailor for help. A prisoner doesn't beg another prisoner to set him free. A pauper knows better than to beg from another pauper. He knows he needs someone who is stronger than he is.

Jesus' message through the Cross is simply this: "I am that person. Trust me."

VIDEO SEGMENT NUMBER 9

My name was in the sports section of the newspaper this week. You had to search to find it, but it was there. Four pages into Tuesday's edition, midway down the sheet at the end of the article about the Texas Open Golf Tournament, there was my name. All nine letters' worth.

It was a first for me. Wow, my name has appeared in other parts of the paper for a variety of reasons, some of which I'm proud of, some of which I'm not. But this was my first time in the sports section. It took over forty years, but I finally made it.

Here's what happened. My friend Buddy is the director of golf at the course that hosts the PGA Texas Open. He asked if I'd like to play in the annual Pro-Am Tournament. I thought about it for about three or four seconds and then accepted.

The Pro-Am has a simple format. Each team has a pro and some amateurs. The low score from each of the amateurs is recorded. In other words, even on the holes where I stunk, if one of my partners did well, I did well. And that is exactly what happened on, oh let me count, seventeen out of the eighteen holes.

Now, imagine the joy of such a game. Let's take my typical hole where I score an eight. But Buddy, or one of the other fellows, scores a three. Guess which score is recorded? The three! Max's eight is forgotten and Buddy's birdie is remembered. A person could get used to this! I get credit for the good work of someone else simply by virtue of being on his team.

Now, hasn't Christ done the same for you?

What my team did for me on Monday, your Lord does for you every day of the week. Because of his performance, you close your daily round with a perfect score. Doesn't matter if you sprayed a few into the woods or shanked one into the water. What matters is that you showed up to play and joined the right foursome. In this case, your foursome is pretty strong; it's you, the Father, the Son and the Holy Spirit. A better team doesn't exist.

And you are given a prize, not because of what you do, but because of who you know.

When you and I stand in heaven to receive our prize, only one will know of all of our sins, but he won't tell—he has already forgiven them.

So enjoy the game, my friend, your prize is secure.

But you might ask the Teacher for some help with that swing.

VIDEO SEGMENT NUMBER 10

People often ask me about the pronunciation of my last name. Is it Lu-KAY-doh or Lu-KAH-do? Remember the verse in the song? "Some say po-ta-to, some say po-tah-to." Well, the same can be said about my name. "Some say Lu-KAY-doh, some say Lu-KAH-doh." For the record, we say "Lu-KAY-doh."

But confusion over the name has created some awkward moments. A notable one occurred when I visited one of our church members at his office. One of his co-workers spotted me. She'd been in our church and read a few of my books. "Max Lu-KAH-do!" she exclaimed, "I've been wanting to meet you."

Well, it seemed rude to correct her before I'd even met her, so I just smiled and said hello, thinking that would be the end of it. But it was just the beginning. She wanted me to meet a few of her friends. So down the hall we went, and with each introduction came a mispronunciation. "Sally, this is Max Lu-KAH-do." "Joe, this is Max Lu-KAH-do." "Bob, this is Max Lu-KAH-do." "Tom, come here! Meet Max Lu-KAH-do." I would smile and cringe, unable to maneuver my way into the conversation to correct her. Besides, after a half a dozen times, we reached the point of no return. It would be too embarrassing. So, I just kept my mouth shut.

But then I got caught. We finally met a fellow who beat her to the draw. "I'm so glad to meet you," he said, as we entered his office, "My wife and I visited your services last Sunday, and we left trying to figure out how you say your name. Is it Lu-KAY-do or Lu-KAH-do?"

I was trapped. Tell the truth, she'll be embarrassed. Lie, he will be misinformed. She needed mercy. He needed accuracy. I wanted to be kind with her and honest with him, but how could I be both? I couldn't. So I lied. For the first time in my entire life I answered, "Lu-KAH-do, I pronounce the name, Lu-KAH-do."

May my ancestors forgive me.

But the moment wasn't without its redeeming value. The situation provides a glimpse into the character of God. You see, on an infinitely grander scale, God faces with humankind what I faced with the woman. How can he be both just and kind? How can he dispense truth and mercy? How can he redeem the sinner without endorsing the sin?

Can a holy God overlook our mistakes? Can a kind God punish our mistakes?

You see, from our perspective there are only two equally unappealing solutions. But from his perspective there is a third. It's called "The Cross of Christ." The cross. Can you turn any direction without seeing one? Perched atop a chapel. Carved into a graveyard headstone. Engraved into a ring or suspended on a chain. The cross is the universal symbol of Christianity. Odd choice, don't you think? Strange that a tool of torture would come to embody a movement of hope. The symbol of other faiths are more upbeat: the six-pointed star of Judaism, the crescent moon of Islam, a lotus blossom for Buddhism. Yet a cross for Christianity? An instrument of execution?

Why is the cross the symbol of our faith? Well, to find the answer look no further than the cross itself. Its design couldn't be simpler. One beam horizontal, the other vertical. One reaches out like God's love. The other reaches up as does God's holiness. One represents the width of his love, the other reflects the height of his holiness. The cross is the intersection of both. The cross is where God forgave his children without lowering his standard.

How could he do this? Well, in a sentence: God put our sin on his Son and punished it there.

"God put on him the wrong who never did anything wrong, so we could be put right with God" (2 Cor. 5:21, Message).

Envision the moment. God on his throne. You on the earth. And between you and God, suspended between you and heaven, is Christ on his cross. Your sins have been placed on Jesus. God, who punishes sin, releases his rightful wrath on your mistakes. Jesus receives the blow. But since Christ is between you and God, you don't. The sin is punished, but you are safe. You are safe in the shadow of the cross.

VIDEO SEGMENT NUMBER 11

At some point in everyone's life, tragedy walks in the door. Sooner or later, we all face difficult times. What's more, we've all received symbols of the tragedy. Yours might be a telegram from the war department, an ID bracelet from the hospital, a scar, or a court subpoena. We don't like these symbols, nor do we want these symbols. Like wrecked cars in the junkyard, they clutter up our hearts with memories of bad days.

Could God use such symbols, such things for something good? How far can we go with verses like this one? ". . . in everything God works for the good of those who love him" (Rom. 8:28). Does "everything" include tumors and tests and tempers and terminations?

Could he take what today is a token of tragedy and turn it into a symbol of triumph?

You know, he did for my friend Rafael Rosales. Rafael is a minister in El Salvador. The Salvadoran guerrillas viewed him as an enemy of their movement. They tried to kill him. Left him to die in a burning automobile. Rafael escaped the car and the country. But he couldn't escape the memories. The scars would not let him.

Every glance in the mirror reminded him of his tormentors' cruelty. He might have never recovered had the Lord not spoken to his heart. "They did the same to me," he heard his Savior say. And as God ministered to Rafael, Rafael began to see his scars differently. And rather than serve as a reminder of his own pain, they were a picture of his Savior's sacrifice. In time he was able to forgive his attackers. He's returned to his country to plant a new church.

Can God turn tragedy into triumph? Rafael would say "yes" and so would the apostle John.
John would tell you that *God can turn any tragedy into a triumph, if only we will wait and watch.*

And to prove his point, he would tell you about one Friday in particular.

Could there be a greater tragedy for John than a dead Jesus? Three years earlier John had turned his back on his career and cast his lot with this Nazarene carpenter. A week earlier John enjoyed a ticker-tape parade as Jesus and the disciples entered Jerusalem. But oh how quickly things had turned! The people who called him king on Sunday called for his death on Friday. And now these linens are a tangible reminder that his friend and his future are about to be wrapped in cloth and sealed behind a rock.

You see, John doesn't know what you and I know. He doesn't know that Friday's tragedy will be Sunday's triumph.

That's what makes what he did on Saturday so important.

Now, we don't know much about John's actions, but we do know this: when Sunday comes, John is still present. When Mary Magdalene comes looking for him, she finds him.

John doesn't leave. Jesus is dead. The Master's body is lifeless. John's friend and future are buried. But John has not left. Why? Is he waiting for the Resurrection? No. As far as he knows, the lips are forever silent and the hands forever still. He's not expecting a Sunday surprise. Then why is he here?

Perhaps the answer is pragmatic. Perhaps he's taking care of Jesus' mother. Or perhaps he didn't have anywhere else to go. Could be he didn't have any money or energy or direction . . . or all of the above.

Or, or maybe he lingers because he loves Jesus.

You see, to others, Jesus was a miracle worker. To others, Jesus was a master teacher. To others, Jesus was the hope of Israel. But to John, he was all of these and more. To John, Jesus was a friend.

And you don't abandon a friend—not even when that friend is dead. John stayed close to Jesus.

What about you? When you are in John's position, what do you do? When it's Saturday in your life, how do you react? When you are somewhere between yesterday's tragedy and tomorrow's triumph, what do you do? Do you leave God—or do you linger near him?

John chose to linger. And because he lingered on Saturday, he was around on Sunday to see the miracle.

Could such a change happen to you? I have no doubt. You simply need to do what John did. Don't leave. Hang around.

Remember the second half of the passage. "God works for the good of *those who love him*" (Rom. 8:28). That's how John felt about Jesus. He loved him. He didn't understand him or always agree with him, but he loved him.

And because he loved him, he stayed near him.

I'd like you to try a simple exercise. Look at that Romans verse again. ". . . in everything God works for the good of those who love him." Now, remove the word *everything* and replace it with the symbol of your tragedy. How would Romans 8:28 read in your life?

In hospital stays God works for the good.

In divorce papers God works for the good.

In a prison term God works for the good.

If God can change John's life through a tragedy, could it be that he will use a tragedy to change yours?

As hard as it may be to believe, you could be only a Saturday away from a resurrection. And you could be only hours from that precious prayer of a changed heart, "God, did you do this for me?"

VIDEO SEGMENT NUMBER 12

I grew up playing football in the empty field next to our house. Many a Sunday afternoon was spent imitating Don Meredith or Bob Hayes or Johnny Unitas. (Of course, I didn't have to imitate Joe Namath; most of the girls thought I looked like him already.)

Empty fields in West Texas have grass burrs. Grass burrs can hurt. You can't play football without falling, and you can't fall in a West Texas field without getting stuck.

More times than I can remember, I pulled myself out of a sticker patch so hopelessly covered that I had to have help. Kids don't rely on other kids to pull out grass burrs. You need someone with skill. I would limp over to the house so my dad could—one by painful one—pluck out the stickers.

I wasn't too bright, but I knew this. If I wanted to get back into the game, I needed to get rid of those stickers.

Every mistake in life is like a grass burr. You can't live without falling, and you can't fall without getting stuck. But you know? We aren't always as smart as young ballplayers. We sometimes try to get back into the game without dealing with the stickers. It's as if we don't want anyone to know we fell, so well, we pretend we never did. Consequently, we live in pain. We can't walk well, sleep well, rest well. And, oh, we are so touchy.

Does God want us to live like that? No way. Listen to his promise: "This is my commitment to my people: removal of their sins" (Rom. 11:27, The Message).

God does more than forgive our mistakes; he removes them! We simply have to take them to him.

He not only wants the mistakes we've made. He wants the ones we are making! Are you making some? Are you drinking too much? Are you cheating at work or cheating at marriage? Are you mismanaging your money? Are you mismanaging your life?

If so, don't pretend nothing is wrong. Don't pretend you don't fall. Don't try to get back into the game. Go first to God. The first step after a stumble must be in the direction of the cross. "If we confess our sins to God, he can always be trusted to forgive us and take our sins away" (1 Jn. 1:9, CEV).

And when you confess your sins, you're leaving them at the foot of the cross. You're abandoning them so that God can take care of them. Each of us could leave something at the cross.

Why don't you spend a minute or two thinking about what you would like to leave at the cross today?

VIDEO SEGMENT NUMBER 13

There is nothing impressive about the stationery. No embossed letters. No watermark. No heavy stock paper. No logo. Just a sheet of yellow legal paper, the top of which is jagged from the tear.

There is nothing impressive about the handwriting. There used to be. As a child I tried to imitate it. But you wouldn't want to imitate this penmanship; you'd be hard pressed to decipher it. Angled lines. Irregular letters and inconsistent spacing.

But it was the best my father could do. Lou Gehrig's disease had so weakened his hands, he could scarcely bring a fork to his mouth, much less write words on a page. Imagine writing with all your fingers wrapped around the pen, and you're close to understanding his challenge.

It was the final letter he ever wrote us. The ALS and cold weather nearly killed him. Denalyn and I rushed home from Brazil and spent a month eating hospital food and taking shifts at his bedside. He rebounded, however, and so we returned to South America. A day or so after arriving, we received this letter.

January 19, 1984

Dear Max and Denalyn,

We were glad you all made it home. Now settle down and go to work.
We enjoyed your trip to no end. Even your spending the nights with me.
Max, you and Denalyn always stick together, whatever happens.

Well, there is no need of me scribbling. I think you know how much I love you both. You all just live good Christian lives and fear God.

I hope to see you all again on earth—if not, I will in heaven.

Lots of love,

Dad

I've envisioned my father writing these words. Propped up in a hospital bed, pen in hand, pad on lap. Thinking this would be his final message. Do you suppose he chose his words carefully? Of course he did.

Can you envision trying to do the same? Can you imagine your final message to those you love? Your last words with a child or spouse? What would you say? And how would you say it?

Even if you can't answer the first question. Even if you don't know what you would say, you know how you would say it. You would say it deliberately. Precisely. Carefully. Wouldn't you go as Monet to a palette—searching, not just for the right color, but the perfect shade, the exact hue? Most of us have only one chance to make our last statement.

That's all Jesus was given. Knowing his last deeds would be forever pondered, don't you think he chose them carefully? Deliberately? Of course he did. There were no accidents that day. Jesus' last moments were not left up to chance. God chose the path, he chose the nails. Our Lord planted the trio of crosses and painted the sign. God was never more sovereign than in the details of the death of his Son. As deliberately as my father wrote the letter, so your Father left this message:

"I did it for you. I did it all for you."

VIDEO SEGMENT 14

Epilogue

Just wanted to take a minute before we say good-bye and thank you for being part of this "He Chose the Nails" study series. It means a lot to all of us that you gave your time and your thoughts and your attention to this very important subject. A lot of different people have been behind this. And it's our prayer that something has been said or heard or mentioned or read that will just bring you a step closer to the cross.

I have an idea for you. I want you to think about this, please? What would you like to leave at the cross? We know what Jesus brought. We see the forgiveness we have because of the scars in his hands, the love that he showed through the path he took. We wear a garment of grace because he took on a garment of sin. We see what Jesus brought to the cross. But you know, for the cross of Christ to become the cross of our life, we need to leave something, too. What would you like to leave? Many people never do. Many come and do what we've done—they look at the cross, they think about the cross, but they don't allow the cross to touch their hearts. And that's because they never leave anything there.

May I suggest two or three things you might consider leaving at the foot of the cross? Why don't you begin with your bad moments? Those mistakes, those failures, those regrets that you have. Why don't you leave them there and let God do what he wants to do, cast them into the ocean of his grace. Why

234

don't you leave your anxious moments?

After you've left some of the past, why don't you leave some of the future? What are you worried about? Next week? Next month? Next year? Take those anxious moments to the cross. Go to the cross, and spend some time there. Hold the spike in your hand. Finger that braided crown once again. Reach down and touch the moistened dirt, moistened with the blood that Christ bled for you, the crown he wore for you, the spikes he took for you. And remember, thinking about all the things that God did for you on the cross then, don't you think he's proven he can take care of you now? Or as Paul said, "He who did not spare his own Son, but gave him up for us all, will he not also along with him graciously give us all things?"

Give God your bad moments. Give him your anxious moments. Give him your past. Give him your future. And give him your last moment. Many of us fear that final breath, that final moment, that final step from this world to the next. But you don't have to be afraid. You see, the death and resurrection of Jesus is proof and preview of our own. Just as he died, unless the Lord returns first, we'll die too. But just as he was raised from the dead, we will be as well. You don't need to be afraid of that moment. Give it to God.

Give him your bad moments, your anxious moments, and your final moments. Now someone is thinking, "Well, if I give all those moments to God, I won't have anything left except for good moments." Well, what do you know. I suppose you won't.

CREDITS

CHAPTER 1
1. Max Lucado, "The Gift Is God—Given" in *Grace for the Moment* [Nashville: J. Countryman, © 2000], 385.
2. Max Lucado, "God Loves You Dearly" in *Grace for the Moment* [Nashville: J. Countryman, © 2000], 340.
3. Max Lucado. "God's Good Gifts" in *Grace for the Moment* [Nashville: J. Countryman, © 2000], 30.
4. Max Lucado. "God's Great Gifts" in *Grace for the Moment* [Nashville: J. Countryman, © 2000], 388.
5. John MacArthur. *Romans, MacArthur Bible Study Series* [Nashville: Word Bibles, © 2000], n.p.

CHAPTER 2
1. Max Lucado, "A Meeting of Moments" in *Grace for the Moment* [Nashville: J. Countryman, © 2000], 110.
2. Max Lucado, "Tipped Scales" in *Grace for the Moment* [Nashville: J. Countryman, © 2000], 118.
3. Billy Graham. *Unto the Hills: A Daily Devotional* [Dallas: Word Publishing, © 1996], August 5.
4. Max Lucado. "The Soul Killer" in *Grace for the Moment* [Nashville: J. Countryman, © 2000], 369.

CHAPTER 3
1. Count Nicholas Ludwig von Zinzendorf. Quoted by Max Lucado in *He Chose the Nails* [Nashville: Word Publishing, © 2000], n.p.
2. Max Lucado. "One Incredible Plan" in *Grace for the Moment* [Nashville: J. Countryman, © 2000], 107.
3. John MacArthur. *Romans, MacArthur Bible Study Series* [Nashville: Word Bibles, © 2000], n.p.
4. Max Lucado. "You Were in His Prayers" in *Grace for the Moment* [Nashville: J. Countryman, © 2000], 107.
5. Max Lucado. "The Strength of God's Love" in *Grace for the Moment* [Nashville: J. Countryman, © 2000], 391.
6. Billy Graham. *Unto the Hills: A Daily Devotional* [Dallas: Word Publishing, © 1996], January 8.

CHAPTER 4
1. Steven Lawhead. Quoted in *Tough Choices* by Len Woods [Sisters, OR: Multnomah Publishers, © 1998], 11.
2. Count Nicholas Ludwig von Zinzendorf. Quoted by Max Lucado in *He Chose the Nails* [Nashville: Word Publishing, © 2000], n.p.
3. C.S. Lewis. Quoted by Max Lucado in *He Chose the Nails* [Nashville; Word Publishers, © 2000], n.p.
4. Donald Bloesch. Quoted by Max Lucado in *He Chose the Nails* [Nashville: Word Publishing, © 2000],n.p.
5. Billy Graham. *Unto the Hills: A Daily Devotional* [Dallas: Word Publishing, © 1996], May 7.

CHAPTER 5
1. Charles Spurgeon. Quoted in *All of Grace* [©1981 by Whitaker House, 30 Hunt Valley Circle, New Kensington, PA 16068. Available at your local Christian bookstore.], 29—33.
2. Billy Graham. *Unto the Hills: A Daily Devotional* [Dallas: Word Publishing, © 1996], May 12.
3. Max Lucado. "God is Crazy About You" in *Grace for the Moment* [Nashville: J. Countryman, © 2000], 87.

CHAPTER 6
1. C.S. Lewis. *Mere Christianity*, © 1952, 62.
2. Charles Stanley. *The Source of My Strength* [Nashville: Thomas Nelson Publishers, © 1994], 101—102.
3. Billy Graham. *Unto the Hills: A Daily Devotional* [Dallas: Word Publishing, © 1996], 315.
4. Max Lucado. "Not Perfection, But Forgiveness" in *Grace for the Moment* [Nashville: J. Countryman, © 2000], 127.

CHAPTER 8
1. C.S. Lewis. *Mere Christianity*, © 1952, 154.
2. Billy Graham. *How To Be Born Again* [Dallas: Word Publishing, 1989], 114—115.

CHAPTER 9
1. Donald Bloesch. Quoted by Max Lucado in *He Chose the Nails* [Nashville: Word Publishing, © 2000], n. p.
2. John MacArthur. *Romans, MacArthur Bible Study Series* [Nashville: Word Bibles, © 2000], n.p.

CHAPTER 10
1. Richard Baxter. Quoted by Paul Lee Tan in *Encyclopedia of 7700 Illustrations* [Rockville, MD: Assurance Publishers, © 1979], 1232.
2. Billy Graham. *Unto the Hills: A Daily Devotional* [Dallas: Word Publishers, © 1996], April 21.
3. A. W. Tozer. *The Root of Righteousness* [Harrisburg, PA: Christian Publications, Inc., © 1955], 66.

CHAPTER 11
1. Max Lucado. *God Came Near* [Portland, OR: Multnomah Publishers, © 1987], 81.
2. C.S. Lewis. Quoted by Max Lucado in *He Chose the Nails* [Nashville: Word Publishing, © 2000], n.p.

CHAPTER 12
1. Billy Graham. *Unto the Hills: A Daily Devotional* [Dallas: Word Publishing, © 1996], September 26.
2. C.S. Lewis. *Mere Christianity*, © 1952, 167—168.
3. A.W. Tozer. *The Root of Righteousness* [Harrisburg, PA: Christian Publications, Inc., © 1955], 49—51.

MAX LUCADO
HE CHOSE THE NAILS

A LIVE WORSHIP EXPERIENCE FEATURING KIM HILL, SONICFLOOD, WES KING, TWILA PARIS AND NATALIE GRANT, WITH WORSHIP LEADER JEFF NELSON

Share in the joy and mystery of the cross of Jesus. Pick up your copy of *He Chose the Nails*—the new original live recording featuring narration by Max Lucado and brand new songs of worship and praise based on the themes of Max's best-selling book. It's on sale now at your favorite Christian music retailer.

www.hechosethenails.com   www.HereToHim.com

WHEN CHRIST COMES

Wouldn't it be refreshing to discuss the end of time and feel better because of it? Or to hear some truly comforting words regarding the return of Christ? As only master storyteller Max Lucado can do, he takes readers on an unforgettable journey to show what will happen on the glorious day *When Christ Comes*.

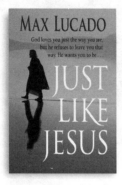

JUST LIKE JESUS

"What if, for one day, Jesus became you," asks master storyteller Max Lucado. With this simple premise, Lucado tells how God loves you just the way you are, but he refuses to leave you that way. He wants you to be . . . *Just Like Jesus.*

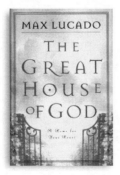

THE GREAT HOUSE OF GOD

God's greatest desire is to be your dwelling place—the home for your heart. Warm your heart by the fire in the living room. Nourish your spirit in the kitchen. Step into the hallway and find forgiveness. No house is more complete, no foundation more solid. So come into the house built just for you... *The Great House of God.*

IN THE GRIP OF GRACE

In his most theologically challenging book yet, Max Lucado shows how you can't fall beyond God's love. "God doesn't condone our sin, nor does He compromise His standard. Rather than dismiss our sin, He assumes our sin and incredibly, incredibly sentences Himself. God is still holy. Sin is still sin. And we are redeemed."

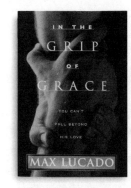

A GENTLE THUNDER

How far do you want God to go in getting your attention? Don't answer too quickly. What if God moved you to another land? (as He did Abraham.) What if He called you out of retirement? (Remember Moses?) How about the voice of an angel or the bowel of a fish (Gideon and Jonah.) God does what it takes to get our attention. Softly shouting, gently thundering…whatever it takes to get us home safely.

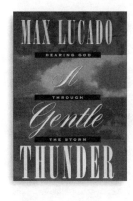

WHEN GOD WHISPERS YOUR NAME

Perhaps you've never seen your name honored. And you can't remember when you heard it spoken with kindness. If you're struggling to find your way, Lucado offers the inspiration to believe that God has already bought the ticket—with your name on it. This book affirms that God can move you along on your journey with power from beyond.

HE STILL MOVES STONES

Why does the Bible contain so many stories of hurting people? Lucado reminds us that the purpose of these portraits isn't to tell us what Jesus did—but rather to remind us what Jesus still does. He comes to do what you can't. He comes to move the stones you can't budge. *He Still Moves Stones.*

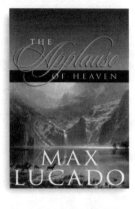

THE APPLAUSE OF HEAVEN

It is what you always dreamed but never expected. It's having God as your dad, your biggest fan, and your best friend. It is having the King of kings in your cheering section. Max Lucado shows you how the Beatitudes provide what we need to discover the joy of God. Much more than a "how-to" book on happiness; *The Applause of Heaven* is an encounter with the Source of Joy.

IN THE EYE OF THE STORM

Come face-to-face with Jesus when He experienced more stress than any other day of his life aside from his crucifixion. With keen insight and exacting clarity, Max Lucado shows us the secret of transforming panic into peace, stress into serenity, and chaos into control.

COSMIC CHRISTMAS

Was the birth of Jesus a quietly profound event? Or could it have included heavenly battles, angel armies, and a scheming Satan? Come along as Lucado takes us on a journey into his imagination—pulling back the curtain as we see what might have taken place one *Cosmic Christmas*.

THE CHRISTMAS CROSS

The Christmas Cross is a story about finding your way home for the holidays, told in the context of one man's journey in a small Texas town. Unique interactive elements inside this book—including envelopes with pullout letters and surprises—make this a one-of-a-kind Christmas treasure.

THE INSPIRATIONAL BIBLE

Imagine studying the Bible with Max Lucado. He sees the Bible as "stories of real people, real problems, real joy, and a real Savior." Edited by Max Lucado, *The Inspirational Bible* includes:

- 700 "Life Lessons"
- Introductions to each book of the Bible
- 48 color pages that address topics from Forgiveness to Victory